CANADA and the MIDDLE EAST

P9-APP-966

The Centre for International Governance Innovation (CIGI) was founded in 2001 to provide solutions to pressing governance challenges. CIGI strives to build ideas for global change through world-class research and dialogue with practitioners, which provide a basis for advising decision-makers on the character and desired reforms of multilateral governance. CIGI's purpose is to conduct research of international significance, and to strengthen the intellectual capacity to understand and propose innovative solutions to global challenges. For more information please visit www.cigionline.org.

CIGI — The Centre for International Governance Innovation — Centre pour l'innovation dans la gouvernance internationale

CANADA and the MIDDLE EAST

In Theory and Practice

Paul Heinbecker and
Bessma Momani, editors

Wilfrid Laurier University Press
[WLU]

We acknowledge the financial support of the Government of Canada through the Book Publishing Industry Development Program for our publishing activities. We acknowledge the financial support of the Centre for International Governance Innovation.

Library and Archives Canada Cataloguing in Publication

Canada and the Middle East : in theory and practice / Paul Heinbecker and Bessma Momani, editors.

Includes bibliographical references.
ISBN 978-1-55458-024-8 / 1-55458-024-2

1. Canada—Foreign relations—Middle East. 2. Middle East—Foreign relations—Canada. 3. Canada—Relations—Middle East. 4. Middle East—Relations—Canada. I. Heinbecker, Paul, 1941– II. Momani, Bessma, 1973–

FC244.M53C28 2007   327.71056   C2007-906014-5

Co-published with the Centre for International Governance Innovation.

© 2007 The Centre for International Governance Innovation (CIGI) and Wilfrid Laurier University Press

Cover image based on a photograph by Carroll Klein. Text design by Pam Woodland.

∞

This book is printed on Ancient Forest Friendly paper (100% post-consumer recycled).

Printed in Canada

CONTENTS

ACCC	Association of Community Colleges of Canada
AHLC	Ad Hoc Liaison Committee
AKP	Justice and Development Party (Turkey)
ARIJ	Applied Research Institute of Jerusalem
AU	African Union
AUCC	Association of Universities and Colleges of Canada
BRIC	Brazil, Russia, India, and China
CABC	Canada-Arab Business Council
CAF	Canadian Arab Federation
CARICOM	Caribbean Community and Common Market
CBC	Canadian Broadcasting Corporation
CCIC	Canadian Council for International Cooperation
CEAD	Centre d'études arabes pour le développement
CEDRI	Comité européen pour la défense des réfugiés et immigrés
CIC	Canada-Israel Committee (Chapter 10)
CIC	Citizenship and Immigration Canada (Chapter 11)
CIDA	Canadian International Development Agency
CIFTA	Canada-Israel Free Trade Agreement
CIIRDF	Canada-Israel Industrial Research and Development Foundation
CIGI	Centre for International Governance and Innovation
CIJA	Canadian Council for Israel and Jewish Advocacy
CJPAC	Canadian Jewish Political Affairs Committee
COMTRADE	United Nations Commodity Trade Statistics Database
DFAIT	Department of Foreign Affairs and International Trade
DND	Department of National Defence
EASF	Middle East Expert and Advisory Services Fund (of the International Development Research Centre)
EDC	Export Development Canada
EFTA	European Free Trade Association
EOV	Explanation of Votes (on United Nations resolutions)
EU	European Union
FIPA	foreign investment protection and promotion agreement
GCC	Gulf Cooperation Council

GDP	gross domestic product
GERPA	Gender and Economic Research and Policy Analysis
GNP	gross national product
IAF	Islamic Action Front
ICCS	Islamic Center Charity Society
ICISS	International Commission on Intervention and State Sovereignty
ICRC	International Committee of the Red Cross
IDEA	International Institute for Democracy and Electoral Assistance
IDRC	International Development Research Centre
IECI	Independent Electoral Commission for Iraq
IRB	Immigration and Refugee Board of Canada
IRFFI	International Reconstruction Fund Facility for Iraq
IRPA	*Immigration and Refugee Protection Act*
JD	Jordanian dinar
MAP	Medical Aid for Palestine
MCC	Mennonite Central Committee
MDG	Millennium Development Goal
MEGGF	Middle East Good Governance Fund (of the International Development Research Centre)
MEWG	Middle East Working Group
MFO	Multinational Force and Observers
MOSA	Ministry of Social Affairs (Egypt)
MP	member of Parliament
NAFTA	North American Free Trade Agreement
NATO	North Atlantic Treaty Organization
NCCAR	National Council on Canada-Arab Relations
NDP	National Democratic Party (Egypt)
NECEF	Near East Cultural and Education Foundation
NGO	non-governmental organization
OAS	Organization of American States
ODA	official development assistance
OECD	Organisation for Economic Co-operation and Development
OPEC	Organization of the Petroleum Exporting Countries
PLO	Palestinian Liberation Organization
PNGO	Palestinian Non-Governmental Organization Network
PRRA	Pre-Removal Risk Assessment
PRT	Provincial Reconstruction Team (Kandahar, Afghanistan)
R2P	Responsibility to Protect

RWG	Refugee Working Group
SALW	small arms and light weapons
SCFAIT	Standing Committee on Foreign Affairs and International Trade
SINT	Subcommittee on International Trade, Trade Disputes, and Investment of the Standing Committee on Foreign Affairs and International Trade
SMEPOL	Small and Medium Enterprises Policy Development
START	Stabilization and Reconstruction Task Force
TFPR	Task Force on Palestinian Reform
UAE	United Arab Emirates
UNDG	United Nations Development Group
UNDOF	United Nations Disengagement Observer Force
UNDP	United Nations Development Programme
UNEF	United Nations Emergency Force
UNFC	United National Front for Change
UNGA	United Nations General Assembly
UNHCR	United Nations High Commission for Refugees
UNRWA	United Nations Relief and Works Agency for Palestine Refugees in the Near East
UNSC	United Nations Security Council
UNSCOP	United Nations Special Committee on Palestine
USAID	United States Agency for International Development
WMD	weapons of mass destruction
WTO	World Trade Organization

Canada and the Middle East:
Ambivalence or Engagement?

n July 2006, the Middle East took violent and unprecedented centre stage for Canadians as war unexpectedly broke out between Israel and Hizbullah. This was no ordinary, remote crisis. Relatives and loved ones of Canadians in both Lebanon and Israel were at mortal risk as the fighting raged and bombs and rockets rained down. Some 40,000 Canadian citizens were trapped in the fighting and nine Canadians died, including a Canadian peacekeeper. On the day before help began to arrive in the port of Beirut, officials in the "war room" of the Canadian embassy in Lebanon received 8,400 phone calls and 5,600 emails from frantic Canadians seeking help.[1] At the cost of nearly $62 million, the Canadian government leased vessels and aircraft and mobilized hundreds of officials to evacuate the desperate citizens, in what was to become the biggest evacuation in Canadian history. Canadians, including their government, learned first hand just how quickly this volatile corner of the world could ignite and engulf them.

The Middle East, particularly the violence in Iraq and the ongoing grind in the West Bank and Gaza, had tended to be seen and understood in most Canadian family homes through television's often antiseptic images of rubble and twisted metal, devoid of the gruesome evidence of the charnel house that modern war has become. These conflicts were seen as intractable and thankfully distant, of little immediate consequence to most Canadians or their government. Not this time. The 2006 conflict in Lebanon brought home to all of us the complexities of the Middle East in ways that were urgent and impossible to ignore and, more importantly, to dismiss.

As the situation in Lebanon evolved, analysts started to question the nature and relevance of Canadian involvement in Middle East affairs. What was Canada's Middle East foreign policy? What were Canadian interests in the Middle East? To what extent were Canadian values engaged? What role had

Canada played historically in the region? Those seeking to develop informed answers to these questions, however, were hindered by serious gaps in the academic literature and an absence of documented institutional memory among Canadian practitioners involved in the region. While a number of scholars had tackled the subject of Canada and the Middle East throughout the 1970s, 1980s, and sparingly in the early 1990s, the Middle East Discussion Group of the Centre for International Governance and Innovation (CIGI) was surprised to discover that the issue had not been adequately examined post-September 11. While libraries of books, studies, and analyses had been written about the Middle East since September 11, mostly by Americans, there was a near void of expert Canadian analysis of our country's role in the region and our government's related policies.

Our motivation in producing this book was to fill this gap. With support from CIGI, a group of practitioners and academics from Canada and the region met to discuss the Canadian relationship with the Middle East, guided by their own practical experience and their academic research. This edited collection is unique on this subject: practitioners with extensive first-hand experience reflect on Canada's role and opportunities in the region and academics speak from their expertise on the Middle East. Canadian foreign policy experts have shied away from in-depth studies of the Middle East due to the sheer complexity of the topics involved and the great sensitivity of the subject matter to diaspora communities. We hope that our approach, which marries academic and practitioner insights, will help Canadians understand Canada's role in the region better and not tread on their sensibilities.

Today's Middle East is in great turmoil and its issues cannot be resolved or contained even by the most powerful country in the world acting alone. Why bother examining the role of Canada in the Middle East then? Canada is not a superpower and has rarely played a decisive role in the politics of the region. While we doubt that this volume will settle this issue, there is a near consensus among our practitioners and academics alike that Canada has mattered in the Middle East in the not-so-distant past, that there remain deep wells of respect for Canada among the peoples of the Middle East that can be leveraged by our diplomacy, and, in short, that we can make a positive difference. Assuming Canadian impotence in the Middle East is an excuse for inaction. Our practitioners and academics also remind us that the largest leap in peace negotiations between the Israelis and Palestinians was brokered by Norway, a country with an economy and population a sixth of the size of Canada's. Nevertheless, the basic question for a country with our attributes is not whether we can make a difference but whether we should—whether it serves our interests and values to do so.

This book argues that it does. The Middle East is evidently fraught with conflict and division. Furthermore, the hegemonic role in the region of the United States, our primary economic partner, has at times put Canadian and American governments at cross purposes, not something to be dismissed lightly. More significantly, it can be argued that being circumspect and minding our own business have served us well in the past. In an integrating world, however, as the Lebanon war illustrated, Middle East peace and Canadian well-being are increasingly interconnected. Our security, our economic well-being, and our domestic harmony are all, to one extent or another, linked with the Middle East. A foreign policy of ambivalence and disinterest would, in our view, carry an unaffordable price tag.

The next question addressed by several of our contributors is how Canada should engage. In the Canadian debate on the issue, all can agree that Canada should take a principled approach. From there, the consensus breaks down, with some arguing for frank support for Israel, a fellow democracy facing chronic danger—an approach initiated by the Martin government and followed by the Harper government—and others advocating a case-by-case approach derived from international law, more akin to the policy that had been followed, for the most part, since Lester Pearson. Readers will not be surprised to learn that the contributors to this book did not reach a consensus view on the subject.

Canada's role in world affairs has often been romanticized. This book strives to avoid self-referential and sentimental debates about Canadian identities and values. Instead, it shows where Canadian policies have contributed to tangible outcomes in the Middle East and suggests where Canadian policies can benefit both Canadians and Middle Easterners. Canada's normative principles, its respect for diversity at home, its constructive approach to diplomacy, its support for economic development abroad, its immigration and refugee programs, and the ethics of its business community have earned it the admiration of many in the Middle East. This observation is not meant to inflate our national ego, but rather to draw attention to the positive legacy Canadians have on which to build.

We begin this book by tracing Canadian contributions to political peace and stability in the Middle East. Four former senior diplomats with direct and vast experience in managing Canada–Middle East relations reflect on a number of pertinent issues on the matter. Former ambassadors Michael Bell and Michael Molloy of Canada, David Sultan of Israel, and Sallama Shaker of Egypt contribute individual sections of the chapter, each covering the challenges and opportunities encountered during their tenure. All four contributors offer their own perspectives on how Canada has been involved in the region and what Canada can do to enhance its participation. Among them there is a consensus that Canada can do more and that Canadian actions would be welcomed in the region.

Nathan Funk begins with a reflective view of a debate in Canadian foreign policy theory between traditional liberal internationalists who call for multilateralism and newer neo-conservatives who embrace a far more combative response to global insecurity. He suggests reinvigorating a "human security" approach that addresses the neo-conservatives' concerns about insecurity and that recognizes the ways in which religious radicalization in the Middle East has been fed by regime repression and protracted regional conflict. Funk prescribes an alternative to military interventions in the Middle East and suggests ways to help enhance hope and prevent violence in the Middle East.

Marie-Joëlle Zahar critically assesses one of Canada's proudest achievements in promoting human security abroad: the Responsibility to Protect (RSP). She provides an assessment of Canadian performance with respect to R2P and contrasts the approaches to the issue of the Chrétien, Martin, and Harper governments. Zahar argues that the tendency toward increased rhetoric and decreased action is not due to a lack of capacity, as commonly argued, but rather a preference on the part of the Martin and Harper governments to align policies with the United States, while creating an illusion of commitment to action.

Rex Brynen examines Canada's historical role in and policies toward the Israeli-Palestinian conflict and peace process. Canada's initial support for the creation of Israel in 1948 and sympathy for Israel in the 1967 Arab-Israeli war began to erode in the 1970s and 1980s, accompanied by increasing, albeit still measured, criticism of the Israeli occupation of the West Bank and Gaza, of the expansion of Israeli settlements there, and of the annexation of West Jerusalem. After initial peace talks between Israelis and Palestinians in Madrid in 1991, the stakeholders asked Canada to assume responsibility as "gavel holder" of the Refugee Working Group. He reflects on Canada's "benign" image among Palestinians and Israelis, which has helped the Canadian government navigate in complicated diplomatic waters, and on the recent pro-Israel tilts under prime ministers Paul Martin and Stephen Harper. Brynen argues that Canadian foreign policy toward the Middle East is shaped by a myriad of domestic and international factors, including Canadian leaders' views of the region, interested community groups' views, the media, and our relationship with the United States.

Janine Clark delves into an important question facing Canadian policy makers and the international community more broadly: can the promotion of democracy in the region lead to the rise of Islamists and should we engage Islamist political parties in the Middle East? Canadian efforts to promote democracy in the region, like those of other western governments, feed into the already rising anti-western sentiments there. Clark identifies an irony in the Middle East that is of policy importance: Islamist organizations exhibit more democratic forms of decision making and governance than their secular civil society counterparts. Clark recommends that Canada should aim to be consistent in its democracy promotion policies. Consistency could improve Canada's image in the region; hypocrisy could contribute to heightened anti-westernism.

We then turn to examine Canadian efforts to promote development in and economic relations with the Middle East. Paul Kingston looks at the Canadian

International Development Agency's (CIDA) attempt to bolster Middle East non-governmental organizations (NGOs) in the 1990s. CIDA sponsored the creation of the Middle East Working Group (MEWG), and supported dialogue, communication, and capacity building among and within Canadian and Middle Eastern NGOs. The MEWG, however, failed both to function as a foreign policy instrument and to elevate the voices of NGOs in their respective Middle East communities. Kingston finds that CIDA's support insulated NGOs from their respective communities and limited their effectiveness in promoting community organization and mobilization. Political and social conditions, moreover, were not conducive to NGO mobilization in the region. The chapter demonstrates some of the limitations of Canada's policy on official development assistance (ODA).

Bruce Muirhead and Ronald Harpelle examine the engagement of a lesser-known Canadian development agency, the International Research Development Centre (IDRC), in the Middle East. IDRC's role has been a discreet and quiet one, but very valuable to researchers in recipient countries and to Canada's "underground" reputation as well. IDRC has supported researchers in the region to develop strategies that address local concerns about governance, geography, the economy, and social relations, to name a few issues. IDCR's arm's-length relationship with the Canadian government, moreover, is an asset both for IDRC and for the government when dealing with politically sensitive issues.

Bessma Momani and Agata Antkiewicz study Canada's economic relationship with the Middle East and find that the region is too often neglected but still promising regarding Canada's overall economic growth. Canada–Middle East trade flows represent a small part of Canada's overall trade, but Momani and Antkiewicz find that there are significant opportunities to foster complementary and very significant value-added trade with the Middle East, particularly with the oil-rich Gulf Cooperation Council (GCC), whose trade volume with Canada and rate of economic growth virtually matches India's. Based on interviews with various stakeholders and government personnel, the authors find that Canada's government and businesses have a positive image in the region, but that the Canadian government has not maximized its branding of Canada to further positive economic ties. Momani and Antkiewicz point to a number of political impediments that warrant government attention in order to enhance trading relations with the Middle East.

Finally, we look at Canada–Middle East relations from the perspective of interested community groups. Brent Sasley and Tami Jacoby turn to the sensitive and under-studied issue of the relationship between domestic lobby groups and Canadian foreign policy. In particular, they examine the question of how to assess the effect of Canada's pro-Israel Jewish organizations and their pro-Palestinian Arab counterparts on Canada's foreign policy toward the Middle East, broadly, and the Israeli-Palestinian issue, specifically. Jacoby and Sasley point to an empirical void and weakness in the academic literature on the issue, despite formal and informal presumptions about the relative influence of the Canadian Jewish lobbies in particular, and suggest the need for an improved conceptual framework and for more research to assess this important subject.

Nergis Canefe examines Canada's refugee policy and points to the need for Canadian policy makers to take greater notice of this neglected group. Refugees from the Middle East have different concerns and experiences in Canada than their immigrant brethren. Having escaped authoritarian regimes and civil wars, refugees from the region want to raise public awareness of human rights violations in the Middle East through refugee advocacy groups and legal frameworks. However, immigrants from the Middle East fear that airing out the Middle East's dirty laundry will stimulate racism toward their ethno-religious groups. Canefe suggests that organized political groups in Canada that represent Middle Eastern immigrants are not as helpful in raising Canadian understanding of the political situation in the region as refugee advocacy groups are. She calls for a more reciprocal flow of information between policy makers and refugees, which would provide the former with a better understanding of the socio-political realities of the Middle East and lead to sounder refugee determination judgments.

Our hope is that this book will be of value to academics, students, policy makers, journalists, and businesspeople who are interested in Canada–Middle East relations. While the contributors' papers have been rigourously challenged by their peers and the editors, the views expressed in this collection are certainly the authors' own. We hope that the chapters contained herein will stimulate new debates and ideas in a controversial policy field that has been neglected for far too long. At the Centre for International Governance and Innovation, we strive to identify and contribute policy relevant ideas to advance global governance. No region presents bigger challenges to global peace and good governance than the Middle East.

Note

1 See Michael Friscolanti and Danylo Hawaleshka, "The Long Road Home," *Maclean's*, July 31, 2006.

Practitioners' Perspectives on Canada–Middle East Relations[1]

Canadians are widely respected internationally, as much for how they live with each other at home as for what they do abroad. Canada is seen as a successful, democratic, and pluralistic society with a strong rule of law, a country that values diversity and that integrates minorities as well as or better than any other country. Internationally, Canada's history as an independent voice, without colonial or imperial encumbrances, and its record of constructive mediation and the promotion of international law are part and parcel of its diplomatic identity. Among Israelis and Arabs alike, Canada has long been perceived as impartial and open-minded. Canada's ability to maintain good relations with both Israelis and Palestinians, as well as with other Arab partners, has been one of the keys to its standing in the region. Recently, however, some observers of Canadian policy have begun to wonder whether its influence is diminishing.

The purpose of this chapter is to re-examine the longstanding relationship between Canada and the countries of Middle East. It also discusses opportunities for strengthening Canadian diplomatic, economic, and security relations with the region. Four practitioners, with ample experience in Canada–Middle East relations and issues, provide insights into what they consider to be the strengths and weaknesses of Canada's ties with the region. They also provide recommendations on how best to contribute to the peace process and to strengthen Canadian relations with individual Middle East countries. The four practitioners are Michael Bell, former Canadian ambassador to Israel, Egypt, and Jordan; Michael Molloy, former Canadian ambassador to Jordan and former Peace Process Envoy; David Sultan, former Israeli ambassador to Canada; and Sallama Shaker, former Egyptian ambassador to Canada.

The Experience of Michael Bell, Former Canadian Ambassador to Israel, Egypt, and Jordan

Michael Bell holds the opinion that Canada's traditional approach to the Arab-Israeli issues can best be described as fair-minded. This refers to a foreign policy dating back to former Canadian prime minister Lester Pearson in the 1960s and is based on the promotion of Canadian values including tolerance, democracy, respect for diversity, and the rule of law. Bell believes that to describe Canada's role in the Middle East as neutral or even even-handed would indicate an abandonment of any value-based position. Fair-minded-ness is a better term, as it contains an element of morality wherein one makes conscious judgments. Fair-mindedness as a Canadian leitmotif has been well understood and accepted by the parties in the region.

Historically, Canada has sought to recognize the need for a legitimate and independent state for the Palestinians and a secure and peaceful Jewish state for the Israelis. In doing so, it has long called for the protection of civilians on both sides and supported the right to self-determination for both peoples. Canada has also been a strong proponent of negotiation over the resort to force.

Bell observes that Canadian approaches to the Middle East have evolved over the past several years. The perception of change in Canadian policy exists among the parties in the Middle East and on the domestic front because of altered voting patterns at the United Nations on issues related to Israel and Palestine. These changes were initiated by the Martin government and have been continued by Prime Minister Stephen Harper. The votes in the United Nations General Assembly (UNGA) on the Middle East have traditionally been seen as one of the few areas where Arab states could legitimately vent their frustration. The language of the resolutions was frequently confrontational but ultimately accepted by Canada because of the deemed validity of a given resolution's substance. In opposing this confrontational tone, Canada now votes against or abstains on certain key texts, most often in the limited company of Israel, the United States, and Australia. Notably, Canada has voted against a text recognizing the Palestinian right to self-determination. This change in approach also extends to other fronts: for example, government representatives have in public referred to Palestinian "aspirations" rather than Palestinian "rights." Given the evolution of rights language in the current era, this change in terminology has for many an archaic feeling that suggests regression.

Bell believes that Canada's involvement with the Refugee Working Group (RWG) should be highlighted as an important historic success in Canadian foreign policy. Canada's involvement with the Palestinian refugee issue began at the 1991 Madrid peace conference. This was followed by an international conference in Moscow in 1992 aimed at finding practical solutions to regional problems, including that of Palestinian refugees. Chaired by Canada, the RWG was formed to discuss ways of improving the living conditions of refugees and displaced persons without prejudice to their rights and future status, to support the process of achieving a viable and comprehensive solution to the refugee issue, and to ease and extend access to family reunification. The RWG achieved considerable success, which today serves as the basis for virtually all discussions on the issue.

Looking at Canada's role in Afghanistan, Bell believes that Canada has played a constructive role by investing considerable resources in post-conflict reconstruction initiatives. In terms of resource allocation, Canada's effective disengagement from the failing Iraq enterprise has provided the flexibility and resources necessary to enable substantial involvement in peace operations in Afghanistan. Although not geographically part of the Middle East regional security dimension, the continuing conflict in Afghanistan has had a far-reaching and destabilizing effect on the broader Middle East. The Canadian presence in that country, as part of a mission sanctioned by the UN and led by the North Atlantic Treaty Organization (NATO) to help build a stable and pluralistic society, has given that venture enhanced international legitimacy. This is in marked contrast to the unilaterally imposed American actions in Iraq. As part of its mission in Afghanistan, Canada assumed responsibility for the Kandahar Provincial Reconstruction Team (PRT) in August 2005, which, while a riskier proposition than its previous engagement, is essential if there is to be any chance of stabilizing the country. Without security the Afghan state will fail.

Bell believes that Canadian leaders need to focus on cultivating relationships with Middle Eastern and western counterparts and developing the human ties and trust necessary to be effective in its engagement. Canada's presence in the region can be lethargic. Canada must be more determined. For example, the dialogue fund established by the Canadian International Development Agency (CIDA) had great potential to be used as a bridge-building tool between Palestinians and Israelis at a critical time, but the fund was never used during Bell's last period of duty in Tel Aviv (1999–2003). It was subject to a time-consuming and politically costly redesign at CIDA headquarters in Ottawa. If Canada is to be a player in the region, this sort of opportunity cannot be missed.

Bell notes the ease of rhetoric in contrast to the long and arduous nature of working on the ground. As ambassador, he always tried to instill a strong sense of focus and purpose, beyond a diplomatic mission's standard functions. He tried to challenge his embassies' teams to think about the broader meaning and purpose of Canada's role in the region. For instance, the embassy in Egypt had a large aid and development assistance presence that he sought to adjust to focus on promoting pluralism as a basic human right. He warns, however, that if not carefully calibrated, such activities risk edging toward a type of neo-colonialism, similar in substance to the current American administration's economic and political agenda for Iraq, even if on a much smaller scale. For this reason, Bell prefers to use the term "pluralism" to describe Canada's engagement in regional democratization. "Pluralism" is a less threatening word and broader in scope than democracy, yet it is a prerequisite to achieving full democracy—a process that can take many decades.

Bell firmly believes that Canada can play a more constructive role as promoter of peace and development in the Middle East. He argues that Canada's policy should focus on a clear and realizable agenda that includes refugees and peace building. Canada continues to enjoy, to a considerable degree, the confidence of states in the region.

He points out that few international players are undertaking substantial work on the issue of refugees in the region. Although a number of organizations are willing to participate in some form of activity, few are doing any serious planning. The first frank, open, and serious discussion on the refugee issue did not occur until December 2000, and yet the refugee issue has still to be properly addressed as part of Israeli-Palestinian peace negotiations. Latest estimates of the number of Palestinian refugees in the region have been put at 4.4 million, most living in neighbouring Jordan, Lebanon, and Syria. This includes 1.7 million Palestinians displaced in 1948 and 1967 from Israel proper, who are registered refugees in Gaza and the West Bank with the United Nations Relief and Works Agency for Palestine Refugees in the Near East (UNRWA). Canada, with interested countries, has sought to find practical solutions to this predicament. It has acknowledged that the plight of refugees depends heavily on the ability of the warring parties, with the assistance of the international community, to find a solution to the conflict.

Despite the challenges that have hampered Canada's engagement in the region, the former diplomat strongly believes that Canada now has an opportunity to reassert itself as a serious partner in the peace process given the dire situation in Gaza. If Canada can establish itself as fair-minded and trustworthy in the view of both parties, it could play an important role. Bell argues that Canada's position should not be modelled after that of the United States. Similarly, Canada should not aspire to be seen in the region as a supporter of either the United States or, for that matter, the European Union (EU) countries. Rather, Canada should act as an independent third party with the expertise, determination, and staying power to support those who take risks for peace.

Canada's ability to play a constructive role in the Middle East peace process depends on a determined agenda based on clear policy priorities and values. If Canada fails to communicate its ability to engage on the issues and cannot look beyond domestic interests, it risks losing credibility on the international stage as both a leader and a serious player. Michael Bell believes that Canada has a clear national interest in doing so and that includes promoting the values of freedom and justice, supporting international development, protecting energy supplies on the world market, meeting the terrorist threat, and ensuring global security.

The Experience of Michael Molloy, Former Canadian Ambassador to Jordan and Former Peace Process Envoy

Like Michael Bell, Michael Molloy believes that Canada's policy in the Middle East has shifted in recent years. While he agrees that it may not have shifted definitively and that the longstanding fundamentals are intact, he sees a more pro-Israel stance. Certainly, that is the perception in Israel and in the Arab countries. Changes in the Canadian voting pattern at the UN may well have important and valid messages at their core, but resolutions have been notoriously unbalanced at least insofar as they singled out only Israel. Canada's problems in trying to influence the annual resolutions have been compounded by the EU's efforts to speak with one voice in New York, which had the effect of excluding Canada and other non-European western countries from the negotiating table, and leaving Canada in a "take it or leave it" situation.

According to Molloy, Canada's shift away from a long-established voting pattern—especially regarding votes on issues that had not changed over the years but were still germane to the conflict, such as UNGA resolution 61/119 on Israeli practices affecting the human rights of the Palestinian people—has sent a message. However, the message perceived by Arab and most other governments at the UN, and by the public, has not necessarily been the message Canadian policy makers intended to send. The conflict in the Middle East is fought as much with symbols as it is with guns. The annual UNGA Middle East resolutions are among the most important of these symbols. When these change, as in the case of Canada's shifting voting pattern, the results, shorn of nuance and explanation, are telegraphed as far as the remotest refugee camp. In the Middle East words matter, as George Schultz noted. Consequently, when the words change, countries such as Canada have little control over the new meanings at the point of reception. It may well be that the reasons for the change in voting pattern are carefully laid out in Canada's Explanation of Votes, but few people on the planet have ever heard of an EOV, let alone had the opportunity to read one. Nor have even attentive audiences, particularly at the UN, found them persuasive.

Canadian policy with regard to the Middle East conflict has deep roots. It began with the horror Canadians felt at the fate of so many of European Jews in the Second World War. It is easy to lose sight of the fact that in 1948 Canada identified itself internationally and primarily as a member of the Commonwealth and the British Empire, that the process of decolonization had scarcely begun, and that the notion of (mostly) European people colonizing the territory of another (so long as the territory was not in Europe) was still perceived as part of the nature of things.

Molloy believes that over the long term, the perception of the relative merits of Israelis versus Palestinians and Arabs appears to have evolved differently in North America than it has in Europe. An element of primal sympathy for Israel seems to be common to the North American perception. This sympathy has resulted in muted reactions to Israeli acts that would otherwise be loudly criticized by North American governments and people. The Europeans, on the other hand, have been much more willing to take Israel publicly to task for the consequences of their occupation of the West Bank, East Jerusalem, and Gaza.

What Canada's Foreign Affairs department has characterized as a fair-minded approach to the Israeli-Arab conflict began during the Mulroney era in the 1980s, when Joe Clark was foreign minister, despite Mulroney's staunchly pro-Israeli stance. Clark, who as prime minister in 1979 had had to backtrack on an election promise to move the Canadian embassy from Tel Aviv to Jerusalem, went to great lengths to master the Middle East file. Consequently he was confident enough in his judgment to be willing to disagree publicly with Israeli leaders and to reflect this in Canada's UN votes when he believed the Israelis were in the wrong.

The trajectory established by Clark was largely maintained during the Chrétien years. For example, when the Israelis sent agents in 1997 to assassinate Hamas official Khalid Mishal in Jordan under the cover of forged Canadian passports, the Canadian government reacted with a vigour that took the Israelis by surprise. Canada recalled its ambassador from Tel Aviv and restored normal relations only when the Israelis undertook to refrain from using Canadian documents in the future.

The process of changing longstanding Canadian voting positions at the UN began during the Martin government and attracted considerable attention. At the same time, and less well known, was the launching of a well-coordinated "all of government" approach to assistance to the Palestinians. This involved a concerted effort to bring to bear the expertise of eight to ten Canadian departments and institutions on strengthening Palestinian institutions in key sectors, including justice and border administration. This initiative seems to have ended with the election of the Hamas government in 2006 and has not been taken up under the Harper government.

It is difficult to generalize how Canadians as a whole regard the Arab-Israeli conflict, but polling by the Canada-Israel Committee some years ago indicated a shift away from "we support Israel" to "we support peace." Interestingly, in Norway, a country that has played an important role in the Middle East, the public has gone one step further: from "we support Israel" to "we support peace" to "we support the Palestinian underdogs."

Molloy points out that Canada is not a superpower and cannot expect to be a major player in the Middle East. Nonetheless, it is critically important for Canadian security and domestic harmony that Canada be seen to play an effective role rooted in Canadian values. With a large and ever-growing Arab and Islamic population (attracted primarily by Canada's reputation of fairness, rule of law, and pluralism), it is essential that Canadian foreign policy on Middle Eastern issues be one with which this new population can identify. This is critical if this complex community is to be fully and peacefully integrated into the Canadian body politic. While this does not entail abandoning Israel, it does require a clear commitment to the creation of a viable Palestinian state, with all that that entails, as well as fair-mindedness in both Canada's declaratory policy and in the programs and projects it funds and executes in the region. It also requires that Canada hold both sides up to the same high standards of conduct that it expects of itself and its other friends.

To realize how Canada's domestic and foreign policy interests vis-à-vis the Middle East are intimately entwined, one need only look at how the promising relations between Canadian Arab and Jewish communities were dashed with the commencement of the Second Intifada, or look at how the satisfaction and comfort Arab immigrants had felt in Canada was compromised in the wake of September 11. The discontent, violence, and frustration that characterize much of the Middle East at present is not only brought home via television broadcasts, but also in the form of refugees, displaced people, and (unless we are lucky) terrorism.

Molloy stresses that while Canada may not be a superpower, it is also not irrelevant. The country has enormous moral authority, an enviable reputation, and a highly talented population. There is a myriad of issues requiring leadership rather than power, and there are numerous examples, large and small (e.g., landmines, human security), where Canada has managed to have a profound impact in the face of superpower indifference or even opposition. Canada's diplomats, its development community, and its non-governmental organizations (NGOs) have a talent for identifying critical niches and addressing them with an efficacy few can match. It matters enormously that the government itself has a clear sense of what it wants to accomplish. Unfortunately, Canadians also have a talent for hiding their light under a bushel. For example, the many solid accomplishments racked up by a potent partnership of government institutions, academics, and NGOs during the 15 years since Canada was charged with responsibility for the Palestinian refugee file under the multilateral peace process has rarely been exploited for the purposes of mainstream Middle East diplomacy.

With respect to opportunities for Canadian involvement in the Middle East, Molloy argues that to some extent Canada's leverage depends on the perception of its distinctiveness from the United States. Reality requires a reasonable degree of consultation and, occasionally, coordination with the Americans, but there is no payoff for Canada in being too closely associated with the United States. This is not about anti-Americanism; it is about the usefulness and broad appeal of a distinctive Canadian "brand."

Molloy observes that a large source of frustration in serving in the Middle East is a lack of interest on the part of the Canadian business community in the region. This lack of interest stems from factors such as proximity to other larger, safer, more predictable, and more accessible markets in, for example, the U.S. or in Asia and Europe. In some parts of the Middle East, the private sector and supporting legal and financial infrastructure are poorly developed or open to manipulation, to the disadvantage of foreigners trying to do business. Countries such as Jordan, Syria, and Egypt continue to lose out to the more savvy and entrepreneurial regimes in the Persian Gulf. In addition, small business people in Canada are often discouraged by the perception that the whole of the Middle East is simply unsafe.

Few Canadians realize how important the Middle East and the Islamic world have become as a source of immigrants—although the need to evacuate tens of thousands of Canadian citizens from Lebanon delivered a rather complex set of messages to Canadians during the summer of 2006. Despite the problems (including even overt discrimination) faced by immigrants in North America since September 11, overall the Arab immigrant experience in Canada is positive and Canada remains the destination of choice for Middle Easterners seeking to emigrate, find refuge, study abroad, or acquire the security of a second, respected nationality and passport. There are also sizable expatriate Canadian communities (of both local origin and otherwise) throughout the Arab and Islamic world from Morocco to Iran.

As part of its humanitarian tradition, Canada prides itself on playing a leading role in protecting refugees and people in need of protection. Canadian values and interests have been well represented in multilateral and bilateral international forums including those relating to human rights and refugee protection. Canada takes more than 20,000 refugees annually, a large portion of them originating in the Middle East and Africa.

Molloy argues that one of the real impediments to resolving the refugee situation is the issue's deep roots in both the Israeli and Palestinian identities. Complicating matters even more are the myths and taboos surrounding the issue that make rational discussion and dialogue, even within each society, painful, dangerous, and difficult. It is widely recognized that the Palestinian national identity was formed by the refugee experience and the belief that blame for their plight rests exclusively with Israel. For their part, the Israelis' assertion that they bear no responsibility for the creation of the refugee problem is summed up in the expression "Israel was not born in sin." Both the Palestinians and the Israelis must come to a new understanding of what really happened in the past and what is realistically attainable in the future. This requires a huge investment in time and the creation of negotiation processes and safe places for real, respectful, but frank discussion. In order to move forward it will be crucial for the Palestinians to think about the problem with their heads and the Israelis to do so with their hearts. Canada can fill an important gap by facilitating and promoting this dialogue and understanding between and among Palestinians and Israelis as a sensitive, non-judgmental, and fair-minded third party.

Aside from its capacity as a peace broker and facilitator in the Middle East, Canada has a role to play in promoting and assisting immigrants of Middle Eastern origin to integrate more fully into Canadian society. The government can help strengthen the effectiveness of existing policies by analyzing the adjustment process of recent immigrants to Canada and promoting the effective integration of permanent immigrants and by working with immigrant advocacy groups and communities to further integration within the mainstream society. The Afghan community, for example, has shown remarkable initiative and an amazing ability to build alliances with other institutions, including Canadian churches. Canada needs to encourage public engagement and capacity-building initiatives with immigrant communities.

Regarding Palestinian asylum seekers, Molloy noted that there have been calls by some advocacy groups to facilitate the admission of a particular group of Palestinian refugees, despite longstanding opposition by Palestinian leaders to the migration of their people. The background of the group provides an interesting illustration of just how complex matters have become. John Manley, on his first trip to the Middle East in 2001 as Canada's foreign minister, publicly suggested that Canada might resettle some Palestinian refugees as part of a comprehensive peace agreement. This prompted enormous anger in various refugee camps where protest rallies were organized and people were asked to sign pledges not to immigrate under any circumstance. (One group made a polite request to the Canadian office in Ramallah for a Canadian flag they could burn.) Despite or perhaps because of the outcry, within six weeks of Manley's statement, young Palestinians began appearing at the border between New York and Quebec, responding to what they perceived as his offer. Sadly most were rejected by the Refugee Board of Canada.

Michael Molloy is of the opinion that Canada's effectiveness as a peace broker in the Middle East can be enhanced if it allocates resources, develops clear objectives, and ensures that federal departments work together. Canadian officials must also have the courage to make more use of unconventional forms of diplomacy, like "track two" activities, which engages local academics, think tanks, NGOs, and other civil society institutions in addition to government representatives. The Canadian experience in working on the Palestinian refugee issue over the last decade and a half shows that Canada has the credentials and the skills to work successfully on complex and controversial problems.

The Experience of David Sultan, Former Israeli Ambassador to Canada

David Sultan argues that the so-called shift in Canadian policy in the Middle East should actually be perceived as a shift toward neutrality. He argues that an examination of the history of Canada's voting record at the UN reveals that Canada has tended to support Arab-drafted resolutions that criticized Israel. This was not even-handedness. Recently, however, Canada has instead abstained from Arab-drafted UN votes, arguably indicating a shift toward real even-handedness.

Despite Canada's own internal discourse regarding the question of whether Palestinians have rights or aspirations to statehood, the reality is that these terms have no practical importance when the international community, including most Israelis and Palestinians, are speaking about a two-state solution. People are speaking about establishing two states through a negotiated peace process. Israel, however, also needs a viable peace partner. To most Israelis the Hamas-led government has proved that it is not a peace partner and that it fundamentally threatens the existence of Israel. A two-state solution is the ultimate goal, but the state of Israel must preserve its Jewish identity. This clearly raises the issue of Palestinian refugees, and Sultan, like many Israelis, argues that these refugees should not return to Israel and distort its character as a Jewish state, but rather that Palestinian refugees should return to their own prospective state. Again, this is important to ensure the future of a two-state solution: a Jewish state in Israel and an Arab Palestine.

In terms of the success of Canadian Middle East foreign policy, Sultan refers to the countless economic agreements ratified between Canada and Israel designed to promote trade and investment. In the fall of 1996, he found himself lobbying for the ratification of the Canada-Israel Free Trade Agreement (CIFTA). This agreement has continued to help boost trade to significant levels (see Chapter 9).

In addition to the economic importance of CIFTA, Sultan also recognizes benefits accruing in a completely different area: the intensification of interaction between Canadians and Israelis. Although far from having exhausted its potential, CIFTA has contributed to Israeli awareness of the importance of Canada's role in North America. Another agreement, having a similar effect, is the Canada-Israel Industrial Research and Development Foundation (CIIRDF). Its program is a modest one, but it did a wonderful job of matchmaking between high technology companies in Canada and Israel, which are now working together to develop new technologies. The CIIRDF has been so successful that the province of Ontario initiated and funded its own program with Israel. Four more provinces are currently in discussions to follow suit, namely Alberta, Manitoba, Quebec, and Newfoundland.

The former Israeli diplomat also recalls some of the challenges presented by past Canadian initiatives and involvements in the Middle East. When Sultan arrived in Canada to take up his role as Israeli ambassador, he assumed, rightly, that his challenge would be to cultivate and develop relations between the two countries by working with the Canadians who represented the various components of the country's multifaceted society.

However, he soon realized that an additional challenge of no lesser importance would be to take home to Israel an understanding that North America consisted of more than the United States. His task was to convince more and more people in Israel that Canada could play a positive role in the region and represented a huge potential for bilateral relations. Even today, much remains to be done in this respect. This undertaking still requires efforts on behalf of both Israelis and Canadians.

Sultan argues that Canada could do much more in terms of bringing the Canadian reality to Israel and defying both the geographical distance and the perception that separates the states. It may well be that the same is true with respect to other Middle Eastern countries as well. Canada must understand the importance of bringing the Canadian reality closer to the countries and people of the Middle East, and must be prepared to allocate adequate resources for the job. During his period of service in Canada, Sultan was not convinced that that was indeed the case.

With regard to peacekeeping, Sultan says that whereas he appreciates the Canadian contribution in this field very much, he regretfully observes that Canada's role in Middle East peacekeeping has diminished over time. In the past, Canada's presence among peacekeeping forces in the region was sizable. During the 1990s, when Israel learned of Canada's decision to withdraw its air force unit from the MFO (the MFO constitutes the force and observers monitoring compliance with the military annex of the peace treaty between Egypt and Israel ratified in 1979), they asked the Canadian government to reconsider. The Canadian government upheld its decision, citing budgetary constraints. Today, according to MFO sources, Canada currently has 29 soldiers stationed between Egypt and Israel in the framework of the MFO.

The Canadian battalion in the United Nations Disengagement Observer Force (UNDOF) between Syria and Israel was withdrawn in 2006. In that case, too, Israel asked the Canadian government to reconsider its decision. Again, the response was negative, this time citing the military commitment in Afghanistan as explanation. There has been no Canadian presence in the forces stationed in the south of Lebanon next to the Israeli border. These actions lead Sultan to believe that Canada's diminishing role in peacekeeping efforts in the region runs contrary to the wish of Canadian policy makers to see Canada play an active role in the region.

In terms of Canada's readiness to allocate the required resources for an active and meaningful role in the Middle East peace process, its record is also less impressive. Sultan notes, on a related point, that while there now appears to be attempts to revive peace efforts, the rise of Islamic extremism in the region and weak leadership on both sides leave little hope of that happening.

Sultan is confident that Israeli-Canadian relations will remain strong, although this bilateral relationship is far from having exhausted the potential in terms of economic and other forms of cooperation. Bilateral relations will continue to develop, as they are based not only on common interests but also on a solid foundation of shared values, such as democracy, the rule of law, and identical or similar views on many issues.

Sultan believes that Canada has many qualities that should contribute to an active, effective, and useful role in the Middle East. It is a major country that has demonstrated much goodwill and decency in its international behaviour, and it has a good reputation in the region. Canada has the will to play an important role in the Middle East, and also has a sense of mission and the resources required for sustaining such a role. All of these qualities combined indicate a strong potential and, yet, what Middle Eastern analysts witness today falls far short of what could be.

In Sultan's view, there are two prerequisites for a successful Canadian role in the Middle East. The first is to avoid controversy and enjoy the confidence of people in the region. The second is to have, and to be ready to allocate, the resources required for an active role. With regard to the first prerequisite, Sultan argues that to this day, by and large, Canada has not been a controversial entity in the eyes of Middle Easterners. During the 1990s, Israel enjoyed a positive experience with Canada as the gavel holder of the RWG. At that time, during the negotiations to promote peace between Arabs and Israelis, the Israeli government often suggested to the Canadian government that they avoid points of disagreement between the two sides, and instead identify and build on points of agreement, even modest ones. Israel encouraged Canada to continue working toward alleviating the plight of refugees while a solution to the conflict was being sought. Indeed, Canada's activities in that area were appreciated by all parties. Good examples of Canadian efforts are the rehabilitation of a refugee camp in the vicinity of Aleppo in northern Syria and the construction of houses in Canada Camp in the city of Rafah.

Beyond the subject of refugees, on a number of occasions in the 1990s Israel suggested that Canada take a leadership role in the region by attempting to build confidence between Palestinians and Israelis and diminish animosity through people-to-people dialogue. The Canadian response was positive, but the realization on the ground was rather modest, largely due to hesitation and inadequate funds. Sultan believes that Canada could do much more: it could have a stronger presence and play a more prominent role in the peace-making process, with more decisive policy and a more sizeable financial budget.

Sultan believes that if the road map to peace, an Arab League initiative, or any other initiative is given a chance, Israelis would welcome a Canadian decision to increase its role in the Middle East. Although he does not believe that it could realistically be one of decisive importance, he stresses that such an increased role would make a positive difference. Sultan suggests that Canada could focus on refugee protection, in particular on the issues of rehabilitation and compensation. With a resumption of the peace process, Canada could resume its work as chair of the RWG. But, even before peace talks resume, Israel would welcome Canada's good office and contributions toward the improvement of the atmosphere between Palestinians and Israelis by contributing creative ideas in the framework of people-to-people activities.

When internal conditions enable the Palestinians to benefit from benevolent cooperation, Canada could play a meaningful role in training members of the Palestinian administration in all aspects of good governance. Indeed, activities in that area would answer an acute need. Specifically, Canada could choose a subject such as vocational education or health services and help upgrade the existing systems. In the 1990s, when the atmosphere between Israelis and Palestinians was more positive, Israel organized courses for hundreds of Palestinians on subjects including agriculture and water management. If conditions were to make it possible once again, trilateral cooperation among Canada, Israel, and Palestine could improve Palestinian conditions through similar courses. The benefits to be derived from such trilateral cooperation would be multiple: improving Palestinians conditions while, at the same time, improving the atmosphere between Israelis and Palestinians, thus contributing to peaceful coexistence between the two peoples.

In terms of international efforts to promote peace in the region, Canada does not form part of the Quartet (which comprises the UN, the US, the EU, and Russia). However, Sultan does not believe that Israel would object to Canada joining this group. In fact, the Israeli government has even made it known to the members of the Quartet that it holds a positive view of Canadian participation. But the Israeli government realizes that the decision is not its to make. For the time being, Sultan suggests that Canada might coordinate its policy with that of the Quartet, and in doing so become more involved in promoting peace in the region. Beyond working to resolve the Arab-Israeli conflict and the Palestinian issue, Canada could usefully contribute to promoting civil society activities. This type of contribution would, in the long run, advance a more representative political reality in some of the countries in the region.

To sum up, Sultan would like to see increased Canadian involvement in the region with a higher profile presence. This would benefit not only Israel, but also the entire Middle Eastern region as well as Canada.

The Experience of Sallama Shaker, Former Egyptian Ambassador to Canada

As Egypt's ambassador to Canada from 2000 to 2004, Sallama Shaker expressed her unequivocal support for Canada's continued and uninterrupted role in the Middle East, dating back to the Arab-Israeli conflict of the 1940s. She has often reflected positively on the role that Canada played during the 1956 Suez war, when Lester Pearson, as secretary of state for External Affairs and later winner of the Nobel Peace Prize in 1957, established the peacekeeping forces, known as the Blue Helmets or Blue Berets, who helped bring about a peaceful end to the crisis.[2] Over time, the Canadian flag became a symbol of peace and fairness in the Arab world.

Shaker notes that as a soft regional power in North America, Canada has been perceived by the Arab world as a multicultural and diverse country that is a strong supporter of human rights and proponent of international law. Canada was among the first North American countries to welcome immigrants from Lebanon, Palestine, Egypt, Morocco, and Tunisia. In 1948, Canada voted in favour of the UNGA resolution 194, in support of the return of Palestinian refugees. And later on, from the 1950s to 2004, Canada played a prominent role in the search for a fair and comprehensive solution to the Palestinian refugee problem, including the adoption of UN Security Council (UNSC) resolutions 242 and 338. She adds that as gavel holder of the multilateral RWG, Canada emphasized the importance of alleviating the plight of the four million Palestinian refugees. In 1994, in collaboration with other donor countries, Canada earmarked assistance for the cause of the Palestinian refugees, for example providing funds to support the Canada Camp, which assisted with the repatriation of Palestinian refugees. These acts, in Shaker's opinion, were carried out on humanitarian grounds—a fact that was very much welcomed by the Arab world and that strengthened the image of both Canada and Canadians in Arab eyes as activists for peace.

Because Canadian policy makers supported UNSC resolutions 242 and 338 and ultimately recognized the Palestinian right to self-determination and the creation of a sovereign, independent, viable, and democratic Palestinian state, Canada earned a respected position in the Arab world. Shaker believes that this enhanced the image of Canada as a peace-loving nation, with a foreign policy based on objectivity and an understanding of the need for human security. Canada also supported UNSC resolutions 446 and 465, which referred to Israeli settlements in the occupied territories as a violation of the Fourth Geneva Convention. Canada was regarded as a pivotal negotiator in the many humanitarian problems arising from the Arab-Israeli conflict and was encouraged to become more involved. Shaker believes that the Arab world was, and continues to be, ready to welcome a stronger Canadian role, as Canada is still regarded as a champion of multilateralism and an honest broker, an image fortified by Canada's decision not to go to war with the U.S. against Iraq.

Shaker believes strongly that Canada has experienced much success in its Middle Eastern foreign policy initiatives. In her opinion, the fact that Canada has no colonizing past and no imperial ambitions has underpinned the success of Canadian foreign development assistance programs. These factors also facilitated Canadian learning about the culture and traditions of the Middle East. The success stories of CIDA programs in Egypt and elsewhere have demonstrated Canada's potential for helping developing countries achieve the UN Millennium Development Goals (MDGs).

Shaker recalls some of the highlights of her time as Egypt's ambassador to Canada. After the tragic events of September 11, 2001, the Muslim diplomatic corps in Ottawa, together with representatives from the Muslim community, spearheaded a campaign to raise awareness about Islam and disseminated factual information about the message of the Quran. The goal was to overcome misconceptions and bring about a better understanding of Islamic values. In March 2002, she spoke at a conference entitled "Beyond the Images" on the need to address the root causes of terrorism, to bridge the gap between the East and West through sustainable dialogue, and to correct misconceptions. The speakers at this conference, which was held in the Canadian Parliament in March 2002, emphasized "the need to work hard on inter-faith dialogue and cross-cultural understanding, maintaining that 'true jihad' was the effort to generate integrity and tolerance, which constitutes the heart of Islam." According to Shaker, the conference was a reminder of the need to reach out to one other and, as one of the speakers asserted, to do so in the spirit of "the genius of Canadian pluralism, reaching out to the world."

This conference was followed by another in 2003, organized by Women Engaging in Bridge Building and titled "Diversity and Islam: Bridging the Gap," which was, in Shaker's opinion, another foundation stone in the a bridge between Canada and the Muslim world. The conference statement echoed the words of Lester Pearson: "We are moving into an age when different civilizations will have to learn to live side by side in peaceful interchange. Learning from each other, studying each other's history and ideals of art and of culture to mutually enrich each other's lives The alternative in this over-crowded little world is misunderstanding, tension, clash, and catastrophe."

These two events were significant in highlighting Canada's multicultural principles and its positive attitude toward Islam and Muslims compared to many other western nations. The construction of a solid foundation for the Egyptian-Canadian relationship was enhanced by the unique understanding by Prime Minister Jean Chrétien, by the importance of Canada's role as a mediator and partner in the peacekeeping efforts, particularly with regard to the refugee problem, and by saying no to the war in Iraq. The last was both a declaration of Canada's full respect for international law and a legacy of its history as a peacekeeper.

With respect to positive developments in Egyptian-Canadian relations, Shaker recounts a time when young diplomats from both countries exchanged visits to learn more about foreign policy and domestic issues. In her opinion, a highlight of the young diplomats' visit in 2003 came when Prime Minister Chrétien welcomed them to his office, assuring them of the excellent relationship between Canada and Egypt and emphasizing Canada's pride in having a dynamic Egyptian community woven into the Canadian fabric. Shaker had the privilege of holding constructive meetings with leading Canadian parliamentarians, including senators Landon Pearson, Marcel Prud'homme, Pierre De Bané, and Mobina Jaffer, who were instrumental in building bridges between Canada and Egypt.

According to Shaker, the presence of 250,000 Egyptian Canadians in Canada has been an important pillar in this relationship. They are the true ambassadors of Egypt to Canada, facilitating the establishment of educational and cultural exchange programs between the two countries. Building such bridges entails explaining the cultural heritage of Egypt as the cradle of civilization and the land of peace. The commemoration of the 50th anniversary of the establishment of diplomatic relations in 2004 began in Toronto and continued in Montreal and Calgary with the opening of the exhibition of "Eternal Egypt," and then returned to Mississauga with an elaborate three-day celebration in a Coptic cathedral. Mayor Hazel McCallion, a Canadian icon, inaugurated the photography exhibition entitled "Common Ground between the East and the West," donated by Canadian photographer Michelle Tremblay. Meanwhile, in Ottawa, the Egyptian Cultural Organization celebrated the occasion and the Egyptian National Association held a special festival at the Canadian Parliament. In recognition of Lester Pearson's legacy of peace, as Egyptian ambassador Shaker dedicated a papyrus scroll in his name and presented medals to veterans of the peacekeeping forces of 1956. All Canadian ambassadors to Egypt over the past 50 years were recognized for their pivotal roles in enhancing relations between the two countries.

Shaker and her Canadian counterpart, Michel de Salaberry, who had been Canada's ambassador to Egypt since 2000, were instrumental in the two countries becoming partners in development. In 2003, a Canadian school was established in Cairo, and 2004 witnessed the foundation of the first Canadian-Egyptian University in Egypt. The university developed its curriculum in collaboration with the University of Alberta, École Polytechnique de Montréal, McMaster University, and Carleton University.

The former Egyptian diplomat worked with CIDA to enhance its human development programs in Egypt, as reflected in the basic education program and the community schools project, which ensure sustainable and equal learning opportunities for girls and boys. It was gratifying, after long sessions and much dialogue, to have CIDA actively collaborate with local communities to eradicate poverty and promote better employment opportunities through small business development. The joint commitment of Egypt and CIDA, as articulated in CIDA's country development program framework (2001–2011), registers the intention to enhance the participation of women in the development process.

This is a very brief account of an ongoing process of collaboration and understanding between these two countries. Shaker maintains that her contribution in consolidating historical relations between the Egyptian and Canadian people could never have been achieved without the full cooperation of the leaders of both countries.

As the first Egyptian female ambassador to Canada, Shaker found it essential to put a human face on all multilateral and bilateral relationships. She travelled to various provinces and reached out to the Egyptian-Canadian communities to underline the image of Egypt as a peacemaker and to enhance the political, cultural, and trade relations between Canada and Egypt. Her interaction with policy makers and Canadian parliamentarians was instrumental in changing the stereotype images of the Muslim world and bringing about a better understanding of the need for a comprehensive solution to the Arab-Israeli conflict, as well as Egypt's pivotal role in the peace process.

In terms of future opportunities for Canada to play a more active role in the Middle East, Sallama Shaker believes that Canada's legacy as a peace-loving nation and as an even-handed mediator, without any colonial history, can be essential to transcending the barriers of fear and psychological phobia that prevent other countries from playing a significant role as mediators and honest brokers in the Middle Eastern conflict. However, given Canada's long-standing legacy as a peacekeeper and a promoter of peaceful resolution of problems, and in light of its more contemporary human security diplomacy, the former Egyptian diplomat believes that Canada can build bridges and restore confidence in its willingness to pursue a well-balanced policy in the Middle East, in fulfillment of its pledge at the UN to support a two-state solution and given the need to promote an enabling environment to achieve sustainable peace in the Middle East. She argues that over the years, Canada has established many strong partnerships in the Arab world, and will continue to do so. The Arab community in Canada could play an important role in enhancing the relationship between Canada and the Arab world, at a time when all are stakeholders in a globalized world.

Conclusion

Canada has been involved in the Middle East since the decision to partition Palestine in 1947. Canada's engagement has been political, economic, and military in character, especially since the Suez crisis of 1956. In the years following the Madrid peace conference in 1991, Canada played a crucial role in the RWG. But over time, partly for budgetary reasons, Canada's military profile has diminished. Domestic issues inevitably preoccupied Ottawa in the 1990s and again this century, with consequences for Canada's prospects of becoming a reliable global player in many international forums.

Arguably, over the past decade, Canada's absolute and relative diplomatic influence in the region has declined. Meanwhile, European states, the Scandinavian states in particular, have played an increasingly active role. Policy makers and academics around the country have begun to ask whether the country has chosen to withdraw from Middle East diplomacy and, if so, whether Canada should—or could—act to reclaim its lost status as a competent peace broker in the region.

Several practitioners and former diplomats who worked on Canadian–Middle Eastern relations have outlined their answers above. They all agree on the need for Canada to become more involved in unlocking the solution to a viable and sustainable two-state solution. They agree that Canada's reputation as an honest broker in the region is still largely intact and can be leveraged if there is the political will to do so.

Note

1 The editors acknowledge the work of Hany Besada in helping to synthesize this chapter based on the co-authors' comments and writings.
2 The Suez war began on October 29, 1956, when Israel, the UK, and France attacked Egypt, after it had decided to nationalize the Suez Canal because the United States and the UK had withdrawn their funding of the construction of the Aswan Dam.

Applying Canadian Principles to Peace and Conflict Resolution in the Middle East

Contemporary Debates

As Canadians seek to define their international role for the early 21st century, they find themselves confronted by divergent visions of their country's identity, values, and fundamental interests. Events in the Middle East—from the war in Iraq to the hostilities between Israel and Hizbullah in the summer of 2006—have a remarkable capacity to sharpen discussions about national interests and purposes. The search for national consensus on foreign policy remains elusive, with advocates of a traditional, liberal internationalist position calling for a balanced or even-handed foreign policy that seeks diplomatic solutions within frameworks imbued with broad, multilateral legitimacy and proponents of a newer, more insistent approach emphasizing military preparedness and support for key allies.

Among advocates of the liberal internationalist vision, Canada's foreign policy identity is that of a principled middle power with strong commitments not only to western and North American alliance structures, but also to the institutions and norms of an emergent United Nations system (Cooper 1997, 19, 75; Keating 1993). Canada's status as a bilingual and multicultural democracy prevents settled attachment to a narrowly defined cultural or linguistic identity, and brings with it a predilection for inclusive universalism within which national values find new expressions as dialogue proceeds in a global context. Domestic commitments to peace, order, and good government correlate closely with external priorities: advancing human security through persistent diplomacy, encouraging respect for international law, supporting humanitarian action, and promoting economic and social development. Canada mediates crises, works for consensus, and—whenever possible—avoids one-sided, bellicose stands. Canada's internal security, in turn, is enhanced by international regard for the "peacekeeping nation."[1]

According to a rival perspective, which we shall hereafter refer to as "neo-conservative," Canada's self-image as a "principled middle power" and "peacekeeping nation" is either outdated or spurious (Granatstein 2007). Contemporary critics of the liberal internationalist model argue that, whatever the merits of past Canadian enthusiasms for mediation, international institutions, lightly armed observer forces, and a generally low-profile approach to conflicted regions such as the Middle East, the time has come for returning to the methods and loyalties of a simpler, pre–Cold War era. The shocking events of September 11, 2001, demonstrate that we live in an unpredictable and dangerous world—a world in which it is impossible to maintain neutrality between rival forces (Segal 2006, 30–31). Canada should therefore define itself in particularistic terms as a western power and prepare to stand with allies in a militarized struggle against international terrorism (Stuart 2007). To be a full and respected partner of more powerful nations—and to guarantee the country's economic and political status in North America and the broader anglophone world—Canada should become preoccupied with pulling its own weight and maintaining a united military and diplomatic front against enemies of liberal democracy. In the search for historical guidance, Canada's engagement in World War I and World War II is more instructive than its role in managing the Suez crisis or in formulating the post–Cold War human security agenda.

Taken together, these two positions do not exhaust the diversity of Canadian foreign policy discourse, nor should either position be construed as monolithic. Each is most appropriately understood as an ideal type—as an intellectual position that, although consistent with categories of international relations and political science, cannot fully encapsulate the many shades of opinion about Canada's role in the world. Nonetheless, debate concerning the continuing relevance of Canada's traditional self-image in an "age of terrorism" has become a mainstay of newspaper op-eds, nightly news programming, and political speech. Increasingly, proponents of the liberal internationalist vision find themselves on the defensive. The reasons for this are many, and at least some credit must be given to the vigour and passion with which advocates of the neo-conservative perspective have articulated their convictions. Whereas the liberal internationalists seek to stay the course by patiently applying diplomatic, political, and economic resources to multilateral peace- and security-building efforts, neo-conservatives underscore new forms of insecurity wrought by the politicization of cultural and religious identities and the proliferation of modern military technologies. In their insistence that the world has changed and that Canadian policy must not remain static or disengaged, exponents of the neo-conservative position have articulated an argument that some Canadians find quite plausible.

Although in many respects the purpose of this chapter is to present a new case for a traditional Canadian policy paradigm, it must be conceded from the outset that the liberal internationalist model is not without weaknesses, among the most notable of which is an imperfect integration of precept and practice (Valpy 2007). With respect to the Middle East in particular, Canada has at times been more concerned with abstaining from new entanglements and keeping a safe distance from battles that are not its own than with the consistent application of a set of national and international principles. Nonetheless, there is considerable scope for a more active and engaged approach—an approach that responds to the urgency of the neo-conservatives without succumbing to their particularism and preoccupation with military solutions.

There is much at stake for Canadians in the turbulent politics of today's Middle East. Contemporary Canadian policy makers face important choices not only between the traditional liberal internationalism and the neo-conservative alternatives, but also between isolationism and proactive engagement. By embracing a recalibrated liberal internationalist vision and electing to play a robustly activist (but non-militaristic) role in the region, Canadian diplomats and civic leaders can update their country's historically emergent strategy for advancing world order values while also responding to new threats and opportunities. What is needed is a clear understanding of how steady work in support of peacemaking in the Middle East is in the Canadian interest, and is best practiced through nonviolent instrumentalities.

Canada and the Middle East: The Ongoing Search for a Suitable Role

What should a country like Canada be doing in a place like the Middle East? Although not often formulated in such terms, this question is implicit in contemporary debates about Canadian policies in the region. It is unfortunate that, in the search for answers, many discussions of national policies quickly become mired in simplified, essentialist views of Canada's historical role and involvement in the region and its conflicts. These discussions seek to identify a consistent foreign policy track record, and propose that past precedents (balanced diplomatic engagement in the case of liberal internationalists, and assertive partiality in the view of neo-conservatives) should determine present policies.

This competition to define past precedents is most evident in debates about the Arab-Israeli-Palestinian conflict, which has been among the region's most internationally salient axes of conflict for well over half a century. As David Taras and David H. Goldberg (1989, 7) argue in *The Domestic Battleground: Canada and the Arab-Israeli Conflict*, Canadian policy toward Israel, the Palestinians, and the surrounding Arab states has been the subject of "fierce domestic battles that have at times shaped aspects of Canada's foreign policy."

Although foreign service officers at the Department of Foreign Affairs and International Trade (DFAIT) have sought to insulate Middle East policy from the vicissitudes of domestic political contestation (while taking implications for Jewish and Arab Canadians into account), recent years have brought new challenges to a tradition of policymaking that is best described as "multi-partial": Canada has been, at various times and sometimes simultaneously, both pro-Israeli and pro-Palestinian or pro-Arab.

At present, many advocates of the neo-conservative position are seeking to reframe Canadian Middle East policy in relation to a "clash of civilizations" or "struggle for democracy" thesis (Warren 2007). Accordingly, they argue that current Canadian policies should accord preferential status to Israel as a country with western roots and a competitive electoral process. To establish the credibility of this position, they point to the decisive role played by Canadian diplomats—including Lester Pearson himself—in the United Nations partition plan of 1947.[2] In contrast, those who argue that Canada should act as an honest broker between Israelis and Arabs—an idea that has come to be associated with liberal internationalism—note that, in addition to its early support for the creation of Israel, Canada was out in front in international efforts to support refugees through the United Nations Relief and Works Agency for Palestine Refugees in the Near East (UNRWA). Pearson's contribution to preventing the escalation of the 1956 Suez crisis is itself a decisive event not only in the formulation of Canada's traditional foreign policy vision, but also in the formation of modern Canada's national identity (Pompa 1970; Melady 2006).

Although neo-conservatives are correct in challenging inaccurate notions of Canadian neutrality toward Middle Eastern conflicts—Canadian multi-partiality appears to be as much a consequence of improvisation and periodic "corrections" as of deliberate design—efforts to redefine Canada as a narrowly partisan player make selective use of history. A close analysis of historical policies reveals that Canada has been on both sides of the Arab-Israeli divide. Canada has been a midwife to Israel and a nurse to Palestinians, an architect of the United Nations Emergency Force (UNEF) in the Sinai and the first country to withdraw support from the Palestinian Authority after Hamas won the elections of 2006. Prime Minister Pierre Trudeau argued against the Israeli invasion of Lebanon in 1982; Prime Minister Stephen Harper acted as a vocal supporter of Israel's summer 2006 offensive against Hizbullah.

A virtue can be made of seeming inconsistencies in Canadian Middle East policy, but the effort to induce principles for policy making from past actions is likely to prove problematic if it is not informed by careful explanations for historical variation, and by reflection on current Canadian values and interests. Historically, Canada became involved in Middle Eastern politics through efforts to act as a mediator between allies with divergent views of regional politics, particularly the United States and the United Kingdom. Canada has also sought to act as a mediator within the alliance of the North Atlantic Treaty Organization (NATO), the Commonwealth, and the UN system, playing a classic "middle power" or "helpful fixer" role (Cooper 1997, 38). Ismael (1973, 12) remarks that, during the decades immediately following World War II, Canada "had, in essence, no Middle East policy beyond a desire for peace and balance"; this policy "evolved as a reaction to the changing relations among its allies and associates, rather than in response to the situation in the Middle East." With the rise of U.S. influence in the region and the decline of European powers such as England and France, Canada's room to manoeuvre as a mediating middle power narrowed, and Canadian policy makers began to take greater interest in social and economic development, trade ties, and humanitarian affairs (Ismael 1994), while seeking a low-profile niche in efforts to advance regional peacemaking through quiet advocacy of an enduring settlement to the painful Israeli-Palestinian conflict. Canada willingly participated in the first Gulf War of 1991, at least partially on the basis of geopolitical expediency (Miller 1994), but in 2003 abstained from the second Gulf War and the "coalition of the willing" for principled as well as pragmatic reasons.

Canada's role in the Middle East is evolving and emergent, not constant. It reflects Canada's journey within a changing international system, as well as shifts within Canada as an increasingly multicultural (and not merely bilingual) nation-state with its own legitimate interests in the region. Allan J. MacEachen's 1983 statement concerning the rationale for Canadian relations with the Middle East remains highly applicable to the present situation:

> Canadians individually and collectively are greatly aided in developing relations with the region by the linguistic duality and the cultural and religious diversity of our country. For example, we share membership in the international French-speaking community with three states of the area: Tunisia, Morocco and Lebanon, and there are several others where French is much used. There are strong adherents in Canada of all three of the great religions which have their spiritual centres in the Middle East. The several Canadian ethnic communities with links to the Middle East and North Africa are intensely interested in the evolution of events in the region. We should be able to build on these varied ties with the area. (MacEachen 1983, 2–3)

Formulations of values and interests to guide Canada's engagement with the Middle East in the early 21st century need not be static. They can draw upon the lessons of past experiences, while incorporating new insights into the nature of contemporary conflict in the region, the character of Canadian domestic society, and insights into the many ways in which Canada's government and civic leaders can "make a difference" in this vital yet increasingly troubled region. Canadians can and should draw inspiration from the diplomatic courage and initiative that accompanied intervention in the Suez crisis, while also seeking new opportunities for relevance that may or may not incorporate aspects of the classical peacekeeping model. Although responding to the Arab-Israeli conflict will remain an important priority, Canada's interests and potential contributions will ultimately need to be defined within a broader regional context.

Values and Interests: Human Security as an Integrative Framework

As Canada seeks a dynamic framework, analysts and policy makers would be well advised to revive and update the human security paradigm of the 1990s. It is unfortunate that, in the Canadian context, the notion of human security has been misunderstood as an invention of the Liberal Party. Jennifer Welsh (2004, 183–86), for example, identifies the human security agenda with the tenure of foreign affairs minister Lloyd Axworthy and sets it aside in favour of a more traditionally state-centric program: supporting weak states to prevent state failure. While there are indeed valid critiques of any program that seeks to replace the national security paradigm with an unrealistically anti-statist or aggressively interventionist approach to human rights protection, the basic objectives and constructs of the human security paradigm are arguably better suited to an age of transnational security threats than approaches to security rooted in realpolitik, military power, and an undisciplined national security state. In the present era, national security and human security have become interdependent and complementary goals, predicated on accountable and empowering domestic governance as well as on an enlightened conception of national interest that recognizes the need for broad-based multilateral cooperation in the formulation and implementation of international economic, environmental, and public safety policies (Homer-Dixon 2001; Kaul, Grunberg, and Stern 1999).

A multilateral approach to international security based on policy coordination through international institutions can be greatly enriched by applying an integrative human security approach to the problems of terrorism and political violence. This framework has a number of virtues: it recognizes that radicalization festers in situations of repression and unresolved conflict; it places a strong emphasis on law enforcement, development, and protection of civilian populations rather than on large-scale (and deeply polarizing) military campaigns; and it affirms the importance of efforts to work toward a uniform standard of human rights, understood to include not only civil and political but also economic, social, and cultural rights. It redirects policy from a narrow focus on empowering state security and military apparatus, toward a more proactive concern with the protection of individual human beings from harm and deprivation (Maclean, Black, and Shaw 2006).

Human security may be a goal that is deeply consonant with Canadian values, but it is not a uniquely Canadian project, nor is implementing the Responsibility to Protect (R2P) the sole or primary expression of human security. Policy literature and expertise on human security are internationally distributed, and provide impetus to innovating thinking about governance and social change as well human rights, violence prevention, sustainability, and development. By emphasizing the need to evaluate security policies in light of overall contributions to the safety and life chances of individuals, the human security paradigm provides an invaluable corrective to over-militarized and repressive state security policies, which are a major affliction in the Middle East and many other world regions beset by political violence. While recent catastrophes in Rwanda and Darfur have focused international attention on R2P and the challenges of humanitarian intervention, the human security paradigm is arguably just as relevant as a basis for comprehensive conflict resolution efforts that include confidence- and security-building measures, mutual security guarantees, movement toward democratic governance, support for human rights, and programs to promote sustainable development. Instead of replacing traditional forms of security analysis, the human security framework underscores the need to conceptualize security within a broader causal and prescriptive context. Rather than diluting conceptions of national or state security, human security calls for greater conceptual clarity about the ends of security policy (enhanced well-being and safety of individual human beings) as well as the means.

If allowed to inform policy thinking and Canada's strategic vision for international engagement, the human security agenda can provide a basis for a richer policy dialogue, as well as for attempts to move beyond the "values versus interests" debate that underpins much of Canadian ambivalence toward a more engaged and proactive Middle East policy. By linking human rights abuses, radicalization, and festering conflict abroad to potential for political violence at home, the human security framework provides a clear sense of how values and interests are connected, while also suggesting constructive policy options far richer than the "fight fire with fire" default position of classical security thinking. From a human security perspective, fire can and should be fought with water whenever possible, as well as with trenches, fire codes, and diverse fire-proofing measures. Terrorism—a human security issue par excellence—comes to be seen not as an autonomous, existential threat to nation-states but as a threat to people, a symptom of a deeply dysfunctional regional and international security system in the greater Middle East region.

Though the neo-conservative perspective is sometimes articulated as a defence of western values—and therefore as a basis for participating in a collaborative international program—its animating vision is polarizing in nature. This significantly limits potential for dynamic, multi-level engagement in regions such as the Middle East. When framed in more concrete terms through an appeal to Canadian interests in North America, neo-conservative prescriptions for active military engagement in theatres such as Afghanistan and Iraq are prone to three forms of miscalculation: (1) overestimating the futility of negotiation, (2) underestimating the potential domestic and international consequences of militarized solutions, and (3) misjudging the likelihood that domestic support for a militarized foreign policy will prove unsustainable, both in Canada and in the domestic politics of major allies such as the United States. Canadian neo-conservatives share with American neo-conservatives the important insight that maintenance or restoration of the status quo will do little to solve the problems of the Middle East, yet the experience of the last several years offers little support for the thesis that democratic transformation or consolidation can be achieved by military means.

There are limits to Canada's capacity to singlehandedly affect policy reform within and toward the Middle East region, yet taking the initiative and leading by example is in Canada's national interest. Canada needs an autonomously defined (rather than subcontracted) Middle East policy every bit as much as its traditional allies do, not only to protect long-term interests and prevent derailment by short-term miscalculations, but also to ensure the peace of domestic multicultural society. A carefully formulated Canadian Middle East policy permits Canada to play a significant middle power role in the region, in ways that are consistent with core Canadian values and ultimately beneficial to allies. Canada's role during the Iranian hostage crisis in 1979 provides an intriguing illustration of an instance when, by representing Canada, Kenneth Taylor was able to advance the interests of U.S. diplomats far more effectively than would have been possible if Iranian revolutionaries had perceived no distinction between the U.S. and its northern neighbour (Thompson and Randall 2002, 265). The world—America included—can benefit more from an autonomous, principled, purposeful Canadian foreign policy than from a rudderless policy that drifts with prevailing winds or lacks a clear destination.

The traumatic events of September 11, 2001, add urgency to the subject of Canadian Middle East policy, but it would be an overstatement to claim that a fundamental shift in nature of international relations has occurred. Post–Cold War policy principles developed during the 1990s, both by Canadians and by transnational policy networks, remain relevant to the search for peace and security in the Middle East and other regions, and to the evolutionary development of Canadian foreign policy. Canadian contributions to international thinking about soft power, global governance, and human security remain relevant, and should be refined rather than discarded.

Strategic Priorities: Preventing Violence and Creating Hope

The recent decline of the liberal internationalist approach to foreign policy has less to do with intrinsic defects—or, as Andrew Cohen (2003) has suggested, insufficient military clout—than with the lack of an energetic vision for updating and applying Canadian principles in the post-9/11 era, particularly in relation to the difficult realities of the Middle East. In the absence of a compelling argument about how Canadian internationalism applies to contemporary dilemmas, imitation and isolationism become more attractive options. Canada's alternatives are not, however, limited to taking sides in a clash of civilizations or wishfully seeking to shield Canada from what might be construed as blowback from decades of problematic foreign policies pursued by great powers and superpowers.

During the last several years, over-militarization of the "war on terrorism" has contributed far more to the destabilization of the Middle East than to the cultivation of a basis for sustainable peace (Heinbecker 2006). The result has been an incoherent policy that enjoins democracy on the one hand, while devaluing negotiation and upholding practices of state repression (including torture) on the other. Although many democratic reformers in the Middle East initially took heart at U.S. president George W. Bush's acknowledgment of past U.S. complicity with oppressive states, turbulence created by the Iraq war has made genuine transformation a more distant goal.

As U.S. intelligence agencies have acknowledged, the war on terrorism (and particularly the choice to invade Iraq) has heightened the appeal of radicalism in many parts of the Middle East (Office of the Director of National Intelligence 2006).[3] Overconfidence in the utility of military force for resolving contemporary problems of non-state political violence has brought increasing turbulence to the region, and has also elevated the level of tension in western multicultural societies. War appears highly ineffective for destroying the taproot of terrorism, particularly insofar as it reinforces the "us versus them" dynamics of contemporary identity conflict and gives an unmerited advantage to historical narratives that grant exclusive weight to Islamic-western rivalry (Funk and Said 2004). It is simply not possible to impose upon the Middle East (or, indeed, the larger Islamic world) a set of political, cultural, and economic solutions that are viewed as inauthentic and humiliating. The resort to military force feeds perceptions of confrontation and injustice, and is ultimately self-defeating. Because of the transnational character of Islamic identity, the escalation of conflict overseas also has negative consequences for inter-religious relations in North America and Europe.

Although intercultural conflict has indeed become part of the contemporary international security environment, talk of an inescapable confrontation obscures the causes of contemporary conflict to which Canadian policy can respond: frustrated aspirations for dignity and change in Middle Eastern societies, historical patterns of misgovernance and human rights abuse, problematic majority-minority relations, a general absence of political space, economic stagnation, and a pattern of asymmetrical, antagonistic relations between western and Islamic peoples.

Among the most important root causes of contemporary Islamic-western strain is a tension between the foreign policy of the most powerful western society, the U.S., and the aspirations of Arab Muslims in the Middle East—historically the most influential identity group within a larger, transnational Islamic community. Efforts on the part of the U.S. to fill a Middle Eastern power vacuum following the withdrawal of colonial powers, combined with a crisis of political development in regional states and a strong U.S. influence on outcomes in the deeply tragic, symbolically charged Israeli-Palestinian confrontation, have been among the more potent determinants of Muslim disaffection in the modern era. These factors, amplified by wars with Iraq and the escalation of Muslim conflicts with western powers in Afghanistan, the Balkans, and Chechnya, have fed radicalization among young Muslims seeking to advance revisionist political objectives that various state actors have been unable to fulfill. The Middle East's many deteriorating conflicts have now begun to feed on one another in a manner that is deeply destabilizing, with wars in Iraq, Afghanistan, and Israel-Palestine exacerbating popular disaffection with compromised government structures and spilling over into conflict-prone environments such as Lebanon.

It is not an exaggeration to state that, in most contemporary Middle Eastern communities, a thick web of political problems and unresolved conflicts creates a deep sense of powerlessness and humiliation. The popularity of conspiracy theories attests to the deep disempowerment that is born of domestic authoritarianism, unaccountable security agencies, economic stagnation, and inability to change unpopular western foreign policies. Unemployment and underemployment have a particularly negative impact on young men in much of the Middle East, and anti-establishment political movements feed upon the resultant despair and hopelessness. When social services and economic empowerment come through participation in radical organizations, the appeal of combative ideas becomes stronger.

Over the long term, one of the most important tasks for peace building is depriving violent extremism of legitimacy. Canada, together with other countries that support international peace building (for example, Japan, Demark, the Netherlands, and Norway), can help to advance this objective by becoming more proactive in its efforts to foster conflict resolution, through efforts to address root causes of conflict as well as through persistent diplomatic engagement premised on consensus building and international law. In a world that has become far too polarized, Canada can help to foster a "third way" that is dynamically progressive, actively multicultural, committed to multilateralism, and supportive of peaceful conflict resolution. Canada's commitment to these principles over the long term is vitally important, and deeply relevant to Canadian security concerns (Standing Committee on Foreign Affairs and International Trade [SCFAIT] 2004).

Prescriptions for a Constructive Canadian Role

Should Canadian leaders seek to revitalize their country's role in Middle East peacemaking, principled independence and alignment with global public opinion will be essential. The complex problems of the Middle East region—as well as the troubled legacy of interactions between the Middle East and the West—can indeed be transformed, but only if there are concerted efforts to foster a new international and regional consensus on conflict resolution, and to create conditions conducive to incremental "change from within" in Middle Eastern states. If Canada embraces this path of dialogue and bridge building, there are several positive steps that can be taken.

1   Strengthen Diplomatic Preparedness

Although federal institutions such as DFAIT, the International Development Research Centre (IDRC), and the Canadian International Development Agency (CIDA) already possess impressive (and sometimes underutilized) expertise on Middle Eastern issues, efforts to develop a more proactive Middle East policy could nonetheless benefit from programs designed to augment cross-cultural diplomatic capacity and deepen specialization. A greater degree of cultural and religious literacy is essential in the diplomatic corps, supported by professional education programs designed to provide deeper historical context for current events, as well as information about multiple voices and political currents in the Islamic world. It is crucial for Canadian officials to have a well-informed, street-level perspective on the complex mix of political frustration and intercultural alienation that feeds radicalization within the region. Ensuring that Middle Eastern diaspora communities are appropriately heard within government policy-making processes is one way to advance this objective.

Diplomatic discourse intended to win trust in Middle Eastern contexts could give increased weight to multiculturalism, multilateralism, conflict resolution, respect, consensus building, and inclusion. The many (past and present) Islamic contributions to western culture could be acknowledged. By granting greater salience to these themes, Canadian diplomacy could more effectively convey a vision that people in the Middle East can relate to and embrace.

2   Reaffirm Multilateralism and Internationally Legitimate Standards

As they formulate policies toward the many inter-communal and international rivalries of the Middle East, Canadian leaders should take care to avoid polarizing discourse (e.g., using terms such as "war for civilization," "axis of evil," or "the enemies of democracy") and the demonization of Islamic movements and parties. The stances taken by the U.S., Canada, and some other countries on the tragically counterproductive Israel-Hizbullah war of 2006, like their rejection of the Hamas victory in Palestinian elections the West had pressed for, have resulted in further loss of political capital for the West (not to mention credibility for democracy) in the Arab Middle East. Canadian influence and ability to offer good offices depend on attempting to act in ways that members of both sides in the region's painful conflicts can recognize as principled. International human rights monitoring organizations may be able to provide helpful guidance in this regard.

Given Canada's limited capacities to affect the policies of Middle Eastern governments directly, there is a need to attend carefully to the messages sent by both words and deeds. Canadian policies need to demonstrate steady commitment to the principles of human rights, human security, and international law (including *jus in bello*). Staying out of the Iraq war was a sound and principled Canadian decision that reinforced the respect with which Canada has traditionally been regarded in the Arab Middle East and the wider Islamic world, and indeed far beyond. Care needs to be taken to preserve that respect and to harness it to constructive diplomacy rather than to risk dissipating it in tilts toward one side or the other in complex and tragic Middle Eastern conflicts where none of the parties is blameless.

The events of recent years demonstrate that the United States, Canada, and other western countries have an interest in working through UN institutions whenever possible to advance key security concerns. Abstention from both involvement in and rhetorical support for military activities that have not received UN approval, or at least that do not enjoy overwhelming support at the UN would be a wise and prudential policy for combating the sense of international lawlessness that feeds radicalization and supports terrorist recruitment. Conversely, a strong Canadian stand on the need for a Middle East free of weapons of mass destruction (WMD) as part of a broader and consistent arms control and disarmament policy could help reinforce the UN's significance and preserve the Nuclear Non-proliferation Treaty.

3   Insist on Negotiated Solutions

Although the government of Canada may not wish to trumpet a willingness to engage with non-state armed groups (be they the adversaries of Canadian forces, as in the case of Afghanistan, or irregulars engaged with the governments of Middle Eastern states), negotiation with insurgent forces is often the only way to put an end to civil and regional wars (Regehr 2006). Denying "radical" groups a chance to develop a stake in the political process can make things worse, not better. Working to integrate these groups into negotiation processes in no way precludes the expression of strong criticisms with respect to past actions taken by members of revisionist movements.

Because radicalism feeds on unresolved conflict, patient efforts to bridge divides are necessary if more moderate political dynamics are to have a chance of succeeding in the region. There is a wide range of regional conflicts that Canadian diplomacy can address, whether publicly or through quiet efforts to foster dialogue. These conflicts include the Arab-Israeli conflict, the conflict within Iraq, hostilities between Palestinian refugees and the Lebanese government, tensions between Kurdish minorities and the states within which they live, conflicts between states and Islamic movements, racialized ethnic conflict in Sudan, ethno-religious tensions in Lebanon and Egypt, and longstanding tensions surrounding the status of the western Sahara. Given Canada's historically "multi-partial" role in the Israeli-Palestinian conflict, Canadian diplomats may find it possible to make unique contributions to dialogue on such "final status" topics as the uncertain destiny and tenuous condition of Palestinian refugees. Canada's francophone diplomatic capacity and vibrant Arab communities may provide a special niche in efforts to address conflicts involving Syria and Lebanon; Canadian federalism and bilingualism, in turn, provide a helpful comparative case that can be brought to the fore when facilitating "track two" and "track one and a half" dialogues among stakeholders in regional conflicts.[4]

4 Support Change from Within

Fostering incremental change from within in the Middle East is among the most vital tasks facing western nations as they seek to adjust and redefine relations with the region. Canada and other western countries can best support positive internal developments by promoting political participation within structures appropriate to the needs and culture of the people, and not by unreflectively promoting the transplantation of western models or supporting authoritarian regimes.

By shaping the conditions within which internal debates proceed, western policies have exerted a significant—but often unrecognized—impact on prospects for democracy in the Middle East. Insofar as past policies have turned a blind eye to repressive practices and to the suffering associated with major regional conflicts, western powers have inadvertently helped to create conditions that are favourable to anti-liberal, reactive action. More recent policies linking democratization to the Iraq war have been even more problematic, fostering the impression that democracy is a Trojan horse for western conquest and political manipulation.

This impression is quite damaging, as democracy in Middle Eastern countries must grow from local soil, and be nourished by the aspirations of local citizens. Although regional democratic projects may derive important ideas and insights from western practices of democracy, their language and forms of expression will reflect regional culture and Islamic values. As Jeremy Jones has argued, democratic change will stand the best chance of success in the Middle East if it is conceived as a genuinely indigenous enterprise:

> Democracy in the Middle East may not only be possible, it may already be under construction. In the diverse institutions and conversations, the traditions and experiments with which the people of the region conduct their daily lives, manage their social relations and organize their politics there might be all kinds of practices that ought to be recognized as democratic in nature. It may be these practices, rather than those that have developed in the West ... that will form the foundations for the further development of democratic political institutions. (2007, 5–6)

By becoming sensitized to ongoing experiments with democratic change in Middle Eastern countries, western policy makers stand a much better chance of finding means to strategically nourish change from within.

Despite their differing cultural and religious heritage, industrialized nations can indeed assist Middle Eastern efforts to develop authentic democratic forms that respect Islamic precepts, by expressing support for regionally grounded approaches. In addition, it is worth pointing out that while some grievances of Islamic movements are widely shared, others are highly localized. We should not repeat the errors of the Cold War, by painting all movements with the same brush or adopting a totalizing agenda of ideological confrontation. Instead, the goal should be to disaggregate and address local conflicts, and thereby reduce the appeal of transnational extremism.

5 Leverage the Soft Power of Multiculturalism

One of Canada's greatest assets in the Middle East is still the soft power of the Canadian example. Although much has changed since March 2004, SCFAIT made many valuable points on this theme in its report entitled "Exploring Canada's Relations with the Countries of the Muslim World." Among many Middle Eastern Muslims, Canada still represents the best of the West—political pluralism, tolerance, and opportunity—without the political baggage associated with countries such as the U.S. and the UK (SCFAIT 2004, 29, 33).

To support democratic change and human rights abroad effectively, Canada and other countries in the western cultural sphere have a strong interest in practicing what they preach on matters pertaining to cultural and religious diversity. Fortunately, Canada's historical commitment to multiculturalism gives it an important resource that can be utilized in the effort to engage Middle Eastern publics, so long as policies remain free from anti-Muslim or western exclusivist rigidities. Advocates of Canadian multiculturalism need to be articulate about the values upon which their efforts are based (recognition, dialogue, equality, pluralism), which culminate in a principled respect for others and commitment to coexistence.

Because diaspora links are strong, a visitor to the Middle East should not be surprised to meet taxi drivers, business people, and middle class professionals with relatives in Toronto or Chicago, and who may well have developed a positive view of North America insofar as relatives abroad have encountered economic and educational opportunity, rule of law, and freedom of religious expression far more consistently than prejudice, exclusion, or corruption. Though U.S. (and increasingly Canadian) foreign policies are indeed a source of grievance and concern, the importance of immigrant experiences in shaping Muslim perceptions of the West should not be underestimated.

6 Facilitate Transnational Alliances

Deliberate efforts to increase scholarly and professional as well as youth contact have the potential to significantly enhance Canadian understanding of the Middle East and vice versa, while also expediting the construction of transnational alliances and networks. Visible partnerships across cultural, religious, and political divides are not a panacea for complex political conflicts, but they symbolize goodwill and prefigure the possibility of peace. They are an invaluable corrective for the sort of groupthink that led to damaging and counter-productive post-9/11 policies in the U.S., and their mere existence helps to undermine the "us vs. them" logic that threatens to shred the fabric of contemporary societies, with their deep-rooted cultural, ethnic, and religious pluralism.

Given the role that misappropriated religious symbols play in current conflict dynamics, the Canadian Government faces a dilemma. On the one hand, any Canadian Government would have great difficulty representing the diverse beliefs and non-beliefs of Canadians, and government-sponsored interreligious dialogue efforts could undermine the principled autonomy that gives religious outreach initiatives their value and legitimacy. On the other hand, Al Qaeda's support correlates with the belief that Islam is under attack in the post-9/11 era, and it makes sense to actively seek civil society perspectives on policies that have the potential to either feed or ameliorate disaffection among Middle Eastern publics (Lynch 2003). Structured consultations with civil society actors involved in transnational dialogue can allow government officials to gain new insights into possible impacts of policy decisions, and can provide a means of accessing the views of Muslims who are broadly affirmative of both Western and Islamic aspects of their own identities, and who are capable of thoughtfully critiquing actions taken in the name of both Islam and the West:

7 Form Peace and Development Partnerships among Governments, Universities, and Civil Society Actors

As policy makers consider ways of reviving public diplomacy and expediting people-to-people linkages, government officials may wish to consider increasing support for projects that promise to develop international partnerships among universities and civil society actors. Partnerships could focus on a range of potential topics, including development, human rights documentation, preparation for government service, human security, international law, refugee support (Iraqi as well as Palestinian), cluster bomb removal (in the case of Lebanon in particular), journalism, peace building, ecology, sustainable agriculture, regional security systems, social development, and interfaith dialogue. Such programs would underscore the importance of intercultural communication and cooperation in a world that needs principled bases for action by members of diverse groups.

With their diverse and highly international student bodies, universities are living laboratories for intercultural dialogue and experiential learning. In addition to their functions in the domain of research and knowledge dissemination, universities have the potential to become resource centres for peace-building efforts, as well as forums for convening policy dialogues and fostering skill development. Universities have a vital role to play in contemporary peace efforts, both as forums for domestic and transnational dialogue and as institutions that equip future professionals with the tools they need to engage interculturally while pursuing careers in development, conflict resolution, public policy, and diplomacy. Efforts to support the field of conflict resolution in regions such as the Middle East and South Asia through university-to-university partnerships may bear more fruit than those sponsored directly by government-affiliated foundations; the same partnerships could also bear fruit for Canadian universities seeking to enhance expertise in the area of Middle Eastern studies.

Conclusion

Since September 2001, it has become commonplace for analysts to suggest that western relations with the Middle East have reached a point of crisis. On the one hand, the momentum of current events appears to be leading toward heightened conflict and violence, and the policies of nations outside the region appear to be making greater aggregate contributions to radicalization than to reconciliation. There is a very real danger that, by acting on superficial and unbalanced readings of Middle East politics, western nations will increase the risks of state failure in the region and entrap themselves in an escalatory and open-ended cycle of asymmetric conflict with non-state actors. On the other hand, the unsustainable nature of the status quo is challenging those who formulate western Middle East policies to revisit, rethink, and re-imagine their role in efforts to prevent systemic breakdown and cultivate constructive dynamics. The Canadian liberal internationalist tradition offers important resources for such efforts, and is most likely to bear fruit if policy makers build upon and extend this legacy by embracing the goals of the human security paradigm and creatively exploring new ways of engaging Middle Eastern realities.

Canada's capacity to act alone is quite limited, but the country's historical prestige as a middle power committed to multilateralism and peacemaking places diplomats in an excellent position to formulate an independent, principled Middle East policy that allows the country to exercise leadership (Byers 2007). Some of the policies suggested here may require willingness to accept short-term political risks in exchange for a hope of long-term benefits. Yet the alternatives of temporary (and unsustainable) isolationism or partisan entrapment in escalating regional conflict are even more unattractive. Given Canada's past significance in Middle East politics and the considerable reserves of regional expertise in government and civil society, there is no reason to believe that Canada cannot reassert itself with effectiveness and impact.

There are many creatively pragmatic options available to resourceful Canadian diplomats and policy makers—options through which Canada can join other nations in taking meaningful steps toward goals that are vitally important. While no single policy initiative is likely to dissipate culturally charged political confrontations that have been in the making for many years, it is never too late to reclaim and augment the best elements of Canada's foreign policy tradition.

Notes

1 For an explication of the origins of Canada's liberal internationalist tradition, see Keating (1993) and Dewitt and Kirton (1983, 17–28, 48–58). Although Dewitt and Kirton are attentive to what they regard as historical departures from liberal internationalist principles, the paradigm itself remains remarkably vibrant in Canadian national identity and foreign policy thinking (see also Kirton 2007, ch. 3).

2 For details on Canada's role in the partition of Palestine, see Ismael (1994, 10–13).

3 Now-declassified sections of the National Intelligence Estimate produced by U.S. intelligence agencies read as follows: "We assess that the Iraqi jihad is shaping a new generation of terrorist leaders and operatives; perceived jihadist success there would inspire more fighters to continue the struggle elsewhere. The Iraq conflict has become the 'cause celebre' for jihadists, breeding a deep resentment of U.S. involvement in the Muslim world and cultivating supporters for the global jihadist movement.... The radicalization process is occurring more quickly, more widely,

and more anonymously" (Office of the Director of National Intelligence 2006, 2, 3–4).

4 Track two diplomacy is informal problem-solving interaction between unofficial but "connected" representatives of groups in conflict; track one and a half is still an informal and unofficial transaction, but one or more of the participants may be an official acting in an informal capacity, or the mediating party may have a government link. See Agha et al. 2004 and Davies and Kaufman 2002.

References

Agha, Hussein, Shai Feldman, Ahmad Khalidi, and Zeev Schiff. 2004. *Track-II Diplomacy: Lessons from the Middle East.* Cambridge MA: MIT Press.

Byers, Michael. 2007. *Intent for a Nation: What Is Canada For?* Vancouver: Douglas & McIntyre.

Cohen, Andrew. 2003. *While Canada Slept: How We Lost Our Place in the World.* Toronto: McClelland & Stewart.

Cooper, Andrew F. 1997. *Canadian Foreign Policy: Old Habits and New Directions.* Scarborough: Prentice Hall.

Cooper, Andrew F., and Dane Rowlands, eds. 2006. *Canada among Nations 2006: Minorities and Priorities.* Kingston: McGill-Queen's University Press.

Davies, John, and Edy Kaufman. 2002. *Second Track/Citizens' Diplomacy: Concepts and Techniques for Conflict Transformation.* Lanham, MD: Rowman and Littlefield.

Dewitt, David B., and John J. Kirton. 1983. *Canada as a Principal Power: A Study in Foreign Policy and International Relations.* Toronto: John Wiley & Sons.

Funk, Nathan C., and Abdul Aziz Said. 2004. "Islam and the West: Narratives of Conflict and Conflict Transformation." *International Journal of Peace Studies* 9(1): 1–28.

Granatstein, J.L. 2007. *Whose War Is It? How Canada Can Survive in the Post-9/11 World.* Toronto: HarperCollins.

Heinbecker, Paul. 2006. "Talk Is Mightier Than the Tank." *Globe and Mail*, August 18, A15.

Homer-Dixon, Thomas. 2000. *The Ingenuity Gap: Can We Solve the Problems of the Future?* Toronto: Knopf.

Ismael, Tareq. 1973. "Canada and the Middle East." *Behind the Headlines* 32(5): 1–32.

——. 1994. *Canada and the Middle East: The Foreign Policy of a Client State.* Calgary: Detselig Enterprises.

Jones, Jeremy. 2007. *Negotiating Change: The New Politics of the Middle East.* New York: I.B. Tauris.

Kaul, Inge, Isabelle Grunberg, and Marc A. Stern. 1999. *Global Public Goods: International Cooperation in the 21st Century.* New York: Oxford University Press.

Keating, Tom. 1993. *Canada and World Order: The Multilateralist Tradition in Canadian Foreign Policy.* Toronto: McClelland & Stewart.

Kirton, John. 2007. *Canadian Foreign Policy in a Changing World.* Toronto: Thomson Nelson.

Lynch, Marc. 2003. "Taking Arabs Seriously." *Foreign Affairs* 82(5): 81–94.

MacEachen, Allan J. 1983. "Canadian Relations with the Countries of the Middle East and North Africa: Statement by the Honourable Allan J. MacEachen, Deputy Prime Minister and Secretary of State for External Affairs, to the Standing Senate Committee on Foreign Affairs, Ottawa, February 17, 1983." *Statements and Speeches*, no. 83/2. Ottawa: External Affairs Canada.

MacLean, Sandra J., David R. Black, and Timothy M. Shaw, eds. 2006. *A Decade of Human Security: Global Governance and New Multilateralisms.* Aldershot: Ashgate.

Melady, John. 2006. *Pearson's Prize: Canada and the Suez Crisis.* Toronto: Dundurn.

Miller, Ronnie. 1994. *Following the Americans to the Persian Gulf: Canada, Australia, and the Development of the New World Order.* Toronto: Associated University Presses.

Office of the Director of National Intelligence. 2006. "Declassified Key Judgments of the National Intelligence Estimate 'Trends in Global Terrorism: Implications for the United States' dated April 2006." Washington, DC. www.dni.gov/press_releases/Declassified_NIE_Key_Judgments.pdf (July 2007).

Standing Committee on Foreign Affairs and International Trade. 2004. "Exploring Canada's Relations with the Countries of the Muslim World: Report of the Standing Committee on Foreign Affairs and International Trade." Ottawa. Bernard Patry, chair.

Pompa, Edward Michael. 1970. "Canadian Foreign Policy During the Suez Crisis of 1956." PhD diss., St. John's University. Ann Arbor: University Microfilms.

Regehr, Ernie. 2006. "Afghanistan: From Good Intentions to Sustainable Solutions." *Ploughshares Monitor* 27(3): 19–22.

Segal, Hugh. 2006. "Compassion, Realism, Engagement, and Focus: A Conservative Foreign Policy Thematic." In *Canada among Nations 2006: Minorities and Priorities*, ed. Andrew F. Cooper and Dane Rowlands, 27–33. Kingston: McGill-Queen's University Press.

Stuart, Matthew. 2007. "Canada Rearms." *Western Standard*, January 29, 28–30.

Taras, David, and David H. Goldberg. 1989. *The Domestic Battleground: Canada and the Arab-Israeli Conflict.* Kingston: McGill-Queen's University Press.

Thompson, John Herd and Stephen J. Randall. 2002. *Canada and the United States: Ambivalent Allies*, 3rd ed. Kingston: McGill-Queen's University Press.

Valpy, Michael. 2007. "The Myth of Canada as Global Peacekeeper." *Globe and Mail*, February 28, A8.

Warren, David. 2007. "Scared into Our Wits." *Western Standard*, January 29, 17.

Welsh, Jennifer. 2004. *At Home in the World: Canada's Global Vision for the 21st Century.* Toronto: HarperCollins.

Talking One Talk, Walking Another:
Norm Entrepreneurship and
Canada's Foreign Policy
in the Middle East

Canada's image in the Middle East reflects the perception that Canadians themselves commonly hold of their country's foreign policy: a staunch multilateralist middle power and norm promoter. This image derives from the history of Canada's involvement in the Arab-Israeli conflict: the role of Lester Pearson in the establishment of the Blue Helmets, Ottawa's role in the Middle East peace process, especially with regard to the question of Palestinian refugees in the 1990s as well as Canada's leadership role in the promotion of human security at the turn of the 21st century. This image, shared by Middle Eastern governments and populations alike, is helped along by the Canadian record of perceived fair-mindedness in voting at the United Nations on the Arab-Israeli conflict and by Canada's reception of an increasingly large Middle Eastern immigrant population.

This chapter argues that Canada's Middle Eastern foreign policy fails in practice to match these perceptions. Over the past decade of Canadian involvement in and reaction to events in the Middle East, a gap has grown between discourse and actions. That gap can be traced using the concept of the Responsibility to Protect (R2P), a norm that earned Canada much praise on the international scene. Whereas analysts usually account for such disparities by invoking the capabilities-commitment gap that has severely curtailed Canadian foreign policy since the early 1990s, this chapter argues that the divergences between Canada's discourse on the international stage and its specific attitudes and declarations regarding Middle Eastern events are best explained by the constraints brought about by changes in the international environment and in the relationship between Canada and the United States since the events of September 11, 2001. Moreover, the gap has broadened further with the arrival in power in Ottawa of a Conservative government ideologically much closer to the Bush administration than its Liberal predecessor was. In conclusion, the chapter offers some thoughts about the potential advantages and pitfalls of current Canadian foreign policy in the Middle East not only for the relationship between Ottawa and regional capitals but also for the achievement of Canada's overarching foreign policy objectives—security, prosperity, and the promotion of Canadian values and expertise.

Talk Is Not Cheap: Discourse and Canadian Foreign Policy Since the End of the Cold War

In Canadian foreign policy, discourse matters. While it is naive to assume that countries always do what they say or say what they do, since the early 1990s talk and normative innovations have, for lack of money, sometimes substituted for Canadian action. "The end of the Cold War in the late 1980s was followed by a [decade of] reckoning on Canada's government deficits (federal and provincial). The long march towards fiscal recovery, strongly supported by Canadians and undertaken as of 1994, cut deeply into the Government's domestic and foreign policy instruments" (Malone 2003, 4). Faced with severe economic constraints that drastically reduced its capability in the realm of foreign policy, Canada embarked on what Allan Gotlieb (2005, 17) described as a new mission "to create new norms of international behaviour which, in turn, reflect our values." This was most clearly expressed in the 1995 review of Canada's foreign policy, which called for the realization of an international system ruled by law, not power (Department of Foreign Affairs and International Trade [DFAIT] 1995).[1]

Human Security: Canadian Norm Entrepreneurship in the 1990s

The concept of human security has been the centrepiece of Canadian foreign policy discourse since the end of the Cold War. This people-focused approach was the hallmark of the Department of Foreign Affairs and International Trade (DFAIT) under the stewardship of Lloyd Axworthy, who "soon after his appointment in 1996, began to carve out what Robin Jeffrey Hay described as 'arguably the most ambitious agenda of any foreign minister in history'" (Gotlieb 2005, 22–23). Since his first speech in front of the UN General Assembly (UNGA) in 1996, Axworthy has promoted human security as a "common thread to tie together conceptually a string of single issues, including landmines and the protection of civilians in conflict" (Kenkel 2004, 7; see also Axworthy 1997). At its core, the concept of human security makes two intimately linked assertions: (1) that the theory and practice of international relations during the Cold War era has privileged the notion of national security above all else, and (2) that the pursuit of national security was necessary, but not sufficient, to protect citizens (Heinbecker 1999). Human security thus proposed a theoretical and practical change of focus: putting people first.

"'In putting people at the heart of security policy, Axworthy's vision,' in the words of Canada's former ambassador to the United Nations, Paul Heinbecker, 'was virtually Copernican in its significance'" (Gotlieb 2005, 23).[2] This agenda, construed as a projection of Canadian values onto the international scene, translated into advocacy on a number of issues, including the protection of civilians in armed conflict, the ban of landmines, the question of child soldiers, and so on and so forth. The effectiveness of this advocacy and Canada's ability to forge alliances to further the notion of human security earned Canadian foreign policy a number of remarkable successes: the Ottawa landmines treaty (1997), (modest) progress in combating the spread of small arms and light weapons (SALW), the appointment of a Special Representative of the Secretary-General for Children and Armed Conflicts at the UN, the creation of the International Criminal Court and the Rome Statute (1998), and, last but not least, the International Commission on Intervention and State Sovereignty and the Responsibility to Protect (henceforth R2P).

Not only has human security become a centrepiece of Canadian discourse and foreign policy since Lloyd Axworthy came to office, but it has also reinforced Canada's image as a multilateralist middle power pursuing international peace through norm promotion. Its efforts to reshape the manner in which the international community perceived and pursued international order and security earned Canada the label of norm entrepreneur, a feature of those countries that attempt to change the basic assumptions and functioning of the international system (McKay 2006, 876). Norm entrepreneurship has been said to reflect "the lively social concern with moral principles" that was characteristic of Canadian political culture (Pratt 1989, 196).

Norm Promotion in Action: Canada and the Responsibility to Protect

The R2P is one of the most potent illustrations, if not the most potent, of Canada's norm promotion in action. In the early 1990s, internal conflicts in Bosnia and Rwanda, among other countries, pitted the moral imperative of acting to save human lives against the international norm of non-intervention in the domestic affairs of sovereign states. In his 2000 report, UN secretary general Kofi Annan put the issue in no uncertain terms:

> If humanitarian intervention is, indeed, an unacceptable assault on sovereignty, how *should* we respond to a Rwanda, to a Srebrenica—to gross and systematic violations of human rights? (Annan 2000, 48; italics added)

The charge to come up with a response to Annan's challenge was given to the International Commission on Intervention and State Sovereignty (ICISS), an independent body commissioned by the Canadian government. Canada and "more particularly its far-sighted then foreign minister Lloyd Axworthy" are therefore to be credited for the commission's output (Evans 2007). The ICISS report, "The Responsibility to Protect," was released in December 2001 and proposed no less than a revolution in world affairs. R2P argued that the erstwhile unassailable concept of state sovereignty was, in effect, conditional. Sovereignty implied responsibility. States, it asserted, abdicated their sovereignty when incapable or unwilling to fulfil their responsibility to protect their citizens. In such conditions, the international community temporarily assumed the state's sovereignty/responsibility in order to save lives.

"The Responsibility to Protect" defines the duty of the international community as threefold: to prevent, to react, and to rebuild. The ICISS thus links prevention, intervention, and post-conflict rebuilding, acknowledging in the process that security and development are two faces of the same coin. R2P espouses the notion that socioeconomic marginalization and political exclusion provide the breeding ground for violence and that development problems are an integral part of the "conflict trap" (Collier et al. 2003). This is by no means an exclusively Canadian outlook on what is commonly referred to as the security-development nexus. UN publications, including Secretary General Boutros Boutros-Ghali's 1992 "Agenda for Peace" and 1994 "Agenda for Development," have long since made the same point. In 2005, the American ambassador to Canada, Paul Cellucci, asserted that it was in the joint economic and security interest of the U.S. and Canada to "help countries lift their people out of poverty." That same year, the report of the UN High-Level Panel on Threats, Challenges, and Change "recognised the need for better understanding of the intersection between development and security if the international community [was] to respond effectively to potential threats to collective peace and security" (Zahar 2005). It was similarly echoed by the report of then UN secretary general Annan (2005) in "In Larger Freedom: Towards Development, Security, and Human Rights for All."

Departing from the sacrosanct principle of non-intervention derived from the inalienable sovereignty of states, R2P provides new language in which to discuss humanitarian intervention. Its logic dovetails with Canada's focus on human security (Gänzle 2007). Under R2P, state sovereignty is conditional on the state fulfilling its primary duty to protect its citizens. Intervention, instead of being framed as a violation of sovereignty, is recast as an instrument "to shore up failing states and restore their primary function as protectors of their citizenry" (Zahar 2005).

Endorsed at the UN Summit of 2005, R2P is a prime example of Canadian norm promotion at work. As such, it provides a good perspective from which to evaluate Canadian foreign policy in the Middle East and to interrogate the fit between the discourse of Ottawa and its practices.

Norm Promotion Meets Reality: R2P and Canadian Foreign Policy in the Middle East

A cursory review of recent Canadian stances on Middle Eastern issues reveals a growing gap between the overarching Canadian discourse and specific reactions to developments in the Middle East. Ottawa has respected its overall commitment to rebuild, but it has trailed behind with regards to the other two elements of R2P—intervention and prevention.

The Responsibility to Prevent

In spite of the acknowledgment in "The Responsibility to Protect" of a "responsibility to prevent," this is the least developed of the concept's three pillars. The document affirms that prevention may take many forms including "development assistance and other efforts to help address the root cause of potential conflict," support "for local initiatives to advance good governance, human rights, or the rule of law," as well as "good offices missions, mediation efforts and other efforts to promote dialogue or reconciliation" (ICISS 2001, 19). It notes the existence of a gap between "rhetoric and financial and political support for prevention," especially with regard to the promotion of development assistance as a tool of conflict prevention, while recent years have been marked by a sharp decline in overall assistance levels worldwide (20).

Canada's prevention record in the Middle East illustrates the difficulty of achieving what the ICISS (2001, 20) considers to be the three essential conditions for success: the ability to assess fragility (so-called "early warning"), the understanding of those policy measures available that are likely to make a difference (so-called "preventive toolbox"), and, last but not least, the willingness to apply those measures (i.e., political will).

EARLY WARNING It is easier to acknowledge the need to prevent conflict from erupting than it is to pinpoint those states that are at risk of descending into war and therefore in need of preventive assistance. Recent efforts to develop early warning capabilities abound. These include the Failed States Index, a joint venture of *Foreign Policy* and the Fund for Peace (see Fund for Peace 2007); the Global Forecasting Model of Political Instability developed by Jack Goldstone and his colleagues (2005), or, closer to home, the Country Foreign Policy Indicators project led by David Carment (2003) at Carleton University's Norman Paterson School of International Affairs, which has received funding from DFAIT, the Canadian International Development Agency (CIDA), and the International Development Research Centre (IDRC). Most researchers and practitioners argue that fragility and failure are part of a "developmental continuum." Along this sliding scale, states rank as strong, weak, failed, and collapsed (Carment 2003, 409).

These efforts, while laudable, suffer from empirical problems. The scores used by the Fragile States Index are a composite of 12 indicators, including factors such as demographic pressure, human flight, and increasingly factionalized elites. Failure is, however, primarily identified with the eruption of violence. Nation-states fail "because they are convulsed by internal violence and can no longer deliver positive political goods to their inhabitants" (Rotberg 2004, 1). But violence and breakdown need not be total for a state to be characterized as failed.

> Sudan, the highest ranked country in the *Failed States Index*, is a case in point. Living in Khartoum, an individual might not fathom the extent of state collapse and the magnitude of the violence that convulses the Darfur region. Pakistan, ranked 9th, experiences occasional outbursts of violence; its army has even gained a reputation for cracking down on opposition members, especially Islamists. Analysts are divided over the reasons for the lawlessness in the "tribal regions," including North and South Waziristan. Some argue this is not a sign that the government of Pervez Musharraf has lost monopoly over the use of violence. Instead, they see the lawlessness as part of a political bargain between the centre and peripheral regions. The inclusion, at rank number 16, of Yemen is even more incomprehensible from such a perspective. Apart from the occasional kidnapping of a Western tourist, there is little public violence in the country to justify its description as failed. (Zahar, Desrosiers, and Brown 2007, 2–3)[3]

Likewise, there is a plethora of "fragile" states that, while weak, do not present signs of vulnerability to impending political destabilization. Nor should one necessarily expect such states to become unstable in the medium term. Where, then, are concerned outsiders such as the government of Canada to focus their efforts? At what point are states in urgent need of or, alternatively, beyond the reach of prevention? (And which among them would acknowledge such need and welcome the outside world to intervene?)

PREVENTIVE TOOLBOX   Difficulties associated with early warning are not limited to the identification of countries at risk. They also extend to the policies most likely to prevent conflict. Suggested policies range from official development assistance (ODA) to mediation and good offices. There is no definitive proof of the link between development activities and conflict prevention, and there are multiple examples of poor countries staying out of trouble while richer ones descend into war. Nevertheless, it is still worth reviewing the record of Canada's developmental assistance in the Middle East from the standpoint of the congruence (to the extent it exists) between discourse and practice. If development assistance could help prevent conflict, how does Canada fare in this respect? The record is at best mixed.

Canada has never been a major development player in the Middle East. A quick look at CIDA's yearly expenditures in the region is sufficient to make the point. Throughout the 1990s, the average yearly expenditure hovered around $65 million for the 21 countries of the Middle East and North Africa region. A height of $97.5 million was reached in 1991/92 in the wake of the Madrid peace conference. The spike in disbursements between 2003 and 2007 (reaching the height of $207.5 million in 2003/04) does not reflect more development work upstream. Rather, it speaks to an increase in post-conflict reconstruction commitments linked to developments in Iraq.[4]

A substantial proportion of Canada's development assistance to Middle Eastern countries has recently focused on the promotion and support of local initiatives to advance good governance, human rights, and the rule of law. These are extensively reviewed elsewhere in this volume. In Chapter 6, Janine Clark cogently argues that western funding benefits a small number of organizations with the capacity, skills, and knowledge base that permit them to pose as interlocutors. The legitimacy and representativeness of these institutions are the subject of much discussion in the various Middle Eastern societies as well as among experts.

Canada has also participated in some mediation initiatives, particularly in its capacity as gavel holder of the Refugee Working Group (RWG), which was established in the wake of the Madrid peace conference. As Rex Brynen shows in Chapter 5, these efforts were most successful when informal, as exemplified by the creation and functioning of the so-called No-Name Group. However, Canadian willingness to get involved in such initiatives is hampered by a number of factors, including some discussed below.

Overall, the nature of Canadian developmental assistance is consonant with prevention in as much as it often focuses on projects that seek to enhance accountability, transparency, and democratic practices. But Canada's development aid is lagging behind the standard 0.7 percent target of gross national product (GNP) established in 1969.[5] "Now, 35 years later, Canada gives approximately 0.3 per cent" (Sachs and MacArthur 2005). Its aid as a share of GNP is currently much less than in the 1980s, in spite of substantial increases in Canadian incomes. Moreover, CIDA's budget was slashed by roughly 30 percent in the 1990s (Malone 2003, 9). This led to the drastic downsizing of programs in countries such as Jordan and Lebanon and prevented Canada from playing a significant role in development assistance to the West Bank and the Gaza Strip (see Chapter 5). Given that such activities could have contributed to prevention, the level of resources devoted to development aid makes it unlikely that Canadian assistance has had a significant impact in this realm.

POLITICAL WILL   A serious commitment to prevent requires political will, all the more so because prevention involves activities that are likely to produce results only in the long run and because its success is often difficult to quantify. In other words, a foreign policy focused on prevention runs counter to the logic of national politics, which requires leaders to deliver short-term benefits. These provide tangible results that can be presented to constituents as proof of the effectiveness and wisdom of foreign policy choices and, thereby, contribute to increasing leaders' chances for re-election.

The importance of political will is particularly evident in putting the responsibility to prevent into action. Thus Brynen argues that, with regard to the Arab-Israeli conflict, concern over the impact of domestic lobbies has instilled "a significant degree of caution in Canadian policy, among ministers and bureaucrats alike." Analysts have also made much of the lack of political will in explaining Canada's failure to live up to its commitment to give 70 cents of every $100 of GNP to the poorest countries (Sachs and MacArthur 2005), which in turn limits funds available for the Middle East.

Ottawa's commitment to prevention is further weakened by the criteria used to determine eligibility for foreign aid. In the development portion of "Canada's International Policy Statement: A Role of Pride and Influence in the World" (IPS), the government defined "development partners" as those countries where the need is greatest as per level of income and ranking on the Human Development Index published by the United Nations Development Programme (UNDP) (DFAIT 2005). However, other criteria included the countries' ability to use aid effectively (as per the World Bank's Country Policy and Institutional Assessment) and sufficient Canadian presence to add value.[6] The 25 development partners are described as countries "that have demonstrated they can use aid effectively and the Government can be confident that programs which make effective and prudent use of taxpayers' dollars are possible" (DFAIT 2005).

Not a single Middle Eastern state has made the list of privileged development partners released by CIDA shortly after the publication of the Martin government's IPS in 2005, although Ottawa does list the countries of the Arab Mashriq—Syria, Jordan, Lebanon, Israel/Palestine, and Iraq—as ones that might receive assistance. However, most Middle Eastern states fail to meet one or another of the eligibility criteria. For example, while the West Bank and Gaza might fit the criterion of need, the unravelling of the Palestinian Authority's institutional structure would disqualify the Palestinian territories. But the list of 25 development partners speaks to the importance of political will in investing resources abroad. Indeed, many of the countries on that list should not have been on it on the basis of the declared selection criteria.

The list of Development Partners was not provided in the IPS but was released soon after by CIDA. The respect of human rights is notably absent as a criterion, despite several mentions in the IPS development, diplomacy and overview papers as being a central guiding principle of Canada's international policy, not to mention obligations under international human rights law.

The list includes several authoritarian regimes (including Burkina Faso, Cameroon, Pakistan and Vietnam), one accused of severe domestic human rights abuses (Sri Lanka) and two that have become in recent years increasingly authoritarian, defying international law and fighting sanguinary wars in a neighbouring country (Ethiopia and Rwanda). Not all Development Partners really appear to be among the poorest and most disadvantaged (Indonesia and Ukraine). In fact, financial assistance to one of them (Ukraine) cannot be counted as ODA [official development assistance] because the OECD [Organisation for Economic Co-operation and Development] does not classify it as a developing country. (Brown 2007)

By removing the countries of the Middle East from its list of development partners, the government of Canada has further curtailed its ability to affect developments in these countries and therefore act upstream of crises to prevent the eruption of conflict.

The Responsibility to React against Massive Human Rights Violations

In practice, the R2P agenda has focused overwhelmingly on humanitarian intervention understood as the responsibility to react or "coercive interference in the internal affairs of a state, involving the use of armed force, with the purposes of addressing massive human rights violations or preventing widespread human suffering" (Welsh 2004, 3). The ICISS defines reaction as the protection of civilians in situations of compelling need when preventive measures have failed and when the state is unable or unwilling to redress the situation. It lists measures that include political, economic, and judicial tools and "in extreme cases—but only extreme cases—they may also include military action. As a matter of first principles, in the case of reaction just as with prevention, less intrusive and coercive measures should always be considered before more coercive and intrusive ones are applied" (ICISS 2001, 29). R2P thus suggests the application of an array of escalating targeted sanctions or the indictment of guilty parties in front of the International Criminal Court prior to any military intervention. Although Ottawa was instrumental in bringing the notion of R2P to life, its policies on intervention have only selectively followed suit.

The prime example of Canada's hesitation to put its discourse into practice in the broader Middle East is its stance on the crisis in Darfur. Ottawa pledges concern for the situation and has systematically supported UN resolutions condemning human rights violations in Sudan. Nevertheless, it is quite telling that the government identifies its approach as three-pronged: "using diplomatic channels to pursue sustainable political solutions and to address the root causes of the conflicts; providing humanitarian, reconstruction and peacebuilding assistance to affected populations; supporting both the United Nations and African Union peacekeeping missions in the Sudan" (DFAIT 2007).

Nowhere in this approach is there mention of the spectrum of tools associated with the responsibility to react. Careful examination of Ottawa's involvement in Sudan reveals, further, that reconstruction and peace-building assistance is being delivered to the populations of south Sudan in the framework of the Comprehensive Peace Agreement, which ended the conflict between the Sudanese government and the Sudan Peoples Liberation Movement/Army rather than to the Darfur region. For its part, Canada provided financial, technical, and diplomatic support to the African Union (AU) during the talks that led to the Darfur Peace Agreement. However, albeit through no fault of Canada's, the agreement was never fully implemented on the ground nor did it stem the violence against civilians.

The most active aspect of Canada's involvement is its military support of the AU-UN mission.[7] Juxtaposing Canadian leaders' norm entrepreneurship against their commitments of resources in the specific case of Darfur, David Black wrote:

> Ever so slowly the Canadian government has, in the company of other donor states, ratcheted up its commitments of humanitarian aid and logistical support to the African Union (AU) force that has been deployed to the region. In May 2005 it announced additional commitments, bringing total support to $198 million since 2000, as well as the creation of a special advisory team to promote and coordinate Canadian initiatives.... Nevertheless, this process has been so tardy and so limited in relation to the magnitude of the emergency that Gerald Caplan was moved to publish a powerfully argued op-ed piece in the *Globe and Mail* on 6 August 2004 titled, "To our great shame, 'Canada doesn't do Africa.'" To be sure, situations like that in Darfur are wicked problems, and Canada has hardly been alone in its dereliction. Nor are our contributions—for example, through the supply of chartered helicopters and military equipment to the AU observer force—unwelcome or unhelpful. But the kind of statist logic that keeps our commitments respectably in line with (or even modestly ahead of) those of comparably positioned "friends of Africa" seems a far cry from a response driven by the real needs of Africans. (Black 2005, 9–10)

Not only has Canada been slow to put the responsibility to react into practice in Darfur, but there has also been a notable lack of urgency with respect to several other crises in the Middle East where civilians were seriously put at risk by their state's inability or unwillingness to protect them. While it would be too much to expect a country with Canada's capabilities to act forcefully in each and every instance of massive human rights violations or widespread human suffering, especially given the size of Canadian engagement in Afghanistan, Canada's commitment to and stewardship of the R2P principle did not even translate into consequent declarations of concern for the fate of civilians in Lebanon, Iraq, and the Palestinian Authority where recent events have put populations at risk.

When war erupted between Israel and the Hizbullah on July 12, 2006, it engulfed all of Lebanon. Israeli military operations put civilians at great risk. Indeed, when all was said and done, more than 1,000 civilians had died on the Lebanese side with a full 25 percent of the country's population displaced.[8] More than 160 Israelis also died in the conflict. The war posed a special challenge for Canada as it quickly became clear that around 40,000 to 50,000 dual Canadian-Lebanese citizens were stranded in Lebanon. Yet, on July 17, Canada's prime minister, Stephen Harper, while making it clear that Israel had a right to defend itself under international law, did not also make it clear that that defence had itself to comply with international law, particularly humanitarian law. Prime Minister Harper described Israel's response to the killing of eight of its soldiers and the kidnapping of two more in a cross-border raid by Hizbullah as "measured." While urging Israel and others to minimize civilian damage, he further stated, in reference to the high number of civilian casualties on the Lebanese side, that it was a "challenge for Israel to fight a decentralized organization, such as Hezbollah, when its members are embedded within urban populations in Lebanon" (Canadian Broadcasting Corporation [CBC] 2006a). The prime minister maintained his refusal to question Israel's use of force, in spite of the loss of Canadian civilian casualties, including seven members of a single family killed during an Israeli raid on the southern Lebanese border town of Aitaroun.[9] Nor did he yield to international pressure. At the end of September 2006, at a meeting of the Francophonie Harper vetoed a resolution that "'deplored' the effect of the month-long conflict on the Lebanese civilians it endangered" (Woods 2006).

The prime minister was not alone in his staunch refusal to express concern for the widespread human suffering, even as it became clear that both Israel and Hizbullah were using weaponry in ways that contradicted the laws of war, including the use of cluster munitions in civilian areas by the Israelis and rocket fire aimed indiscriminately at population centres by Hizbullah. Michael Ignatieff, a member of the ICISS and, at the time of the war, a Liberal leadership candidate, went even further. Commenting in the wake of an Israeli air raid that resulted in 28 deaths from the collapse of a residential building onto people seeking refuge in its basement in the town of Qana, he said "Qana was frankly inevitable in a situation in which you have rocket-launchers within 100 yards of a civilian population. This is the nature of the war that's going on.... This is the kind of dirty war you're in when you have to do this and I'm not losing sleep about that" (Bryden 2006).

Canada has also remained silent on the plight of two other Middle Eastern populations that have experienced widespread human suffering in recent years. There is yet to be sustained Canadian action on the precarious situation of the more than 2 million Iraqi refugees living in Syria and Jordan.[10] Likewise, the deteriorating conditions of Palestinians in the West Bank and Gaza as a result of the escalation of fighting with Israel in summer 2006 and of the festering civil war between Hamas and the Fatah, while a concern, seem not to be an urgent preoccupation.

The Responsibility to Rebuild War-Torn Societies

Humanitarian intervention is part and parcel of a social re-engineering project that seeks to prevent the collapse of state power or its arbitrary use and to rebuild functional and responsible states. Indeed, international practice reflects the development of a "responsibility to rebuild" norm. The international community is increasingly involved in nation-building projects that aim to establish or transform state institutions such that they can provide peace, order, and good governance, the three elements of a state's ability to protect its citizens against harm. Canada's record of involvement in the nation-building project is best exemplified by its action in Iraq.

Since early 2003, Canada has provided $300 million of humanitarian and reconstruction assistance to Iraq. To date, more than $250 million has been disbursed—a proportion that stands in stark contrast to the general trend in this regard.[11] In keeping with its multilateralist stance, Canada supports the significant role of the UN in the reconstruction and political transition of Iraq. Indeed, one third of the funds are channelled through the International Reconstruction Fund Facility for Iraq (IRFFI), launched by the UN and the World Bank in 2004. Canada's commitment to the IRFFI is substantial; it ranks third after the European Commission, Japan, and the United Kingdom. Canada chaired the IRFFI donor committee until 2007.

Canada's support for the reconstruction of Iraq is consonant with Canadian values as stated in "Canada in the World." According to CIDA, the money has gone to support education and health services, the promotion of human rights, and the development of Iraq's electoral process. Assistance was also provided to the rehabilitation of Iraqi police, to support the constitutional referendum and subsequent national elections by the International Mission for Iraqi Elections, to develop the capacities of non-governmental organizations (NGOs), and to provide governance support for targeted Iraqi institutions.

Canada's commitment to rebuilding Iraq stands in contrast to its lukewarm response to the summer 2006 crisis in Lebanon. The six-week long conflict between Hizbullah and Israel wiped out Lebanon's post-civil war recovery. The Lebanese government put the cost of damages at US$3.6 billion. The international community mobilized to assist in rebuilding the country, pledging close to US$900 million in assistance at the Stockholm 2 Conference held only two weeks after the end of hostilities (Republic of Lebanon, Ministry of Finance 2006). Canada was noteworthy for its absence from the long list of donors. In August 2006, Ottawa announced the creation of the $25 million Lebanon Relief Fund to be allocated over two years to assist the United Nations, the Red Cross Movement, other multilateral organizations and NGOs to provide for water and sanitation, shelter, protection, medical facilities and repair to essential infrastructure in Lebanon (Office of the Prime Minister 2006).[12] Some Canadian reconstruction aid was specifically earmarked to assist the environmental clean-up of the Lebanese coast and to demining.

The Gap between Canadian Discourse and Foreign Policy Practice in the Middle East

Critics describe the 1990s as the period when Canada went from a do-good to a feel-good policy. They refer mostly to the increase in the commitment-credibility gap (Gotlieb 2005). They point to the fact that as Canada projected its values onto the international scene, it retrenched on the two pillars of its liberal foreign policy: commitments to peacekeeping and development aid.

> Compared to a level of defense spending of some 7.3 percent of gdp [gross domestic product] in the 1950s and some 0.53 percent of gdp in official aid in the 1970s, expenditures declined to a fraction of that by century's end— 1.1 percent of GDP on defense and some 0.22 percent on aid. Canadian spending on defense ranked Canada among the lowest three members of NATO [North Atlantic Treaty Organization], along with Luxembourg and the Netherlands, and 17th in the world in terms of official aid. From being the largest contributor to peacekeeping in the 1970s and 1980s, Canada declined to 32nd in the world by the end of 2001. By 2003, Canada had only 250 military and civilian personnel in UN peacekeeping operations. In Jack Granatstein's assessment: "By the beginning of the current century, shortages of equipment and personnel all but eliminated Canada's military capacity." (Gotlieb 2005, 23)

While an empirically accurate observation, this does not provide an adequate explanation for the gap between discourse and practice. Indeed, if, as argued above, Canadian norm entrepreneurship was a strategy aimed in part at maintaining profile and relevance in spite of increasing financial and human resource constraints, then the commitment-credibility gap cannot be invoked simultaneously as the impulse for norm entrepreneurship and the cause of its failure. Indeed, were Canada's resources so limited that it could not "walk the walk," one would still have to account for its failure to "talk the talk." David Malone put it best:

> During the (necessary) budget-cutting years, the government lulled itself into believing that Canada could continue to matter internationally while its foreign policy instruments eroded and while the country's weight relative to others ... declined. Our approach was to "be there" ... and relying on our many club memberships. The government did very well out of Lloyd Axworthy's "Human Security Agenda," policy driven, imaginative, relevant, and,

importantly, cheap. Observers nevertheless sometimes pointed to the apparently more dynamic diplomacy of Norway. Oslo's success is owed first of all to a willingness to make choices and accept a "niche diplomacy" role (mainly in international mediation) and second to large sums of "walking around money" available to the Norwegian Ministry of Foreign Affairs, reputedly up to US$250 million a year. DFAIT does not dispose of 10 percent of this sum for discretionary diplomatic initiatives. (Malone 2003, 23)

Two main political reasons can be invoked to explain the gap between discourse and practice. First is September 11, 2001, and its impact on Canadian-American relations. Second is the impact of the change of government in Ottawa. In this context, and in the context that the change started under the Liberal government of Paul Martin and deepened under the Conservative stewardship of Stephen Harper, current Canadian foreign policy in the Middle East can be elucidated.

Norm Promotion and Realpolitik: September 11 and beyond

Canadian policies in the Middle East can be viewed as an attempt by Ottawa to address American concerns. Although there is no evidence of direct American pressure on the Canadian government to change its policies in the region, decisions to "get tougher," at least rhetorically, with terrorists and to refocus the bulk of Canada's financial commitments on rebuilding Iraq speak to the efforts of the Martin and Harper governments to display more sensitivity to U.S. priorities in the region and elsewhere.

Since September 11, 2001, security and defence concerns lie at the heart of U.S. foreign policy. Washington has subordinated all other aspects of its bilateral relations to security concerns. For Canada, which shares the longest border in the world with the U.S. and which depends heavily on trade with the U.S. for its economic prosperity, this shift in U.S. priorities was bad news.[13] Concerned about Ottawa's ability to control the presence of "terrorist" elements on Canadian soil and skeptical of the Canadian government's ability to guard the border, the U.S. implemented a number of measures that sent a loud and clear signal to Canada that things would not just go back to the way they were on the eve of the attacks on the World Trade Center and on the Pentagon. Washington also "signalled that not only will it focus with great intensity on any serious security threats it perceives to the U.S. homeland and U.S. citizens elsewhere, but that the political support of its allies for its military ventures abroad will be monitored closely" (Malone 2003, 12).

In this context, Prime Minister Jean Chrétien's decision to oppose U.S. intervention in Iraq seriously strained Canadian-U.S. bilateral relations. A CBC report on the state of the relation summarized the situation thus:

> When Chrétien decided not to join the American-led attack on Iraq in 2003, Bush's schedule suddenly got too busy to accommodate a planned trip to

Ottawa. The schedule did, however, permit Bush to entertain Australian Prime Minister John Howard at his Texas ranch on the days Bush was to have visited Canada. Australia had sent troops to Iraq. (CBC 2006b)

Chrétien's decision on Iraq has variously been explained as a consequence of Canada's strong multilateralist commitments and, alternatively, as the result of a shrewd domestic political calculation revolving around Quebec's opposition to the war and the province's centrality to federal Liberal electoral prospects.

Whatever its real (and probably mixed) motives, the decision highlighted another development of consequence to the Canadian-U.S. relationship. As the U.S. government grew more circumspect about the usefulness of international institutions to pursue American national interests and security, and as Washington became more and more unilateralist, Canada's traditional support of multilateral institutions was increasingly inconsistent with maintaining good relations with the United States, unlike during the Clinton years (Keating 2003). Not only could Canada not expect forbearance from the United States in bilateral security and defence relations, but also it could no longer expect it in case of any divergence over foreign policy. Such forbearance was essential for Canada to be able to carve a role for itself as a "helpful fixer" on the international scene (Malone 2003).

While the situation improved somewhat under Prime Minister Paul Martin, the Canada-U.S. relationship remained beset by a number of contentious issues, including divergences on the proposed U.S. missile defence system and serious trade problems, notably over softwood lumber. However, the Martin government implemented a number of subtle yet important changes that indicated increasing awareness of U.S. security concerns and a willingness to address them. These changes were evident in the Martin government's IPS, which shifted the discourse of the Canadian government from human security to failed and fragile states.

From Responsibility to Protect to Failed and Fragile States: Wither Human Security?

Canada's IPS reiterated Ottawa's commitment to exert efforts to build a more secure world. To do so, the IPS indicated that "in the face of a panoply of challenges, and a range of possible responses, the Government of Canada will seek to make a difference in three main areas: countering global terrorism; stabilizing failed and fragile states; and combating the proliferation of weapons of mass destruction" (DFAIT 2005).

Of the 192 members of the UN, more than a hundred currently experience either violent breakdown or institutional erosion, two dimensions most consistently associated with fragility and failure (Woodward 2005). Canada has made addressing state fragility one of its priorities for action abroad. The government has moved to develop a coordinated, whole-of-government approach, which involves, among others, DFAIT, the Department of National Defence (DND), and CIDA, and relates to work on fragile states being done at the OECD.[14] As it stated in the IPS:

> To help states under stress from becoming failed states—at tremendous human and material cost to their own citizens and others—Canada must consider how it can, in a coordinated fashion with other donors, support countries where the need is great but the capacity to use aid effectively is weak. With our focus in the area of governance, we have the capacity to strengthen the ability of poor performing countries to use aid more effectively. We will, therefore, provide targeted bilateral support directly aimed at improving governance in a limited number of strategically significant poor-performing countries. (DFAIT 2005)

Such an approach is consonant with the empirical observation that Canada, while not living up to its declared commitment to intervene and prevent, is nevertheless upholding its responsibility to rebuild. The Martin government's IPS reserves a special type of bilateral programming for failed and fragile states— countries in or emerging from crisis and that are of overriding strategic importance—where Canada will provide humanitarian and reconstruction assistance, including through its Global Peace and Security Fund. To illustrate this commitment, the IPS cited Canadian involvement in Iraq, Afghanistan, and Haiti, and the decision to help with nation building in Sudan.

The label "strategically significant" deserves further examination. Perhaps top of the current Canadian list is Afghanistan, which as a former and possibly future base of international terrorism and as a state where trade in illicit narcotics plays a prominent role, is important to the United States. Haiti is a member of the Organisation of American States (OAS), and a country whose people have sought refuge in Canada and the United States. As such, stability in Haiti might be considered directly important to Canada both for hemispheric and for domestic reasons. For its part, Sudan has been important to Canadian oil interests, which historically were heavily involved in oil prospecting in the south of the country. From a purely Canadian perspective, the case for Iraq's strategic significance is more tenuous, at least it was prior to the U.S. invasion. It is, however, undisputable that Iraq is strategically significant to U.S. security. It is therefore possible to interpret the choice of strategically significant countries as one way in which the Canadian government attempts to cooperate with and contribute to the American search for international order and stability.

Indeed, researchers and policy makers alike have increasingly linked failed and fragile states to growing threats of violence. Yet this is not limited to internal violence. There has been increasing concern that failed and fragile states provide fertile ground for threats to international security, ranging from the facilitation of drug trafficking to the implantation of criminal and terrorist networks in states where governments cannot ensure a monopoly over the use of violence or effective control on the national territory. Says Michael Ignatieff (2003, 109) of the western intervention in failed states: "Its essential purpose is to create order in border zones essential to the security of great powers."

The Martin government's IPS also committed Canada to actively combat global terrorism. This commitment helps elucidate changes in Canada's foreign policy in the Middle East, notably the trend—started under Martin's leadership in 2003—to abstain or vote against UN resolutions on the Israeli-Palestinian question (see Chapter 5). Official explanations of these decisions highlight the absence in the text of the various resolutions of serious condemnation of Palestinian terrorist actions against Israeli civilians.

Finally, and beyond the IPS, the Martin government's strong endorsement of the high-level panel on UN reform provided an entry point to reconcile Canada's commitment to multilateralism with growing U.S. skepticism of the UN system (UN 2004). Canada thus indicated its willingness to play a role in the renovation of the UN system in such a way as to address the most serious U.S. criticisms levelled at the international organization (Zahar 2005, 733–34).

"Seeing like the United States": The Impact of the 2006 Conservative Electoral Victory

The victory of Stephen Harper's Conservatives in the January 2006 federal election has contributed to deepening changes in Canada's foreign policy in the Middle East. This is partially due to a narrowing of the attitudinal gap between the U.S. and Canadian governments. Harper's views are closer to those of U.S. president George W. Bush on a number of key issues than were his predecessor's. "Harper is a social and fiscal conservative with a deeply religious orientation—all characteristics that should endear him to President Bush," wrote Munroe Eagles (2006, 821) in one of the first assessments of potential changes in Canada-U.S. relations following the Conservative electoral victory. A significant ideological congruence between the new Canadian and the Bush administrations derives from what Bush himself described as mutual values, namely the need to stand firm against terrorism and to address the problem of rogue states. In a letter addressed to the Wall Street Journal on March 28, 2003, then Canadian Alliance leader Stephen Harper and his predecessor Stockwell Day strongly criticized Canada's decision to sit out the Iraq war: "The Canadian Alliance—the official Opposition in Parliament—supports the American and British position because we share their concerns, their worries about the future if Iraq is left unattended to, and their fundamental vision of civilization and human values" (Eagles 2006, 822).

This convergence was further confirmed when Canada became the first country to suspend all aid to the Palestinian Authority on the morrow of

Hamas's electoral victory in early 2006. Having described the group as a terrorist organization, Ottawa acted consequently and cut ties with the Palestinian Authority. The government also substantially modified its stance at the UN, abstaining on resolutions that reaffirmed the Palestinians' right to self-determination and the importance of Israel acceding to the Nuclear Non-proliferation Treaty and refraining from exploiting natural resources in the occupied territories (Edwards 2006; see also DFAIT 2006).

The narrowing in the gap between Canada and the U.S. was also illustrated by a number of decisions taken by the Harper government within a few months of coming into office. Prime Minister Harper endorsed the Martin government's decision to increase Canada's military presence in Afghanistan to more than 2,200 troops and to assume greater responsibility in the troubled Kandahar region. As Eagles wrote:

> Responding to long-standing American criticisms of the erosion of the country's armed forces, Harper's first budget, introduced in May 2006, promised $1.4 billion (US$1.26 billion) in additional spending on policing, border security, and public safety, and another $1.1 billion (US$0.9 billion) over the next two years in increased defense spending. (Eagles 2006, 822)

The government confirmed its predecessor's commitment to concentrate financial resources on the needs of strategically failed and fragile states, with Iraq and Afghanistan gaining the lion's share. The government also forged ahead with an internal revision of its policy with regard to failed and fragile states under the aegis of the Stabilization and Reconstruction Task Force (START), mandated to "plan and coordinate rapid and integrated civilian responses to international crises" (DFAIT 2005). Among its tasks, START focuses its efforts on the articulation of a Canadian whole-of-government approach and on the resulting practical implications for engagement in failed and fragile states (Zahar, Desrosiers, and Brown 2007).

Where Do We Go from Here?

This chapter has reviewed and provided explanations for the gap between Canada's norm-laden discourse on the international scene and its failure to live up to this discourse in the Middle East. This gap needs to be addressed. Canada must not only "talk the talk." It must also endeavour—to the extent possible—to "walk the walk," particularly in view of the potential for increasing entanglement between domestic and international politics. In other words, Canada's ability to achieve security and prosperity at home depends in part on its behaviour abroad. In this respect, it is useful to assess the new direction recently charted by Ottawa's Middle East policy with an eye on its ability to meet two longstanding objectives of Canadian foreign policy: to maintain good relations with the United States and to project Canada's image as a helpful fixer on the international scene.

The World Knocking at the Door

Canada is increasingly multi-ethnic and multicultural. Only one other country in the world, Australia, accepts more immigrants on a per capita basis. This trend has profoundly changed the face of Canada. Today, close to 20 percent of Canadians are foreign-born. They do not hail from Europe as was the case until the 1960s. Most immigrants now come from the developing world, with 58 percent of new immigrants emigrating from Asia and the Middle East (Statistics Canada 2003). Arab Canadians are a large and growing group of immigrants, pushed by continuing instability and economic stagnation in the countries of the Middle East. The approximately 194,000 Arab Canadians counted in the 2001 census are expected to reach between 370,000 and 521,000 by 2017.

What impact does this have on Canadian foreign policy? There is little systematic research on the topic and tentative conclusions are the best with which analysts can come up (Riddell-Dixon 2003). As argued elsewhere in this volume, organized communities are likely to press the government of Canada to take positions favourable to their views on highly contested political issues. These competing pressures are only likely to increase. Organized communities also subject Canadian foreign policy to closer scrutiny. Reactions in the Lebanese and broader Arab community to the Israel-Hizbullah conflict are a case in point. Observers were quick to point out that Canada's attitudes were not consonant with its values and obligations under international law (Crépeau et al. 2006). Some have attributed the initial pro-Israeli tilt of the Harper government to the effectiveness of the pro-Israel lobby, and to the ineffectiveness of its Arab counterpart (Irani 2005). (For a detailed discussion of lobbies, see Chapter 10.)

All of this is happening at a time when Canada's Arab community is feeling increasingly insecure and Canada's domestic commitment to the protection of citizens of Arab and Muslim origin is being increasingly questioned. In the past couple of years, a number of disturbing facts have emerged in this respect. First and foremost is the Maher Arar affair. In addition, there are a number of issues relating to racial profiling, as Elizabeth Riddell-Dixon describes.

> In October 2002, the Bush Administration announced that those born in Iran, Iraq, Libya, Pakistan, Saudi Arabia, Sudan, Syria or Yemen, who were not immigrants to the US, would be singled out and subjected to extra scrutiny at US borders. The Canadian Ethnocultural Council as well as Arab and Muslim communities in Canada were quick to condemn the US position and to urge the Canadian government to protest the discriminatory policy." (Riddell-Dixon 2003, 12)

The debate on dual citizenship triggered by the mass evacuation of Lebanese Canadians in summer 2006 reinforced perceptions in some quarters that, since the events of September 2001, Arabs and Muslims were not equal citizens under the law. In the winter of 2007, similar concerns were raised over Bell Helicopter's decision to sideline 24 employees who had been working on a U.S. security contract because of their place of birth (CBC 2007). To its credit, the government has acted on all of these issues, although not always in as timely or decisive a manner as might have been wished. It has held an inquiry into the Arar affair, lodged complaints with the U.S., and publicly expressed concern over profiling. It not only evacuated Lebanese Canadians at great cost, but it also rejected reopening the dual citizenship file in the wake of the Israel-Hizbullah war.

Nevertheless, these developments point to the growing integration of domestic and international politics. Ottawa must increasingly consider the domestic reverberations of its policies abroad, lest it feed resentment in parts of its population and, in the worst-case scenario, pave the way for potential recruitment of disgruntled Canadians as terrorists. While a complex, multifaceted issue, the highly publicized phenomenon of home-grown terrorism, as experienced in the United Kingdom, does highlight the potentially destabilizing convergence of foreign policy and domestic politics.

At Home on the Continent?

Canadian foreign policy on the Middle East has been experiencing subtle and not so subtle changes. It is increasingly taking into serious consideration American security concerns, both at home and abroad. In this regard, the move from the language of R2P to that of failed and fragile states holds the potential of narrowing the distance between Canada and the United States.

By adopting an uncompromising attitude toward "terrorist groups" and by contributing its part to the reconstruction of Iraq, Ottawa is sending a clear signal to the United States that Canada is sensitive to U.S. concerns about international order and stability and that Canada is willing to do its part in this respect. Paul Martin's government began the process of realigning Canada's foreign and domestic policies (especially in the realm of security) in part to address American concerns. Stephen Harper's government has narrowed the philosophical gap between the two countries. One thing is clear: Canada's foreign policy in the Middle East is contributing positively to Ottawa's efforts to be at home in North America.

At Home in the World?

Can Canada be at home in North America and in the world at once? The reorientation of Canadian foreign policy in the Middle East provides both positive and negative answers.

On the positive side of the ledger, the decision of the government of Canada to focus on failed and fragile states might provide a lens to focus on crises zones. From that perspective, Canadian involvement in the Middle East seems guaranteed in the medium term though Canadian presence and involvement might be limited to the region's conflict zones and to countries of interest to the United States. Should this trend be confirmed, the reorientation of Canadian foreign policy to focus on conflict zones might lend an underlying logic to what now seems like a haphazard set of decisions. The current readjustment of Canadian policies on the Middle East might also bring a different kind of coherence by bringing the values Canada talks in line with the values Canada walks. Canadian policies toward groups labelled "terrorist" have had their critics and supporters, but Ottawa is now behaving in concordance with its discourse.

On the negative side of the ledger, this more ideological set of policies and attitudes can hurt Canada's standing in the Arab world. In her review of Canadian foreign policy in the region, Mira Sucharov concluded in 2003 that the absolute and relative diplomatic influence of Canada had declined from that "of a middle power to a minor power at best." She shared the assessment of both David Malone (2003) and Rex Brynen in this volume that this decline was happening at the same time as other third parties such as Norway or the European Union were carving a larger role in the region.

Although Canada's benign reputation might be an artefact of local ignorance of an otherwise small player, Ottawa runs the risk of seeing its influence wane further the more ideological its policies become. Its policy on Hizbullah and Hamas prevents it from playing a role in mediation and good offices to help resolve current political crises that pit Hamas and Hizbullah respectively against Fatah and the Lebanese government of Prime Minister Fouad Siniora. As Janine Clark argues in Chapter 6, Canada ought to rethink its policies if it wants to continue to undertake preventive activities including mediation and democracy promotion in the Middle East. Although largely absent from the development game in the Middle East, Canada continues to provide aid to assist in rebuilding war-torn societies. However, this is unlikely to earn Ottawa the prestige it has traditionally sought through its aid policy (Nossal 1988). Assistance to the reconstruction of war-torn states and societies is a long and perilous venture on a road fraught with dangers. Success is as much a function of donor resource commitments as it is of the convergence of situational factors over which donors have little control. This was made painfully obvious by the experience of EU assistance to the Palestinian Authority, which, while successful in achieving tangible results until 2000/01, literally went up in smoke when the situation between Palestinians and Israelis deteriorated with the Israel Defense Forces systematically targeting and destroying the entire institutional infrastructure of the Palestinian Authority.

Canadian foreign policy seeks to achieve stability, prosperity, and the promotion of Canadian values. Ottawa's involvement in the Middle East speaks to the difficulty of squaring the circle when resource limitations encourage governments to find inexpensive but powerful alternatives to make a difference. In choosing to privilege norm entrepreneurship, the Canadian government raised expectations among Canadian citizens that Canadian foreign policy would be guided by values rather than interests. The gap between Canada's discourse and its practice was not only predictable; it was inevitable. So was the change in Canada's Middle East policies. Changes in the international environment and the overriding interest in patching up the Canada-U.S. relation could not be ignored. However, Ottawa risks writing itself off the map of international actors in the Middle East should it align itself too closely with the United States. Canada stands to lose any comparative advantage: it is dwarfed by American military power, it cannot compete with European and Japanese financial resources, and it risks the loss of even the perception of impartiality that allows countries such as Norway to act as effective behind-the-scene mediators.

As it navigates the troubled waters of the Middle East and rides the waves of its tumultuous relationship with the United States, the Canadian government needs to consider the domestic reverberation of its actions. Foreign policy in the Middle East has always been a delicate business; it now has the potential, if poorly managed, to trigger instability at home. Home is also where the most useful lessons that might help chart the government's future course of action in the Middle East rest. For pluralism, tolerance, and mutual recognition are the challenges that tear apart the social and political fabric of Middle Eastern societies. They are also the strength and the distinctiveness of the Canadian experience.

Notes

1 The review, entitled "Canada in the World," argued that Canadians "hold deeply that we must pursue our values internationally." It goes on to identify the core elements of Canadian values and culture as human rights, democracy, a law-based international system, sustainable development, and, lastly, culture and education.

2 Axworthy did not only focus on people abroad; he also gave people at home unprecedented access and opportunity to participate in the crafting of Canadian foreign policy. Under his stewardship, government forged closer links than ever with non-governmental organizations (NGOs) and academics notably through the yearly peace-building consultations (a node of interaction with civil society) and the

establishment of the Canadian Consortium for Human Security (a node of inter-action with Canadian academics).

3 While Yemen and Pakistan might not deserve inclusion based on the imminence of a violent breakdown, they do rank very high on other indicators.

4 For example, in 2004/05, Canadian official development assistance (ODA) to Lebanon totalled a mere $7.16 million of the overall $143 million disbursed in the region.

5 The target was established by an international commission headed by former Canadian prime minister Lester Pearson and adopted by the UNGA in 1970.

6 For details about the controversy surrounding the Country Policy and Institutional Assessment criteria, see Powell (2004).

7 For detailed information on the nature of activities and the financial resources committed to help, see www.forces.gc.ca/site/operations/sudan_e.asp.

8 Israel lost 122 citizens and soldiers during the six-week conflict. A full 50 percent of the population of northern Galilee was also displaced by the barrage of Hizbul-lah Katyusha rockets (Zahar 2006).

9 The deaths occurred on July 16; the family held a press conference at noon on July 17. At that time, they had not received word from the federal government. Quebec premier Jean Charest had called them to offer his condolences (see Hamilton 2006). Covering the same story, the BBC stated that "Canadian Prime Minister Stephen Harper offered his condolences to the families of the victims but he refused to criticise Israel or question its use of force" (Carter 2006).

10 The Mennonite Central Committee of Canada is involved in efforts to urge gov-ernments to resettle more refugees from Iraq, although there appears to be no indication of a specific government policy in this respect (see Terichow 2007).

11 Post-conflict aid is usually beset by a substantial gap between pledges of aid and actual disbursements (Forman and Patrick 2000).

12 The fund is in addition to the $5.5 million that CIDA had provided to the Interna-tional Committee of the Red Cross and the United Nations for emergency human-itarian assistance to civilian populations.

13 It is estimated that 80 percent of Canadian exports are sold on the U.S. market.

14 For the OECD's perspective on policy coherence and the whole-of-government approach, see OECD (2007a, 2007b).

References

Annan, Kofi. 2005. "In Larger Freedom: Towards Security, Development, and Human Rights for All." Report of the Security General of the United Nations for decision by Heads of State and Government in September 2005. New York: United Nations. www.un.org/largerfreedom (August 2007).

———. 2000. "Freedom from Fear," chapter 3 of "We the Peoples: The Role of the United Nations in the 21st Century." Millennium Report of the Secre-tary General of the United Nations. www.un.org/millennium/sg/report/full.htm (August 2007).

Axworthy, Lloyd. 1997. "Canada and Human Security: The Need for Leadership." *International Journal* 52(2): 183–96.

Black, David. 2005. "From Kananaskis to Gleneagles: Assessing Canadian 'leadership' on Africa." *Behind the Headlines* 68(3).

Boutros-Ghali, Boutros. 1992. "An Agenda for Peace, Preventive Diplomacy, Peace-making, and Peace-keeping." Report of the Secretary General. New York: United Nations. www.un.org/Docs/SG/agpeace.html (August 2007).

———. 1994. "An Agenda for Development." Report of the Secretary General. New York: United Nations. www.un.org/Docs/SG/agdev.html (August 2007).

Brown, Stephen. 2007. "Creating the World's Best Development Agency"? Confusion and Contradictions in CIDA's New Policy Blueprint." *Canadian Journal of Development Studies* 28(2).

Bryden, Joan. 2006. "Liberal Leadership Hopeful Ignatieff Admits Gaffe over Mideast Conflict." Canadian Press, August 10.

Canadian Broadcasting Corporation. 2006a. "Middle East in Crisis: The Key Quotes." www.cbc.ca/news/background/middleeast-crisis/key-quotes .html (August 2007).

———. 2006b. "So, How's It Going, Eh?" www.cbc.ca/news/background/ canada_us (August 2007).

———. 2007. "Montreal Workers Forced Off Contract over U.S. Security Concerns." January 11. www.cbc.ca/canada/montreal/story/2007/01/11/bell -contract.html (August 2007).

Carment, David. 2003. "Assessing State Failure: Implications for Theory and Policy." *Third World Quarterly* 24(3): 407–27.

Carter, Lee. 2006. "Canada's Shock at Lebanon's Deaths." *BBC News*, July 17. news.bbc.co.uk/2/hi/americas/5189380.stm (August 2007).

Collier, Paul, V.L. Elliott, Havard Hegre, Anke Hoeffler, Marta Reynal-Querol, and Nicholas Sambanis. 2003. "Breaking the Conflict Trap: Civil War and Development Policy." World Bank Policy Research Report. Washington, DC: World Bank. go.worldbank.org/R4ELDCDQE0 (August 2007).

Cellucci, Paul. 2005. Remarks to the "Canada in the World" conference. McGill University, Montreal, February 16–18. misc-iecm.mcgill.ca/canada/ celluci.pdf (August 2007).

Crépeau, François, Marie-Joëlle Zahar, Ryo Chung, Yves Couture, Élise Groulx, Christian Nadeau, Michel Seymour, and David Weinstock. 2006. "Le Canada doit faire respecter le droit international." *Le Devoir* July 22. cerium.ca/article2847.html (August 2007).

Department of Foreign Affairs and International Trade. 1995. "Canada in the World: Canadian Foreign Policy Review." Ottawa. www.international.gc .ca/foreign_policy/cnd-world/menu-en.asp (August 2007).

———. 2005. "Canada's International Policy Statement: A Role of Pride and Influence in the World." Ottawa. geo.international.gc.ca/cip-pic/current _discussions/ips-archive-en.aspx (August 2007).

————. 2006. "Explanation of Vote before the Disarmament and International Security Committee (First Committee) on the Resolution 'Risk of Nuclear Proliferation in the Middle East.'" www.international.gc.ca/middle _east/resolutions/gA61_EOV1-en.asp (August 2007).

————. 2007. "Canada-Sudan Bilateral Relations." Canada: Active in Sudan. geo.international.gc.ca/cip-pic/sudan/cip-pic/library/diplomatic-en.asp (August 2007).

Eagles, Munroe. 2006. "Canadian-American Relations in a Turbulent Era." *PS: Political Science and Politics* 39(4): 821–24.

Edwards, Steven. 2006. "Conservatives Reversing Canada's Position at UN." *National Post*, November 16. www.canada.com/nationalpost/news/story .html?id=a4f26a2f-d325–443a-8e13-cf8ed08b5927 (August 2007).

Evans, Gareth. 2007. "The Responsibility to Protect: The Power of an Idea." Keynote address at the "International Conference on the Responsibility to Protect: Stopping Mass Atrocities," University of California, Berkeley, March 14. www.crisisgroup.org/home/index.cfm?id=4780 (August 2007).

Forman, Shepard, and Stewart Patrick, eds. 2000. *Good Intentions: Pledges of Aid for Post-Conflict Recovery.* Boulder: Lynn Rienner.

Fund for Peace. 2007. "Failed States Index." www.fundforpeace.org/programs/ fsi/fsindex.php (August 2007).

Gänzle, Stefan. 2007. "The Impact of 9/11 on Human Security in Canada's Foreign Policy." Paper prepared for the annual meeting of the Canadian Political Science Association, Saskatoon, Saskatchewan, June 1. www.cpsa -acsp.ca/ papers-2007/Ganzle.pdf (August 2007).

Goldstone, Jack A., Robert H. Bates, Ted Robert Gurr, Michael Lustik, Monty G. Marshall, Jay Ulfelder, and Mark Woodward. 2005. "A Global Forecasting Model of Political Instability." Paper prepared for the annual meeting of the American Political Science Association, Washington, DC, September 1–4. globalpolicy.gmu.edu/pitf/PITFglobal.pdf (August 2007).

Gotlieb, Allan. 2005. "Romanticism and Realism in Canada's Foreign Policy." *Policy Options* (February): 16–27. www.irpp.org/po/archive/feb05/gotlieb .pdf (August 2007).

Hamilton, Graeme. 2006. "Relatives See Hezbollah as Protector: Montreal Druggist Dies from Injuries in Beirut." *National Post*, July 18, A4.

Heinbecker, Paul. 1999. "Human Security." *Peace Magazine* 15(4): 12. archive .peacemagazine.org/v15n4p12.htm (August 2007).

Ignatieff, Michael. 2003. *Empire Lite: Nation-Building in Bosnia, Kosovo, and Afghanistan.* Toronto: Penguin.

International Commission on Intervention and State Sovereignty. 2001. "The Responsibility to Protect: Report of the International Commission on Intervention and State Sovereignty." Ottawa. www.iciss.ca/report-en.asp (August 2007).

Irani, George. 2005. "Canada, Bush II, and the Challenge of Middle East Policy." *Daily Star*, Beirut, January 15. www.royalroads.ca/about-rru/the

-university/news-events/rru-news/canada-bush-ii-and-the-challenge-of -middle-east-policy.htm (August 2007).

Keating, Tom. 2003. "Multilateralism and Canadian Foreign Policy: A Reassessment." Calgary: Canadian Defence and Foreign Affairs Institute. www.cdfai .org/currentpublications.htm (August 2007).

Kenkel, Kai M. 2004. "Whispering to the Prince: Academic Experts and National Security Policy Formulation in Brazil, South Africa, and Canada." Geneva: HEI (unpublished manuscript). Quoted in Gänzle 2007, 6.

Malone, David. 2003. "Canadian Foreign Policy Post 9/11: Institutional and Other Challenges." Calgary: Canadian Defence and Foreign Affairs Institute. www.cdfai.org/currentpublications.htm (August 2007).

McKay, Simeon. 2006. "The Limits of Likemindedness." *International Journal* 61(4): 875–94.

Nossal, Kim Richard. 1988. "Mixed Motives Revisited: Canada's Interest in Development Assistance." *Canadian Journal of Political Science* 21(1): 35–56.

Office of the Prime Minister. 2006. "Prime Minister Announces New Lebanon Relief Fund." Ottawa. August 16. www.pm.gc.ca/eng/media.asp?id=1282 (August 2007).

Organisation for Economic Co-operation and Development. 2007a. "Principles for Good International Engagement in Fragile States." www.oecd.org/ document/46/0,2340,en_2649_201185_35233262_1_1_1_1,00.html (August 2007).

———. 2007b. "Whole of Government Approaches in Fragile States." www.oecd .org/document/4/0,2340,en_2649_201185_35237252_1_1_1_1,00.html (August 2007).

Powell, Jeff. 2004. "The World Bank Policy Scorecard: The New Conditionality?" London: Bretton Woods Project. www.brettonwoodsproject.org/ atissuecpia (August 2007).

Pratt, Cranford, ed. 1989. *Internationalism under Strain: The North-South Policies of Canada, the Netherlands, Norway, and Sweden.* Toronto: University of Toronto Press.

Republic of Lebanon, Ministry of Finance. 2006. "Stockholm Conference for Lebanon's Early Recovery." August 31. www.finance.gov.lb/NR/rdonlyres/ 8B9C27A9-7424-4A34-80E0-FC0C2B7D121A/0/StockholmConference forLebanonForDissemination12Oct2006doc.pdf (August 2007).

Riddell-Dixon, Elizabeth. 2003. "Domestic Demographics and Canadian Foreign Policy." Calgary: Canadian Defence and Foreign Affairs Institute, 2003. www.cdfai.org/currentpublications.htm (August 2007).

Rotberg, Robert I. 2004. "The Failure and Collapse of Nation-States: Breakdown, Prevention, and Repair," in *When States Fail: Causes and Consequences*, ed. Robert I. Rotberg, 1–50. Princeton: Princeton University Press.

Sachs, Jeffrey, and John MacArthur. 2005. "Promises Aren't Enough." *Globe and Mail.* April 22, A23.

Statistics Canada. 2003. "Canada's Ethnocultural Portrait: The Changing Mosaic." www12.statcan.ca/english/census01/Products/Analytic/companion/etoim/ canada.cfm (August 2007).

Sucharov, Mira. 2003. "A Multilateral Affair: Canadian Foreign Policy in the Middle East." In *Canada Among Nations 2003: Dealing with the American Colossus,* ed. David Carment, Fen Osler Hampson, and Norman Hillmer. Toronto: Oxford University Press.

Terichow, Gladys. 2007. "Refugee Resettlement Issues, Private Sponsorship to Be Discussed at UN Consultations." ReliefWeb, June 22. www.reliefweb.int/ rw/rwb.nsf/db900sid/YDOI-74H3AH?OpenDocument (August 2007).

United Nations. 2004. "A More Secure World: Our Shared Responsibility." Report of the Secretary General's High-Level Panel on Threats, Challenges, and Change. New York. www.un.org/secureworld (August 2007).

Welsh, Jennifer. 2004. "Introduction." In *Humanitarian Intervention and International Relations,* ed. Jennifer Welsh, 52–68. Oxford: Oxford University Press.

Woods, Allan. 2006. "Harper Blocks Lebanon Resolution." CanWest News Service. September 29. www.canada.com/topics/news/story.html?id=80d16e11 -b92b-4fe7-a6dd-4a47c26d2e9f&k=28442 (August 2007).

Woodward, Susan. 2005. "Introduction to the Workshop." Prepared for the "Workshop on State Failure: Reframing the International Economic and Political Agenda," City University of New York, May 9–10. www.statesand security.org/_pdfs/Woodward_memo.pdf (August 2007).

Zahar, Marie-Joëlle. 2005. "Intervention, Prevention, and the 'Responsibility to Protect': Considerations for Canadian Foreign Policy." *International Journal* 60(3): 723–34.

———. 2006. "Moyen-Orient: L'année de tous les dangers." In *Les conflits dans le monde 2006,* ed. Albert Legault, Michel Fortmann, and Gérard Hervouet. Quebec: Presses de l'Université Laval and Institut québécois des hautes études internationales.

Zahar, Marie-Joëlle, Marie-Eve Desrosiers, and Stephen Brown. 2007. "Failed and Fragile States: Diagnoses, Prescriptions and Considerations for Canadian Foreign Policy." Discussion paper presented at the workshop "Failed and Fragile States: Diagnoses, Prescriptions, and Considerations for Canadian Foreign Policy," Université du Québec à Montréal, Montreal, May 25.

Canada's Role in the
Israeli-Palestine
Peace Process

Like most of the international community, "Canada is committed to the goal of a comprehensive, just and lasting peace in the Middle East, and the creation of a sovereign, independent, viable, democratic and territorially contiguous Palestinian state living side by side in peace and security with Israel" (Department of Foreign Affairs and International Trade [DFAIT] 2007). The key challenge facing Canadian decision makers, however, has been how to translate general support for a negotiated two-state solution into policies that might make a difference in bringing that solution into being. Does Canada have particular strengths (or weaknesses) to bring to the Middle East peace process? Is there a particular Canadian niche? And what constraints might be imposed on Canada for taking a proactive and innovative role in supporting a peaceful settlement of the conflict?

This chapter will focus on the evolution of Canadian policy since the early 1990s. In doing so, it will first offer a brief history of Canadian involvement in the Arab-Israeli conflict. It will then turn to the contemporary Israeli-Palestinian peace process and Canadian engagement in that process. Several aspects of Canadian policy during this period will be highlighted: Canada's general orientation toward the Middle East peace process, development assistance to the West Bank and Gaza, and the thorny humanitarian and political issue of Palestinian refugees. This will be followed by a discussion of the key variables that have shaped Canadian policy responses. Finally, the chapter will conclude by assessing what role Canada might play in the coming years.

Canada and the Arab-Israeli Conflict

Canada's first substantial involvement in the Arab-Israeli conflict came with the very birth of Israel. As a member of the 11-member United Nations Special

Committee on Palestine (UNSCOP) in 1947, Canada voted in support of the majority report calling for the partition of Palestine into Jewish and Arab states. At the time, Canadian views were shaped by cultural and historical factors rather than realpolitik: many Canadian policy makers viewed the "Holy Land" through the prism of the bible and their predominantly Christian heritage, and had particular sympathy for the Jewish people in the wake of the recent atrocities of the Holocaust. By contrast, the views of the majority of the indigenous Arab population in the territory counted for little. When Israel was established in May 1948, Canadians overwhelmingly supported the nascent Jewish state in the ensuing war with its Arab neighbours.

The next major phase of Canadian engagement came during the 1956 Suez crisis, when Israel, France, and the United Kingdom attacked Egypt. Anglo-French intervention was criticized by Washington, and Ottawa found itself uncomfortably torn between its American and British allies. The Suez crisis also threatened to escalate into a broader East-West confrontation amid the tensions of the Cold War. To resolve the splits in the western alliance and avert the broader crisis, as Minister of External Affairs Lester Pearson proposed the deployment of a UN peacekeeping force in the Sinai. Canadian forces subsequently served in the United Nations Emergency Force (UNEF), which was commanded for a period by a Canadian, Lieutenant-General E.L.M. Burns. For Pearson's contribution both to resolving the Suez Crisis and the development of UN peacekeeping, he was awarded the 1957 Nobel Peace Prize. No other Canadian foreign minister achieved as much, and few even tried to make the issue a personal priority.

With the 1967 Arab-Israeli war, Israel achieved a stunning military victory over its neighbours. The last remaining areas of Palestine—the Jordanian-annexed West Bank, and Egyptian-administered Gaza Strip—fell under Israeli occupation. So too did Syria's Golan Heights. Canadians remained overwhelmingly sympathetic to the Israeli side. At the same time, Canadian policy supported UN Security Council (UNSC) resolution 242 and its call for an Israeli withdrawal from occupied territories and a negotiated settlement among the warring states. The Palestinians and their claims for self-determination, however, did not yet figure as a major element in either UNSC resolution 242 or Canadian policy, other than as amorphous "refugees" in need of a "just settlement" to their plight.

From this point, however, Canadian policy would undergo significant evolution in the 1970s and '80s. One reason for this was the 1973 Arab-Israeli war. This war again illustrated the dangers of regional conflict in a world already fraught with Cold War tensions. The accompanying Arab oil embargo also highlighted the large and growing strategic importance of this resource. While Canada (unlike the United States) was not specifically targeted, the embargo and subsequent oil price increases led Ottawa and most other western capitals to be more mindful of Arab views and sensitivities. At the same time, a number of Israeli actions—notably, illegal settlement activity in the occupied territories, as well as the annexation of east Jerusalem—eroded Canadian support for Israeli policies.

The importance of this was underscored in 1979, when the new Conservative government of Prime Minister Joe Clark proposed, against the advice of the Department of External Affairs, to relocate Canada's embassy from Tel Aviv to Jerusalem. Withering, negative Arab reaction led Clark to appoint former Conservative leader Robert Stanfield to review both the embassy issue and the broader spectrum of Canada's relationship with the Middle East. While stressing Canada's sympathy, friendship, and "strong support" for Israel, Stanfield's report suggested that the embassy not be moved in view of the political sensitivities involved. It also suggested that Canada deepen its bilateral and commercial relations with the Arab world. Significantly, the report offered some recognition of the importance of the Palestinian issue, noting that the Palestinians "have now emerged fully conscious of their identity and anxious to give that identity political expression" (Special Representative of the Government of Canada and Ambassador-at-Large 1980).

The political salience of the Palestinian issue was further highlighted by growing prominence of the Palestine Liberation Organization (PLO), by Israel's 1982 invasion of Lebanon and subsequent siege of PLO forces in Beirut, and by the eruption of the first Palestinian intifada (uprising) against Israeli occupation in the West bank and Gaza (1987-91). Canadian public opinion grew somewhat more sensitive to the rights of the Palestinians. Overall, however, Canadian policy was slower to change in this regard than were the policies of many other western countries (for an overview, see Noble 1985a, 1985b). While support for Israel was much of the reason for this, there was also some concern about the ramifications of supporting Palestinian political self-expression or self-determination at a time when Ottawa faced a growing sovereignist movement in Quebec.

The Israeli-Palestinian Peace Process: A Brief Overview

In October 1991, Israel, Syria, Lebanon, Jordan, and the Palestinians met in Madrid under U.S. and Soviet auspices—a historic meeting that would mark the beginning of the contemporary Middle East peace process. When the multilateral tracks of the peace process started up in January 1992 in Madrid, Canada found itself assigned a formal role, as gavel holder of the Refugee Working Group (RWG). The RWG was not Canada's first choice of assignment—Ottawa would have much preferred to head the working groups on water or arms control and regional security. However, both Washington and Israelis seemed to be more comfortable with a Canadian (rather than a European) chair of the highly sensitive refugee issue. Canada's RWG role would have a significant influence on its subsequent engagement in Middle East affairs for more than a decade.

In September 1993, a major breakthrough in the peace process occurred as Israel and the PLO signed the joint Declaration of Principles, better known as the Oslo Accords. This paved the way for the establishment of the Palestinian Authority in parts of the West Bank and Gaza in 1994.

A Canadian representative office to the Palestinian Authority was opened in Ramallah in 1999, staffed by personnel from the Department of Foreign Affairs and International Trade (DFAIT) and the Canadian International Development Agency (CIDA). Canada—by virtue of its seat on the steering committee of the multilaterals—became a member of the Ad Hoc Liaison Committee (AHLC), a 15-member body established in 1993 to provide overall coordination and coherence to donor efforts in the West Bank and Gaza. Later, Canada also joined the Task Force on Palestinian Reform (TFPR), another small international coordinating body that functioned from 2002 to 2006 to oversee donor support for reform efforts in the Palestinian Authority.

Israeli-Palestinian permanent status negotiations were held in 2000/01. They were tragically unsuccessful. The failure of the July 2000 Camp David Summit, the eruption of the second Palestinian intifada in September 2000, escalating Palestinian-Israeli violence, the February 2001 defeat of Ehud Barak and election of Israeli prime minister Ariel Sharon all marked the accelerating, and often bloody, collapse of the peace process. In an effort to arrest and reverse this collapse, the diplomatic Quartet (the United States, the European Union, Russia, and the United Nations) produced its "Performance-Based Roadmap to a Permanent Two-State Solution to the Israeli-Palestinian Conflict" in April 2003 (U.S. Department of State 2003). The road map, however, made little progress. In November 2004, Palestinian leader Yasser Arafat died and was succeeded in the presidency of the Palestinian Authority by his long-time Fatah colleague Mahmud Abbas.

Amid diplomatic stalemate and continued violence—and in recognition that demographics did not favour the perpetuation of a democratic Jewish state, as well as in the hope of consolidating Israel's territorial control in the West Bank—Sharon adopted a unilateral approach. As a major element of this, Israel withdrew its forces and settlers from Gaza in August 2005. Canadian prime minister Paul Martin (2005) welcomed the move as a "significant decision" and expressed hope that it would be "a historic opportunity for Palestinian Authority President Mahmoud Abbas and his people to make progress toward the eventual establishment of a Palestinian state in the West Bank and Gaza." In support of disengagement, Canadian technical expertise on border crossings management was provided. A few Canadian military personnel (in "Operation Proteus") also assisted the U.S. Security Coordinator in supporting security sector reform and strengthening the capacity of Palestinian (or, to be more accurate, Fatah) security personnel (Department of National Defence [DND] 2007).

In January 2006, however, Sharon suffered a stroke and was succeeded by Ehud Olmert, while in the Palestinian territories the militant Islamist group Hamas won a striking victory over the mainstream Fatah movement in elections for the Palestinian Legislative Council. The Olmert government reacted by isolating Hamas and withholding tax revenues of the Palestinian Authority. Especially after its unsuccessful military campaign in Lebanon the previous summer, and in light of continued rocket attacks from Gaza, the Olmert government proved unable and unwilling to undertake further unilateral withdrawals. Canada, followed by other donors, cut off budget support and direct contact with the Hamas-controlled institutions of the Palestinian Authority, while continuing to work with Abbas, the Fatah president of the Palestinian Authority.

Despite the eventual formation of a Hamas-Fatah national unity government in 2007, the Palestinian Authority continued to be afflicted by severe political paralysis, deteriorating economic conditions, and periodic bouts of internecine fighting. In June 2007, these escalated to full-scale armed clashes in Gaza, in which Fatah forces were routed and Hamas was left in control of the strip. Abbas responded by condemning Hamas's actions as a "bloody coup," consolidating Fatah's position in the West Bank, and announcing the formation of a new (Fatah-controlled) emergency government. While Hamas decried these moves as unconstitutional, Israel, Egypt, Jordan, the U.S., the EU, and Canada all moved to support the Abbas government. In Washington, hope was expressed that the removal of Hamas from the formal government would make it easier to move forward in the peace process. However, a bifurcated Palestinian administration and deeply divided Palestinian society seemed to be a very poor foundation for any optimism at all. Peace seemed as far away as ever.

Canadian Policy and the Peace Process

Canada's general position on the Israeli-Palestinian conflict has—not coincidentally—typically fallen somewhere between that of the U.S. and Europe. Unlike Washington, Ottawa has long characterized Israeli settlement activity in the occupied territories not only as a serious obstacle to peace, but also as a violation of international law. As noted earlier, Ottawa (unlike many European states) was relatively slow to acknowledge a Palestinian right to self-determination, a term that was not employed until after the first Palestinian intifada erupted in 1987. Moreover, through much of the 1980s, Canadian officials expressed vague support for a Palestinian "entity" or "homeland" rather than a Palestinian state (Noble 1985b). Even in the aftermath of the

Oslo Accords, Ottawa tended to state that it "would not exclude" the creation of a Palestinian state if that were decided by the parties through negotiations, rather than actively advocating this as the desirable outcome of negotiations. It was not until after permanent status negotiations in 2000/01, and especially UNSC resolution 1397 of March 2002 (which affirmed "a vision of a region where two States, Israel and Palestine, live side by side within secure and recognized borders"), that Canadian policy makers actively, and rather belatedly, advocated this outcome.

In general, Canada has benefited from a relatively benign image among Israeli and Palestinian officials alike—although, among Palestinians, in particular, this may be as much due to their slight knowledge of Canadian policies as to their warm feelings toward Canada in general. Moreover, while Israeli officials have generally been satisfied with Canadian diplomacy (especially in the Martin and Harper eras), Palestinians have been heard to express disappointment that Canada is not more active, either as a middle power diplomatic activist (as Norway and, to a lesser extent, Sweden have been) or as a major aid donor.

Canadian policy began to tilt more toward Israel, tentatively at first under the Liberal government of Prime Minister Paul Martin, and more assertively under the Conservatives and Prime Minister Stephen Harper. Under Martin, this was marked by a shift in Canadian votes on a number of UN General Assembly (UNGA) resolutions, which the government characterized as unbalanced or excessively politicized, although few other governments seemed to agree. Perhaps the most notable example of this came in July 2004, when Canada abstained on an UNGA resolution calling for Israel to abide by a recent International Court of Justice opinion regarding the illegality of Israel's separation barrier in the West Bank. The vote on the resolution was 150 in favour and six against, with 10 abstentions. While the U.S. and Australia opposed the resolution, every other country in the western world supported it (UN 2004).

This pattern continued, and intensified, under the new Harper government. In 2006, Canada's voting record on UNGA resolutions sympathetic to the Palestinians stood at 8 votes in favour, 4 votes against, and 4 abstentions, compared to 13–0–3 for France, Italy, Germany, Norway, Sweden, and the UK (among other Europeans) and Japan, 5–8–3 for Australia, 0–14–2 for the U.S., and 0–15–1 for Israel (Permanent Observer Mission of Palestine to the UN 2007). Also, the Conservative government was the first country to withdraw aid from the Palestinian Authority following the election of the Hamas government in January 2006. Prime Minister Harper has been sharply critical of past Liberal policy, arguing that "my own assessment of Canada's role in the Middle East in the past decade or so is we've been completely absent. I don't see any evidence we've been playing any role" (CTV 2006).

Canada and the Palestinian Refugee Issue

As noted earlier, Canada was designated the gavel holder of the RWG in 1991, with the start of the multilateral track of the Middle East peace process. Thereafter, the refugee issue would become a major focus of Canadian engagement.

Under Canadian leadership, the RWG held large plenary sessions in May and November 1992, May and October 1993, May and December 1994, and December 1995. Numerous expert and intersessional meetings were also held. However, the challenges facing the RWG, and its Canadian chair, were formidable (for a more detailed account, see Brynen and Tansley 1995; Brynen 1997). The refugee issue was a particularly sensitive one, cutting to the very existential core of the Israeli state and Palestinian self-identity. Unlike some issues of the peace process, there had been little prior discussion of it between Palestinian and Israeli experts. The formal and multilateral character of RWG meetings discouraged frank discussion, and tended to generate agreement only on the lowest common denominator of improving the humanitarian conditions of the refugees. Israel was particularly anxious to steer the RWG away from addressing political issues, while the U.S. tended to be extremely cautious lest the multilaterals complicate progress on what Washington considered the more important, bilateral track. Syria and Lebanon boycotted the multilaterals altogether, with Damascus fearing that such "normalization" of contact with Israel would work to the latter's advantage.

Finally, the RWG, like all of the multilaterals, was profoundly vulnerable to changes in the broader status of Arab-Israeli relations. The deteriorating climate that followed the May 1996 election of a right-wing coalition under Israeli prime minister Benjamin Netanyahu (Likud) made it impossible to hold another RWG plenary. The following year, the Arab League announced a boycott of the multilateral track altogether, although some quiet RWG activities continued. Although the Labor Party returned to power in Israel under Ehud Barak in May 1999, the approach of permanent status negotiations meant there was little interest in formally resurrecting the multilaterals.

Faced with these challenges, Canada adopted a number of alternative approaches. First, it sponsored a range of so-called "second track" research projects, bringing together scholars, civil society, and former officials in what became known as the "Ottawa process" (Rempel 1999; Dumper 2007, 129–31; Palestinian Refugee ResearchNet 2007). This process, first anticipated in a Canadian-authored "vision paper" prepared for the steering committee of multilaterals in 1995, became a major focus after 1996. Through such efforts it was hoped to develop new and innovative ideas that could inform future negotiations, as well as foster a degree of quiet dialogue among well-connected Palestinian and Israeli interlocutors (Brynen et al. 2003). Canada also played an important role in supporting (with both money and technical assistance) policy planning on the refugee repatriation and absorption by both the World Bank and by the Palestinian Authority itself.

Ottawa continued to use its position as RWG gavel to raise awareness of the refugee issue, despite the non-functioning of the working group itself. Perhaps the most noteworthy example of this was the so-called "No-Name Group," an informal group of key international actors (including Canada, the U.S., the UK, Norway, several other western countries, the UN, and the World Bank) that first met under Canadian auspices in Washington in December 2000. In stark contrast to earlier RWG plenaries, the small and very informal setting of the No-Name Group allowed a free and frank discussion of what the international community might do to support any future refugee agreement that might emerge from permanent status negotiations.

Subsequent No-Name Group meetings were held in London, Washington, Geneva, and Brussels from 2001 to 2004. Over time, the group lost some of its focus, both because of the collapse of permanent status negotiations and because an expansion of its membership tended to dilute the quality of discussions. In April 2007, Canada sought to establish a new refugee coordination forum as a replacement, although problems of focus and membership remained.

Canadian Development Assistance

Another major element of Canadian engagement in the Israeli-Palestinian peace process has been through the provision of development assistance, both to the occupied Palestinian territories and to Palestinian refugees in neighbouring countries. Between 1993 and 2004, CIDA (2006) allocated an average of approximately $25 million per year, with total disbursements totalling $333 million by the end of 2005. Canadian aid has been allocated across a number of areas, including initial budget support to the Palestinian Authority, refugees, child welfare, municipal infrastructure and capacity building, and civil society.

How successful have these aid efforts been in promoting peace and sustainable development in the Palestinian territories? Aid can certainly build local capacities, and create a supportive environment for peace (Secretariat of the Ad Hoc Liaison Committee 2000; Brynen 2000). Aid cannot, however, in and of itself buy support for peace. Indeed, polling data show little if any connection between socioeconomic conditions and political attitudes among Palestinians (Brynen 2005a, 130–32). Instead, local attitudes to the peace process are fundamentally driven by political factors, including normative concerns, the level of violence, and the state of the peace process itself. Moreover, there is substantial evidence that many donors—Canada among them—have often used development aid as a safe and non-controversial alternative to addressing the sensitive and difficult political issues at stake in the conflict. This sort of issue avoidance has led many aid officials and other analysts to conclude that "aid may have been part of the problem rather than part of the solution" (Keating 2005, 2).

In addition, the effectiveness of aid in the West Bank and Gaza has been limited by massive exogenous political and economic shocks, which have often offset its positive effects. In particular, Israeli security measures (mobility restrictions and the construction of the separation barrier) as well as the periodic suspension of tax transfers have resulted in severe economic damage to the territories and have rendered sustainable economic development impossible—for the present, at least. Despite being second only to Israel as the largest per capita recipients of aid in the world, Palestinians have also experienced what the World Bank described as one of the most severe economic downturns in modern history, exceeding even that of the Great Depression (World Bank 2004, 1). By 2006, per capita gross domestic product (GDP) had fallen to almost 40 percent from its 1999 (pre-intifada) levels (International Monetary Fund [IMF] and World Bank 2007, 8–9).

There have also been particular challenges facing Canadian assistance in the West Bank and Gaza. CIDA is a relatively small donor relative to others in the Palestinian territories. Between 1994 and 1998, Canada accounted for 1 percent of aid pledges to the occupied territories. Relative to donor gross national product (GNP), this was one of the least generous rates of aid mobilization among substantial donors (Brynen 2000, 75, 84). In the 2002, Canada accounted for only 0.9 percent of aid commitments in the West Bank and Gaza (ranking 11th among donors) and 1.3 percent of aid disbursements (ranking 10th) (Brynen 2005b).

Canada's aid program has also been relatively broadly dispersed across sectors, making it difficult to establish a recognized niche. This would be less of a problem if CIDA had a particular reputation for responsiveness, and the fast and flexible delivery of assistance (which in itself can be a niche). It is fair to say, however, that it does not—although Canada's ratio of aid disbursements to pledges has been above the average for donor agencies (Brynen 2000, 150). At times, Canadian aid responsiveness has also been constrained by bouts of dysfunctional bureaucratic politics between CIDA and DFAIT. Only in the area of refugees has Canada carved out a distinctive niche—and here, some of the value of that niche has declined somewhat as a resolution of the refugee issue has seemed ever more distant.

While most comparably sized European donors are able to get an aid coordination and impact "multiplier" through their membership in the EU, Canada is not able to do so. While Canada has been a member of two exclusive aid coordination bodies—the AHLC and TFPR—it is not large enough to be a member of the so-called "aid politburo" (the U.S., the EU, Norway, the

World Bank) where most strategic aid decisions are made. Moreover, Canada has tended to deliver relatively bland policy statements, rather than offering new information or articulating distinct, controversial, or innovative ideas in donor coordination forums. Indeed, when interviewed by the author in 2003, many aid officials from other countries were unaware that Canada was even a member of the TFPR.

Compounding this problem is the tendency of many Canadian officials to overestimate our role, expertise, contribution, or reputation. In both Israel and the occupied Palestinian territories, it is probably fair to say that Canada is seen as a "nice," but often rather marginal, donor and diplomatic actor.

Canadian development assistance to the occupied Palestinian territories faced new challenges in January 2006, with the electoral victory of Hamas in Palestinian Legislative Council elections. With this and the establishment of a Hamas-controlled cabinet, Canada announced a suspension of direct aid to the Palestinian Authority, a review of all projects involving partnership with the authority, and restrictions on official Canadian contact with Palestinian officials. Four projects (worth $7.3 million) were suspended, and eight others worth $23.9 million were limited or restructured (CIDA 2006). Much of this aid was redirected through international organizations active in the West Bank and Gaza.

In June 2007, the picture changed again as civil conflict enveloped Gaza and the Palestinian Authority split. Canada responded by announcing a resumption of its bilateral assistance to the authority—or, more specifically, to the new West Bank–based, Fatah-controlled emergency government. While some aid to Gaza would continue, it would be directed through channels not under Hamas control.

The Determinants of Canadian Policy

Canadian engagement in the Israeli-Palestinian peace process—like all foreign policy—is the product of a complex mix of factors, both domestic and external. Most fundamentally, Canada has an interest in seeing a peaceful resolution of a conflict that has spurred regional conflict and political radicalization in the Middle East for well over half a century. The strategic importance of the Middle East—an importance rooted in geographic location, petroleum resources, dangers of the proliferation of weapons of mass destruction (WMD), and the contemporary scourge of terrorism—heighten the salience of the conflict still further, and helps to explain why the issue receives a larger share of Canadian diplomacy and aid than do the much needier populations in most countries of sub-Saharan Africa.

Societal Attitudes

Canadian policy is obviously shaped by general societal attitudes to the conflict. These—when Canadians are paying attention—generally support a negotiated, two-state solution to the conflict.

In turn, societal attitudes in Canada on the Palestinian-Israeli conflict are, to some extent, shaped by the nature of media coverage. Some have accused the Canadian Broadcasting Corporation (CBC) of a pro-Palestinian bias, a charge that the network vehemently rejects. Among other media outlets, both Hollinger (former corporate owner of the Southam newspaper chain) and CanWest Global (current owner of the former Southam/Hollinger papers, as well as Global TV) have adopted strongly pro-Israeli editorial positions.

Of particular importance are the views held by those communities and interest groups more closely linked to the region, namely the Jewish Canadians (approximately 340,000 in 2001) and Arab Canadians (approximately 194,000 in 2001, including approximately 20,000 Palestinians). Historically, the Jewish Canadian organizations such as the Canadian Jewish Congress and the Canada-Israel Committee have been among the most effective foreign policy lobbies in Ottawa, by virtue of their skill, resources, and political sophistication. By contrast, Arab Canadians tend to have less political experience and deeper internal divisions. Many have immigrated from countries were policy advocacy and dissent are far from encouraged. For this and other reasons, their lobbying organizations (such as the Canadian Arab Federation and the National Council on Canada-Arab Relations) have been much less effective. It remains to be seen whether this gap will narrow over time. What is known, however, is that the Arab Canadian population, fuelled by continued immigration, will continue to grow substantially over time, with Statistics Canada estimating it will reach between 370,000 and 521,000 by 2017 (Statistics Canada 2005).

The effect of such interest group activism on Middle East issues has generally been to instil a significant degree of caution in Canadian policy, among ministers and bureaucrats alike. This is especially true of positions that might provoke critical reaction from the pro-Israeli lobby. With relatively few Canadian voters (even in the most interested communities) casting their ballots on the basis of foreign policy preferences, this caution often seems well out of proportion to the actual political clout of domestic communities.

Policy Makers and Policy Making

Canadian policy on the Israeli-Palestinian conflict is also shaped by the attitude of governing parties, and especially key policy makers: the prime minister, the minister of foreign affairs, and other influential members of Cabinet. Typically, most Canadian parties contain a range of views on the region. However, the importance of policy-maker attitudes was clearly demonstrated by the modest shift in Canadian policy that occurred between (Liberal) prime ministers Chrétien and Martin, and the much larger tilt that took place under (Conservative) Prime Minister Harper. Harper holds particularly strong ideological views on the Middle East, including sympathy for Israel and support for the basic tenets of the Bush administration foreign policy. These instincts were particularly evident in his handling of the Israel-Hizbullah war in the summer of 2006. Harper has also maintained (through the Prime Minister's Office) a much closer watch (and rein) on Canadian initiatives and policy statements on the region than had his predecessors.

In addition to the influence of political leaders, officials at DFAIT and CIDA also have significant influence on policy content. The bureaucracy filters and packages information for senior policy makers (although politicians also rely heavily on media coverage and other sources of information). They help frame issues and play a key role in developing and proposing policy initiatives. Of course, they do so with a generally cautious eye to what they view as feasible given both the region and the political climate at home. Still, the effect of idiosyncratic factors—the political views of officials and their particular diplomatic and organizational styles—can be substantial, especially in the relatively small universe of Canadian policy in the Middle East.

This has been particularly evident in the significantly different approaches taken by the various diplomats who have served as RWG gavel holder and Middle East coordinator over the years. The first, Marc Perron, was often bluntly outspoken and eager to challenge the various "taboos" associated with the refugee issue. Andrew Robinson was more of a consensus builder, and placed great stock in keeping alive the formal RWG process of plenary and intersessional meetings. Mike Molloy, by contrast, tended to favour more informal approaches, as evidenced in the establishment of the No-Name Group. Jill Sinclair proved particularly dynamic, advocating a significant role in support of Gaza disengagement in addition of the established focus on refugees. However, her views and style also led to serious tensions with CIDA and others during this period. Finally, with Peter McRae there has been renewed attention to the refugee issue.

In addition to the particular roles of policy makers, processes of policy making have also helped to shape Canadian initiatives. On the positive side, tripartite cooperation among DFAIT, CIDA, and the International Development Research Centre (IDRC) was absolutely essential in the Ottawa process, with CIDA providing the funding, DFAIT the political umbrella, and IDRC's Middle East Initiatives unit organizing much of the policy research and second-track activities. On the other hand, bureaucratic turf battles—especially between DFAIT in Ottawa and CIDA across the bridge in Gatineau—can be especially debilitating, with the Ottawa River seeming very wide indeed at times.

External Relations

Canadian policy has also been influenced by Ottawa's desire to maintain a positive relationship with other countries, both inside and outside the region. By far the most important consideration in this regard has been the United States.

The U.S., by simple fact of geography and economics, is by far the most important dimension of Canadian foreign policy. Canada has therefore been reluctant to undertake Middle East initiatives that might not enjoy Washington's full endorsement, a reluctance that sometimes constrains policy independence and innovation. Ironically, it is not always clear that American officials pay much attention to most Canadian activities in the region, providing perhaps more room to manoeuvre than is generally perceived. In turn, this leads to something of a paradox, whereby Canada consults the U.S., the U.S. expresses an opinion, and Canada then feels bound to adhere by it—while had Ottawa not asked in the first place Washington would not have much cared. A good example of this was Canadian support for World Bank policy research on the refugee issue in 2000/01. The U.S. had long signalled that it felt such work was too politically sensitive to undertake. The World Bank, however, systematically under-informed the State Department about the scope of its activities, and Canada did not closely consult Washington while supporting those efforts. Washington's benign ignorance turned out to be a blessing in the spring of 2000 when—in the run-up to the Camp David Summit, the U.S. suddenly shifted positions and asked the World Bank for technical work on refugees. Because the work had gone ahead anyway, seven volumes of reports were on their way to the State Department within a week.

Conclusion

What overall assessment might be made of Canadian support for the Palestinian-Israeli peace process since 1991? One appraisal has noted that "through persistence, pragmatism and a commitment to balance, fairness and even-handedness, Canada has achieved a prominence in the Middle East refugee debate vastly disproportionate to its ranking in the traditional hierarchy on international power and influence" (Goldberg and Shames 2004, 215). A more critical evaluation would suggest that Canada has had little practical influence on the search for peace, on the refugee issue or any other (Spector 2003).

In fact, Canada's influence lies somewhere between the two. Canada has certainly done much more than any other country to promote technical knowledge and original thinking on the refugee issue. In some key areas (notably that of refugee repatriation and compensation), such work has substantially shaped both intellectual and policy approaches. On the other hand, Canada probably could have done somewhat more in 1999/2000 to help prepare the way for permanent status negotiations on this issue.

Canadian policy on the broader aspects of the conflict has been unremarkable, and has had correspondingly little influence. Even when Canada has managed to join significant multilateral groupings—such as the AHLC and TFPR—its presence has had no discernable impact. Domestic and U.S. constraints, and a certain ingrained lack of adventurism, have led Canada to be less frank, outspoken, and proactive than it might have been. The contrasts between Canadian policy, and that of another like-minded middle power—Norway, are particularly striking. It is hard to imagine Canada having assumed the role that Norway has taken in the Israeli-Palestinian peace process (or, for that matter, Norwegian efforts in Guatemala and Sri Lanka). Successive Norwegian governments have understood, inter alia, that successful foreign policy requires independence of mind, confidence, sustained commitment, and the financial resources to underwrite activism.

Canada's willingness to "vote the merits" on UN resolutions—changing its traditional vote if need be to express its opposition to unbalanced or rhetorical resolutions—can be seen as Ottawa sticking by principles even at the cost of critical commentary. In the case of recent votes, the criticism of change came from the Palestinian side. The credibility of the initiatives of the Martin and Harper governments, however, was severely undermined by Canada's unwillingness to be similarly outspoken about other issues, such as the continued expansion of settlements and the separation barrier. Indeed, Canada's opposition to the 2004 reference by the International Court of Justice on the separation barrier—on the frankly ludicrous ground that a court established by the UN Charter to deal with international disputes, moreover a court whose judgments Canada had welcomed in other cases, should not deal with political issues—stands as something of a low point in Canadian diplomacy on the peace process. It also flies in the face of years of Canadian rhetoric on the importance of international law and the need for a rules-based international system.

With the peace process in tatters, and no prospects of a return to serious Israeli-Palestinian peace negotiations any time soon, it is particularly difficult to identify useful directions for future Canadian policy. Work on the refugee issue should certainly continue, since it has become an established Canadian niche. It will also be a central issue in any future peace negotiations, whenever those might occur. Such efforts should be focused on salient current aspects of the issue (such as the status of Palestinians in Iraq and Lebanon, or the challenges facing the United Nations Relief and Works Agency for Palestine Refugees in the Near East [UNRWA]), however, where Canadian leadership could make a real difference. Longer-term work on final status issues can, for now, be kept to the back burner.

There is also a need for a comprehensive review of Canadian policy on how to deal with the challenge posed by Hamas, to assure that policies in this area are underpinned by a clear medium-term strategic vision and not by wishful thinking or an ad hoc reaction to local events. The events of 2006/07 have shown that the Islamist movement has deep social and political roots, and will not simply fade away under western (or Israeli) pressure. Indeed, policies designed to undercut the Hamas-dominated Palestinian Authority and promote Fatah instead—ignoring the niceties of Palestinian democratic institutions in the process—had the effect of spurring the Hamas takeover of Gaza by otherwise denying it the fruits of its electoral victory. This is not to say that Hamas's programmatic commitment to the destruction of Israel is compatible with Canadian values and interests—it clearly is not. However, some way needs to be found to encourage more moderate elements within the Islamist political spectrum that would be willing to accept a negotiated, two-state solution to the conflict. In this, some form of political engagement will be key.

Above all else, Canada needs to be realistic about its capacities, innovative and principled in its approaches, circumspect about local conditions, and pragmatically ambitious (often in concert with other like-minded actors) in its engagement. Middle East peace will not come easily, and at times it may feel like it will never come at all. The stakes for the protagonists, and indeed for the rest of us, however, are potentially so great that the international community, Canada included, has ample reason to keep trying.

References

Brynen, Rex. 1997. "Much Ado About Nothing? The Refugee Working Group and the Perils of Multilateral Quasi-Negotiation." *International Negotiation* 2(2): 279–302.

———. 2000. *A Very Political Economy: Peacebuilding and Foreign Aid in the West Bank and Gaza.* Washington, DC: United States Institute of Peace Press.

———. 2005a. "CIDA and the Middle East Peace Process: The Changing Political Context and Its Implications for Canadian Development Assistance." Paper prepared for Canadian International Development Agency, Ottawa, January 16.

———. 2005b. "Donor Aid to Palestine: Attitudes, Incentives, Patronage, and Peace." In *Aid, Diplomacy, and Facts on the Ground: The Case of Palestine,* ed. Michael Keating, Anne Le More, and Robert Lowe 129–42. London: Chatham House.

———, with Eileen Alma, Joel Peters, Roula el-Rifai, and Jill Tansley. 2003. "The Ottawa Process: An Examination of Canada's Track Two Involvement in the Palestinian Refugee Issue." Paper prepared for the Stocktaking Conference on Palestinian Refugee Research," International Development Research Centre, Ottawa, June 17–20. www.mcgill.ca/files/icames/ottawa .pdf (August 2007).

————, and Jill Tansley. 1995. "The Refugee Working Group of the Middle East Multilateral Peace Negotiations." *Palestine-Israel Journal* 2(4): 53–58.

Canadian International Development Agency. 2006. "Update: Canadian Aid Programs in the West Bank and Gaza." April 1. www.acdi-cida.gc.ca/ CIDAWEB/acdicida.nsf/En/JOS-42618224-U8U (August 2007).

CTV. 2006. "A Conversation with the Prime Minister." 23 December. www.ctv.ca/ servlet/ArticleNews/story/CTVNews/20061221/harper_year_end_061221/ 20061223?hub=TopStories (August 2007).

Department of Foreign Affairs and International Trade Canada. 2007. "Canadian Policy on Key Issues in the Israeli-Palestinian Conflict." www.inter national.gc.ca/middle_east/can_policy-en.asp (August 2007).

Department of National Defence. 2007. "Operation Proteus." www.forces.gc.ca/ site/Operations/Proteus/index_e.asp (August 2007).

Dumper, Michael. 2007. *The Future for Palestinian Refugees: Toward Equity and Peace.* Boulder, CO: Lynne Rienner.

Goldberg, David, and Tilly R. Shames. 2004. "The 'Good-Natured Bastard': Canada and the Middle East Refugee Question." *Israel Affairs* 10(1–2): 203–20.

International Monetary Fund and World Bank. 2007. "West Bank and Gaza— Economic Developments in 2006: A First Assessment." March. siteresour ces.worldbank.org/INTWESTBANKGAZA/Resources/WBGEconomic Developments2006.pdf (August 2007).

Ismael, Tareq, ed. 1985. *Canada and the Arab World.* Edmonton: University of Alberta Press.

Keating, Michael. 2005. "Introduction." In *Aid, Diplomacy, and Facts on the Ground: The Case of Palestine,* ed. Michael Keating, Anne Le More, and Robert Lowe, 1–14. London: Chatham House.

Martin, Paul. 2005. "Statement by the Prime Minister on the Gaza Withdrawal." 23 August. www.pco-bcp.gc.ca/default.asp?Language=E&Page=archiv martin&Sub=statementsdeclarations&Doc=statement_20050823_566_e .htm (August 2007).

Noble, Paul. 1985a. "From Refugees to a People? Canada and the Palestinians, 1973–1983." In *Canada and the Arab World,* ed. Tareq Ismael. Edmonton: University of Alberta Press.

————. 1985b. "Where Angels Fear to Tread: Canada and the Status of the Palestinian People, 1973–1983." In *Canada and the Arab World*, ed. Tareq Ismael. Edmonton: University of Alberta Press.

Palestinian Refugee ResearchNet. 2007. "The Ottawa Process: Conferences, Workshops and Dialogue on Refugees." www.arts.mcgill.ca/mepp/new_prrn/ activities (August 2007).

Permanent Observer Mission of Palestine to the United Nations. 2007. "The United Nations and the Question of Palestine 2006." New York, January 22.

Rempel, Terry. 1999. "The Ottawa Process: Workshop on Compensation and Palestinian Refugees." *Journal of Palestine Studies* 29(1): 36–49.

Secretariat of the Ad Hoc Liaison Committee. 2000. "Aid Effectiveness in the West Bank and Gaza." June. Washington, DC: World Bank.

Special Representative of the Government of Canada and Ambassador-at-Large. 1980. "Final Report of the Special Representative of the Government of Canada Respecting the Middle East and North Africa." Stanfield Report. Ottawa. Quoted in Ismael 1985, 184.

Spector, Norman. 2003. *A War Foretold: How Mideast Peace Became America's Fight.* Vancouver: Douglas & McIntyre.

Statistics Canada. 2005. "Population Projections of Visible Minority Groups, Canada, Provinces and Regions." Ottawa: Statistics Canada. www.statcan .ca/english/freepub/91-541-XIE/91-541-XIE2005001.pdf (August 2007).

United Nations. 2004. "General Assembly Emergency Session Overwhelmingly Demands Israel's Compliance with International Court of Justice Advisory Opinion." Press Release GA/10248, July 20. www.un.org/News/Press/ docs/2004/ga10248.doc.htm (August 2007).

United Nations Security Council. 2002. "Resolution 1397." S/RES/1397 (2002). New York. www.un.org/Docs/scres/2002/sc2002.htm (August 2007).

United States Department of State. 2003. "A Performance-Based Roadmap to a Permanent Two-State Solution to the Israeli-Palestinian Conflict," 30 April. www.state.gov/r/pa/prs/ps/2003/20062.htm (August 2007).

World Bank. 2004. "Disengagement, the Palestinian Economy, and the Settlements." June 23. lnweb18.worldbank.org/mna/mena.nsf/Attachments/ Disengagement+Paper/$File/Disengagement+Paper.pdf (August 2007).

Canadian Interests and Democracy Promotion in the Middle East[1]

In January 2006, Hamas won a sweeping majority in the Palestinian Legislative Council elections. Despite having helped facilitate and monitor the elections, the government of Canada was the first state to cut off funding to the Palestinian Authority following Hamas's victory in the elections for its refusal to recognize Israel and for its terrorist activities.[2] The United States and the European Union followed suit. The issue of Hamas's electoral victory raises some of the most difficult issues and questions for states engaged in democracy promotion in the Middle East, specifically with regard to Islamist groups that have deep roots and popularity within Middle Eastern society.[3] Is the aim of democracy promotion to strengthen democratic structures and procedures or values? What if the structure and procedures Canada supports produce winners with values Canadians do not support? To what extent should Canada engage with actors that have popular legitimacy and support but do not have a liberal democratic agenda? What if, as is the case with some Islamist organizations, they have a military wing in addition to their social and political wings or directly or indirectly support what the government of Canada deems to be terrorist activities? At the very core of these questions, indeed of the notion of promoting democracy itself, are two very basic questions: To whom should one talk? Who are the reformers?

This chapter argues that if democracy promotion is to be successful, then Canada must engage with all political and civil society actors, including moderate Islamist organizations and actors that come to power legally through democratic elections. If the government of Canada is unwilling to engage with moderate Islamist forces, Canada should reconsider democracy promotion as a primary foreign policy objective in the Middle East. This position is taken largely from the perspective of Canadian interests. Namely, an inconsistency in implementing Canadian-promoted values or an inconsistency in how

Canada treats actors only serves to undermine its programs, credibility, and values. Ultimately, in today's political climate of growing anti-westernism, inconsistency not only discredits pro-democracy activists and democratic reforms in the region, but the perceived western hypocrisy it breeds also potentially threatens Canada's security interests by reinforcing a militant Islamist worldview of the West.

To be sure, identifying moderate Islamists, much less engaging with them, is far easier said than done.[4] The International Crisis Group defines Islamism as the active assertion and promotion of beliefs, prescriptions, laws, or policies that are held to be Islamic in character (International Crisis Group 2005, 1). Moderate Islamist organizations are commonly defined as those Islamists who are deemed non-violent and non-revolutionary, as they work within society and within the legal political system by engaging in party politics, for example, and have a political agenda that recognizes and is limited to the nation-state and is not aimed at the creation of a pan-Islamic state. While making important distinctions between moderate and radical Islamism, this definition masks more than it reveals. Finding moderate Islamism according to this definition is a difficult task as Islamist groups are internally diverse, often having factions or streams that include those with moderate and radical religious interpretations and activities they are willing to support or engage. In addition, Islamist networks overlap, resulting in cross-membership among segments of moderate and more radical Islamist groups. Furthermore, the agendas of moderate Islamist organizations are often vaguely stated—with few specifics regarding areas of concern to western governments, such as pluralism, the competition for power, freedom of religion, and rights for ethnic minorities and women. Despite these challenges, engaging with moderate Islamists does not mean agreeing with or funding them. Rather, it entails dialogue and inclusion.

This chapter begins with a brief discussion of democracy promotion in Canada. It is followed by three main sections examining the growing anti-westernism in the region today, the nature of civil society in the Middle East, and the nature of Islamist movements and organizations, respectively. These three factors are integral to understanding the context within which Canadian democracy promotion operates in the region and the implications of this context for Canada's interests and policies. It concludes with advice to the Canadian government in its response to these factors.

Democracy Promotion

The government of Canada identifies democracy promotion, along with human rights and the rule of law, as a core value that guides Canadian foreign policy. Over the past few years, and particularly as a result of the 2005 review of foreign policy priorities and policies by the government, there has been an increased emphasis on democracy promotion as a key to reducing terrorist recruitment, alleviating poverty, and fostering sustainable development in the developing world. Indeed, in early 2007, the Department of Foreign Affairs and International Trade ([DFAIT] 2007) conducted an open online discussion with the public in order to identify the "ways in which Canada can play a more active role on the world stage in promoting democratic principles." These recent initiatives in democracy promotion, such as the Democracy Council created in 2005, build upon existing long-term efforts.[5] The Canadian government has historically engaged in diplomatic and development efforts in support of new or weak democracies and in opposition to democratic violations. Among other initiatives, Canada participates in multilateral organizations engaging in democracy promotion, such as the United Nations. It also is a member of the International Institute for Democracy and Electoral Assistance (IDEA) and has been involved in electoral assistance, such as monitoring, in Iraq, Afghanistan, the Palestinian Authority, and Lebanon. Canada furthermore recently has reasserted the importance of democracy promotion in its aid policy. In 2005, the Canadian International Development Agency (CIDA) targeted more than $375 million toward programs supporting democratic governance (Standing Senate Committee of Foreign Affairs 2007). Toward this end, that same year, CIDA created the Office of Democratic Governance with a mandate to work with both governments and civil society to share knowledge and also to create fruitful partnerships among Canadian and international experts, organizations, institutions, and government departments.[6] As with all of CIDA's programs, the development and support of civil society organizations in the Middle East are seen as an important component in deepening democratic practices and the culture of democracy.

A cursory examination of CIDA's (2007b) website reveals a broad range of activities falling under the banner of democracy promotion and democratic governance. CIDA's work with civil society reflects the widespread belief held by many states and international organizations that indigenous, bottom-up reforms are necessary for the betterment of people's economic, social, and political lives and the sustainability of these reforms. Civil society includes non-profit organizations, religious organizations, labour unions, business associations, interest and advocacy groups, societies, clubs, research institutions, as well as political, social, and religious movements—which generally speaking are independent of the state and market (Hawthorn 2005, 82). Some examples of CIDA's projects dealing with democracy and governance include a 2006 grant that contributed to the United Nations Development Programme's (UNDP) Electoral Law Reform project, which assisted the Lebanese government's National Commission on Electoral Law Reform in developing a new electoral law by engaging all segments of society and political streams and factions and facilitating a process of national dialogue on a range of issues deemed pertinent by the Lebanese to the reform of the electoral law. CIDA also contributed to another UNDP program (2004–06) to assist in the establishment of a voter registry for the 2006 Palestinian elections. Also in the Palestinian territories, the Canadian mission in Ramallah established and managed the Palestinian Election Support Fund (2004–07) to support civil society engagement in elections; it focuses on women's empowerment and more effective participation by women and youth in the electoral process. In Morocco, CIDA contributes to the Gender Equality Support Fund (Phase II, 2004–10), which finances programs and projects to promote gender equality in strategic public reforms while supporting partnerships between government and civil society and raising public awareness.

At the heart of all these projects lie fundamental values such as equality, pluralism, participation, inclusiveness, and accountability, core Canadian values. Indeed, Canada considers itself a legitimate "democracy promoter" presumably because it bases its political system and policies on these values. As foreign minister Peter MacKay (2007) asserted, Canada's partners in the Middle East respect and understand that Canada's "firm and clear positions" are based on principles of "freedom, democracy, human rights and the rule of law" and, for this, Canada is considered a friend and a partner. The fundamental question becomes, however, to what extent can Canada's support for civil society foster the development of these values and of pro-democracy civil society organizations? Closely related to this, to what extent do the organizations Canada supports in the Middle East possess these values?

Growing Anti-Westernism and Its Consequences for Democracy Promotion

Shaping the nature and discourse of reform and the ability of any international body, including DFAIT, to work effectively at democracy promotion or with the region's democratic reformers and organizations is the overarching context of a growing gap (real or perceived) between the East and the West. Anti-westernism has been fuelled by the unpopular invasions of Afghanistan and Iraq, the apparent failure at democracy building and the death and suffering of thousands in these two countries, and the unresolved dispute between Israelis and Palestinians. It is at unprecedented levels throughout the region, even within those states not directly involved in any of the abovementioned issues (Ottaway 2005, 162–63). This larger political and ideological context acts as a lens through which all engagements by western governments and donors in the Arab Middle East are viewed. As many Middle Eastern states struggle with issues of national identity, including the political and economic orientations of their foreign policies, an increasing number of seemingly unrelated issues are being interpreted through this "East versus West" lens with arguments of western imposition of ideas and values overriding the central concerns of the issues at hand. Many non-governmental organizations (NGOS) in the region, including human rights NGOS, refuse to work with states directly involved in these invasions or whose policies are seen as overly biased toward Israel. Some critical NGOS refuse all foreign funding while others accept funding only from the UN (Abdelrahman 2004, 64). Institutions of civil society promoting "western values" are often marginalized due to their presumed co-optation by the West. In Jordan, for example, individuals and organizations working to eliminate honour crimes are accused of helping to impose western alien values and of being too western themselves (Clark 2003, 38–41). The work of organizations such as these, and that of their international donors, is compromised by this East-West gap.

It is not surprising that public and parliamentary debates over greater divorce rights for women or the introduction of computers into the classroom or the decision to support the "war on terror" regularly become engulfed in discussions over the presumed western imposition of ideas, values, and policy. At the same time, this rhetoric cannot be equated with a rejection of democratic values or the rejection of political reform per se. Polling data indicate that Arabs support democracy and rank "civil/personal rights" as the most important political issue, before health care, the Palestinian issue, and economic questions (Gause 2005). These pro-democracy views furthermore are borne out by extremely high voter turnouts at the polls (Gause 2005).

Rather, anti-western rhetoric and the apparent rejection of democratic reforms reflect a larger frustration with western support of autocratic and authoritarian regimes (or at least not their public condemnation), the price for which appears to be Arab states' support for western policies in the region. The anti-democratic rhetoric also reveals a perceived hypocrisy by Arab citizenry on the behalf of western governments. The international isolation of the Hamas government in the Palestinian territories is a case in point from the perspective of many of those who live in the region. While the international community declared the 2006 election in the Palestinian Authority free and fair, successive western governments refused to accept the outcome and cut off political and economic ties with the Hamas-led government, further plunging the Palestinian territories into chaos. Arab support for western policies in the region, including Canada's, also comes at the price of democratic processes, with the gerrymandering of electoral systems and the limiting of freedoms of association and the press to ensure the passage of policies unpopular on the Arab street. An excellent example is Jordan, a state that Canada regards as a key strategic player in the region and singles out as one with which strengthening ties is a priority. Prior to Jordan's 1993 election and the then upcoming parliamentary debate over the peace treaty with Israel, the regime introduced new electoral laws (still in effect today). Critics across the spectrum agreed that the changes to the laws were designed to ensure a parliament supportive of the regime and its foreign policies.[7] Summarizing his 2004 polling data from six Arab countries—Egypt, Saudi Arabia, Morocco, Lebanon, and United Arab Emirates—Shibley Telhami states that the vast majority of people in each of these countries believe that the Middle East has become less democratic than it was before the 2003 Iraq War (Ottaway et al. 2005, 7–9). While there are many reasons for this, he notes that 90 percent of the public was opposed to the Iraq War, believing that it was against Arab interests.

> Arab governments had to make a strategic decision whether they supported the United States or not. They made a strategic decision generally to support the United States, and in the process they became far more insecure. They preempted organizations, they arrested people, they limited freedom of speech—and in the case of Egypt, extended the emergency law on the eve of the war. That's what the public saw, and that is what the public is reacting to. (Ottaway et al. 2005, 8)

Authoritarianism, Arab foreign policies, and western political, ideational, and economic domination have become intertwined in the popular mind as reflected in the local press and street demonstrations.

While Canadian foreign policy is based on a variety of factors, including domestic concerns and constituencies (see chapters 3 and 10), its intent may be perceived differently by those abroad. The terrorism of Osama bin Laden is supported by only a very small minority of Muslims in the Middle East. However, as Dale F. Eickelman (2002, 37–38) points out, bin Laden's message of oppression and corruption of many Arab governments and the blame he places on the West for this oppression and for the violence in Palestine, Kashmir, Chechnya, and elsewhere reach well beyond this minority and into the Arab street. Eickelman (37) cites a poll taken in Morocco in late September 2001 that showed that a majority of Moroccans condemned the September 11 bombings, but 41 percent sympathized with bin Laden's message. As he states, bin Laden's message builds on widespread resentment against the West (38).

As a result, anti-westernism in the Arab world manifests itself in a political cynicism toward perceived western hypocrisy and toward western human rights discourse, a resentment toward the perceived western imposition of values and practices, and a critical approach (often vocal and public) to civil society actors that discredits organizations that are considered "too western" as a result of their funding or agendas.[8] These criticisms emanate from the entire political and ideological spectrum in the region with even some pro-democracy activists questioning the degree to which western efforts at democracy building, such as the training of electoral candidates, are worthwhile within the present larger international context.

Civil Society and Democratization

The role of civil society in democratization has been well documented in academic and policy literature. Essentially, as Amy Hawthorn (2005, 82) states, civil society organizations contribute to the process of democratization by enabling citizens "to carve out independent political space, to learn about democracy, to articulate a democratic alternative to the status quo, to spread this idea within society, and to mobilize millions of their fellow citizens against repressive regimes." For civil society to fulfill this democratizing role, a critical mass of civil society organizations must develop three key attributes: autonomy from the regime, a pro-democracy agenda, and the ability to build coalitions with other sectors of civil society and with other forces, such as political parties in order to push for political reform (92). Hawthorn and others agree that civil society as a whole in the Arab world has not yet developed these three attributes. To the contrary, civil society is weak and divided, and the majority of the region's civil society organizations depend heavily upon the state, are weak institutionally (thus resulting in poor service or project delivery and little to no sustainability), and display little internal democracy in terms of decision-making procedures and management.

Within the Arab world, civil society can be described as small, albeit growing, and dominated by what Hawthorn (87) refers to as five sectors: the Islamic sector (to be dealt with separately in the following section), service-oriented NGOs, professional organizations such as syndicates and unions, informal and formal family and community organizations, and pro-democracy associations. Algeria, Bahrain, Egypt, Jordan, Kuwait, Lebanon, Morocco, the Palestinian territories, Tunisia, and Yemen have a degree of civil society activity in one or more of these five sectors. Morocco, Lebanon, and the Palestinian territories have the most diverse and active civil societies in the region (88–89). Pro-democracy or advocacy organizations, such as human rights NGOs, are generally the only civil society organizations with the direct aim of spreading democratic values or seeking legislative change and political reform. All civil society organizations and political parties in the region share many of the same abovementioned characteristics. However, as demonstrated below, the Islamic sector, and Islamist movements and their affiliated institutions in particular, provide a number of exceptions. Indeed, Islamist movements defy many of the challenges that plague civil society organizations in the region.

In all states within the region, civil society organizations and political parties are highly regulated, monitored, and controlled politically, institutionally, and financially. The autonomy of civil society organizations from the state and their ability to pressure the state for political reform are severely constrained and compromised through both direct and indirect means. In many respects, the legal history of increasing state control over NGOs in Egypt provides the norm for the region. After more than ten years of human rights advocates and other NGOs pressuring for amendments to Law 32 of 1964 that regulated NGO life, in 2002 Law 84 of 2002—which is even more restrictive—was passed. While put forth as laws to regulate and improve NGO work, both laws were clearly intended to monitor and control NGOs and regulate their relations with the state (and specifically the Egyptian Ministry of Social Affairs [MOSA]). Registering an association is an onerous process requiring approval from both MOSA and the Ministry of the Interior. MOSA has wide powers of discretion to deny an association the right to establish, dissolve an association, and to oppose any candidate who runs for the administrative council of an association. It can nominate representatives from MOSA to a NGO's administrative council, and dissolve and nominate new councils in their entirety. The law further enables MOSA to do so according to vague criteria for national security. In addition, NGOs are severely restricted in the type of fundraising they engage in. All foreign funds or donations NGOs receive are also required to be channelled through MOSA (Clark 2000, 170–72, 2004; Abdelrahman 2004, 129–35). In all countries of the region, accusations of foreign funding provide an easy avenue through which governments can arrest and thereby silence civil society activists, such as Saad Eddin Ibrahim in Egypt, or rival civil society organizations can discredit others.

State control over civil society, inhibiting its ability and willingness to organize for political reform, also comes in more indirect means. Civil society organizations in the Middle East are largely populated by the middle class and, given the large state bureaucracies in the region, an overwhelming proportion of volunteers are civil servants. In the case of Egypt, civil servants also are seconded to civil society organizations by MOSA. Indeed, Maha Abdelrahman's study of Egyptian NGOs found that 90.7 percent of the board members of all 60 NGOs she interviewed were civil servants. Furthermore, in 40 cases (66.6 percent), at least one board member of the NGO was a current or retired MOSA official. While many people interviewed argued that these civil service connections influence the work of the NGOs positively and facilitate and accelerate the realization of NGO goals, Abdelrahman (2004, 157, 159) and other researchers have noted the tendency of NGOs to remain as close as possible to professional matters; in other words, to remain apolitical. With their incomes at stake, few civil servants would be inclined to confront the government or state on behalf of their civil society organization.

Hawthorn (2005) observes that, not surprisingly, a critical mass of civil society organizations has not adopted a clear pro-democracy agenda. With the exception of the relatively small pro-democracy sector, civil society organizations are usually reluctant to jeopardize their work by running afoul of the authorities. Few service NGOs, for example, have advocacy campaigns aimed at improving policy on issues on which they work (93). As Hawthorn (94) states: "Beyond the fact that most are financially and administratively linked to the state, their fundamental mission is not to challenge systems and institutions of politics. Rather, it is to provide the services and socioeconomic development necessary to maintain social stability." With few exceptions, service NGOS, such as development organizations, unions, professional organizations, and mutual aid societies restrict their activities to servicing their members and do not prioritize democratic activism (94).[9]

As a byproduct of both the abovementioned prevalent anti-westernism and the practices of state control employed by the region's authoritarian regimes to divide potential opposition and co-opt supporters, civil society in the Middle East furthermore is highly fragmented, if not polarized. The greatest divisions exist between secular, liberal advocacy groups, many of which are engaged in the types of political and social reforms supported by the international community, and Islamist organizations such as charities, schools, hospitals, and political parties. Each represents a very different, if not opposing, vision for political and social reform. Yet each also represents the two most relevant sectors for democracy promotion. The former is directly engaged in liberal democratic change but lacks a popular following (Hawthorn 2005, 95). The latter, as discussed below, has the deep grassroots support and legitimacy (96).

As Marina Ottaway (2005a) states, pro-democracy intellectuals in the region tend to shun political parties and focus on establishing NGOS, often with foreign funding. They have failed to build broad-based constituencies and often "move in a small world, somewhat isolated from their own societies" (153). While they reach other like-minded intellectuals around the Middle East, they fail to reach down and connect to their own public. Ultimately, what is lacking "is a supply of broad-based political organizations pushing for democracy—political parties, social movements, labor unions, large civic organizations" (151).

Within this primary distinction between liberals and Islamists, civil society organizations further can be divided along partisan lines. Arab intellectuals are divided ideologically over the best route to revitalize the region. Civil society institutions are more often than not associated with a political party or movement and, at their core, often are devoted to the political goals of the party. In Lebanon, many NGOS are extensions of clientelist politics. These divisions are exacerbated by the lack of economic resources and, as a result, an intense competition for donor funds. Furthermore, civil society fragmentation is worsened by personal conflicts between the leaders of civil society organizations (particularly NGOS) and political party leaders, resulting in the ongoing splintering and reformulation of organizations and parties. As evidence of this splintering, for example, in Jordan the number of NGOS is increasing but the proportional number of members is not. In other words, new members are not forming or joining NGOS; rather, existing NGOS are breaking apart.

These divisions deeply affect civil society's ability to work cohesively toward reform. In Egypt donors complain of lack of an NGO or civil society movement or even coordinating bodies (Clark 2000, 167). What is more disconcerting, donors must struggle to get organizations to work together on projects in order to avoid unnecessary duplication. In Jordan, donors bemoan the difficulty of getting civil society organizations, specifically pro-democracy NGOs such as women's NGOs, to work together even when the funded project requires joint effort. One donor representative complained of NGO leaders calling her at home in the evening to complain about other NGO leaders' actions.[10] As Hawthorn (2005) states, different sectors of civil society sometimes work side by side but they can rarely do so in a sustained fashion. This hinders the "the ability of civil society to unite groups of citizens around common goals in a way that might generate pressure on regimes" (95).

Just as importantly, a significant number of institutions within civil society as well as most political parties suffer from a lack of internal democratic procedures and acute institutional weaknesses. NGOs are frequently elitist in nature or dominated by one dynamic person running the entire operation. This often results in a paternalistic or fundamentally authoritarian mode of decision making (Clark 2000, 167). In her study of NGOs in Egypt, Abdelrahman (2004, 153) noted that in most Egyptian organizations the general assemblies play little more than an honorary role with no meaningful or actual involvement in decision making. She found that in rural NGOs, boards of directors are dominated by members of the most influential families, while in urban NGOs they are dominated by civil servants (often the two overlap). In both cases, the decision makers comprise local elites who make decisions on behalf of and with little to no input from the community (as represented by the general assembly) or the beneficiaries (154–57, 175–76). More alarming is the fact that despite the multi-member boards of directors of most Egyptian NGOs, one or sometimes two people are in charge of everything, including all decisions and most of the implementation (Clark 2000, 167; Abdelrahman 2004, 161–63). Mudar Kassis (2001, 46) similarly observed the alienation of the Palestinian public from decision-making procedures in civil society organizations. In Jordan, a significant number of NGOs also are what one donor refers to as MONGOS—"My Own NGOs." As in Egypt, these NGOs are established by one person, often for his or her own self-aggrandizement, who essentially becomes the permanent head of a highly centralized organization. As the frustrated acting head of one semi-governmental NGO stated, it is highly common for a leader not to send a replacement if he or she cannot attend an event.[11] Either there is no one else to send or the head simply does not want to share power or knowledge. These complaints were confirmed by a survey of nine women's organizations in Jordan, which found that real decision making generally only takes place at the level of the executive board and not in the general assemblies (al-Atiyat 2003, 108).

Ultimately, individual or centralized decision making within civil society organizations means that the internal turnover within Middle Eastern organizations is extremely low. Repeatedly nominating the same leader regularly is substituted for free and fair elections in some NGOS (Kassim 2006, 18). In his study, Kassis (2001, 46) found that more than one quarter of Palestinian civil society organizations admitted that they do not hold a conference to elect their leadership. That little new blood makes it up the ranks in civil society organizations is confirmed by Abdelrahman's (2004, 159) study of Egyptian NGOS, where she found that, despite a law requiring one third of board members to be elected every year, a considerable number of board members have been in office for more than 20 years and 87 percent have occupied their positions since the NGO was founded. Similarly, the abovementioned survey of nine women's NGOs in Jordan found that six of them have had the same women as activists since the establishment of the organization (Al-Atiyat 2003, 108). Ultimately, Abdelrahman (2004, 196) argues that Egyptian NGOS are undergoing a crisis of democratization. One problem is that few NGO members undergo any form of training, and few found this to be an issue of concern. In short, as Abdelrahman (161) states, Egyptian NGOS in general "reproduce the same models of authority that prevail in the society at large." The same can be said for the region as a whole.

Finally, to the list of challenges for civil society organizations—their dependency on the state, their fragmentation, and the lack of internal democratic procedures—can be added their lack of sustainability, a factor that both exacerbates the abovementioned problems and, to a certain extent, is caused by them. Many civil society organizations are overstretched both in their ambitions and in their trained staff. As a result, plans are often not put into practice and service delivery or project implementation can be inconsistent and unreliable. According to Kassis (2001, 41–42), for example, Palestinian civil society organizations have such great problems with sustainability (due to both a lack of funding and a lack of volunteers) that 37 percent of the organizations in his survey declared that they could continue for only one year.

Funding from the West, including from Canada, tends to exacerbate some of these problems. It tends to be concentrated in a small number of civil society organizations. Similarly, a limited number of voices are consulted for policy advice. The organizations that are granted western aid, repeatedly, are those that have the capacity to research and write funding proposals, are cognizant of the priorities of western aid agendas, and have the institutional capacity to manage and use large funds adequately. The result is an over-concentration of donor funding in a small number of large NGOS that follow western agenda setting (and an intense competition for funds). This further results in making it difficult to hear alternative voices that express contrasting values yet are potentially more popular or effective. In addition, it contributes to a sense of western imposition. Finally, it contributes to the perceived creation of a class of pro-western NGOs promoting alien values. As a result, the very NGOs that western donors support struggle with questions of legitimacy.

Islamic Activism

Within this broader context, Islamist organizations present a number of policy challenges. Taken within the broader context of civil society within the region, Islamist movements, with their affiliated institutions, have the greatest legitimacy and grassroots support of any civil society organization. Their popularity is due both to their long-term social activities, such as charities, granting them deep roots in society, and to their political stances against regime corruption and authoritarianism and, most recently, against the Iraq War. Islamist civil society organizations and political parties have furthermore demonstrated their willingness and ability to work together with secular organizations and parties of opposing ideologies. These instances of cooperation, in the form of protests or joint communiqués, for example, demonstrate a degree of tolerance for other groups. Finally, some Islamist civil society organizations display a fairly high degree of internal democracy as ordinary members have regular input into decision making and leadership elections are regular and transparent and result in healthy changes in leadership.

While the Islamic sector ideologically does not "constitute a prodemocracy force" (Hawthorn 2005, 94), scholars increasingly argue that all these factors strongly point to the need to include Islamists in democracy promotion. As Saad Eddin Ibrahim, the abovementioned liberal pro-democracy activist, who has served a total of seven years in jail for his activities, states:

> Speaking as an activist more than an ideologue, I say Islamists on principle and on pragmatic grounds must be included in any democratic transformation of the region. They are substantial, they are there on the ground, they are disciplined, they are committed. They have been performing very important social services for the poor and the needy, and they have managed to protect an image of a corruption-free political force in contrast to regimes that are plagued by corruption. They have substantial constituencies, and they have to be included in any scheme for governance. (Ottaway et al. 2005, 11)

Furthermore, a small but growing number of scholars argue that these instances of "cross-ideological cooperation" and the movements' internal provisions for debate and leadership change indicate the diverse pressures bearing upon Islamist movements and the potential for "political learning whereby the Islamist movement revises its stances and its actions" (Cavatorta 2006, 210). Indeed, Francesco Cavatorta (203) even regards moderate Islamists as a potential force for democratization.

As Hawthorn (2005, 85) states, the Islamic sector of civil society is made up of a wide array of groups, associations, and movements whose common objective is upholding and propagating the religion of Islam. It is the most active and widespread form of associational life in the region. While Islamic civil society organizations are quite diverse in their forms and political orientations (85–86), those with which democracy promoters are most concerned are those that are affiliated with moderate social movements.[12] Islamist movements themselves, such as the Muslim Brotherhood in Jordan, Hamas in the Palestinian territories, and Hizbullah in Lebanon, also differ quite substantially in terms of the political systems within which they operate, their legal status and their ideologies, activities, and mass base. Egypt, Jordan, and Yemen, for example, are highly centralized states often referred to as liberalized autocracies (Brumberg 2003). These countries share the fact that they have nominal liberal freedoms and democratic rights, such as elections, but political power remains firmly in the hands of the regime. Despite their similarities, their strategies for controlling political opposition—particularly Islamist opposition—differ, with Jordan and Yemen allowing Islamists to establish legal political parties and Egypt maintaining an approximately 40-year ban on the Muslim Brotherhood. In Jordan, the Muslim Brotherhood's political party, the Islamic Action Front (IAF), refers to itself as the loyal opposition. In each of the countries, the dominant Islamist movements comprise the largest opposition group to the regime. Rather than a highly centralized authoritarian state, Lebanon represents the Arab world's strongest democracy—one that is highly decentralized and divided by sectarianism. Hizbullah represents its supporters' needs in a confessional political system that accords political power according to a formula based on the size and historical importance of religious sects. As in the case of the Muslim Brotherhood in Jordan and Egypt, for example, Hizbullah runs an extensive network of charity and other social services and has established a political party that runs in municipal and national elections. However, Hizbullah emerged out of the political and military resistance to Israel's invasion and occupation in 1982 and retains a military wing that is active along the border with Israel. The same can be said of Hamas in the Palestinian territories, which refuses to acknowledge the right of Israel to exist and battles both Israel and its secular Palestinian rivals in the struggle for a future state of Palestine.

As Hawthorn (2005, 95) states, in general, moderate Islamist movements operating within the region's authoritarian regimes, such as Egypt, Jordan, and Yemen, "have not pushed for democracy in a comprehensive fashion. Some emphasize themes of justice, participation, and reform. But they hold vague or negative positions on other aspects of democracy, such as rotation of power and minorities' and women's rights."

Ottaway agrees (2005a, 154), stating that "Islamist parties, even those that profess their commitment to democracy, still struggle to reconcile the concept of the citizen's right to make individual choices and the idea that there are God-given truths that human choices must not contradict." Recognizing the classic tension confronted by all political parties rooted in religion, she goes on to argue that even those Islamist parties that profess to support democracy add the caveat that

> democracy is good as long as it does not lead to choices that go against the *Sharia* [Islamic law]. Since Islamic law is not a code, but a collection of interpretations by different sects and different schools within the sects over centuries, respect for Islamic law can lead to democracy or to its rejection, depending on the interpretation chosen. (Ottaway 2005a, 154)

In his study of civil society and Islamism in Morocco, Cavatorta (2006, 204) observes that conventional wisdom among policy makers and academics alike is that Middle Eastern and North African civil societies are inherently authoritarian because of the role that Islamist movements and associations play. He explains that Islamic activism is perceived to be uncivil rather than civil, and therefore more conducive to authoritarian political and social relationships than to democratic ones (207). There are basically three criticisms of Islamist actors: ideologically their commitment to democracy is not clear, they may engage in or support military activities deemed as terrorist by western governments, and there is a strong suspicion among critics that Islamists are "lying their way to power" by engaging in what is commonly referred to as "one vote, one time."

That Islamist movements throughout the region have been successfully addressing the needs of the poor and the middle classes is a well-established fact. Although the region's Islamist movements arose out of different circumstances and can differ quite substantially in their ideologies and choice of strategies and tactics, most began with social welfare institutions designed to do what their respective governments could not or would not do.

Benefiting from its historically positive relationships with successive monarchs in Jordan, the Muslim Brotherhood's Islamic Center Charity Society (ICCS) is one of the most impressive examples. Established in 1963, today, the revenues and expenditures of the ICCS far exceed most other NGOs in the country.[13] The ICCS had a budget of more than 1 billion Jordanian dinar ([JD], approximately CA$1.5 billion) in 2004–05.[14] Through the services and support it provides in its 4 branches and 55 centres, it spent, for example, 9,880,000 JD (averaging CA$17,009,371 over this period) on services and items for the poor, an additional 2,100,000 JD (CA$3,615,423) and 815,000 JD (CA$1,403,128) on orphans and poor families respectively (both of which are sponsored monthly), and distributed 100,000 JD (CA$172,163) to 880 university students to help cover their educational fees.[15] The ICCS facilities include 2 hospitals, 15 medical clinics, 1 college, and 28 schools. The medical clinics alone received 153,819 patients in 2005 and the number of students in the schools was 12,062.[16] By Jordanian standards, these numbers and sums are enormous.

These accomplishments by Islamists are not limited to Jordan. The social unit of Hizbullah provides social welfare services and technical help to thousands of members and supporters and to the families of members who died in battle against Israel. Hizbullah is a vast organization covering the needs of its supporters from birth to death. Just two of its social welfare foundations are the Mu'assasat Jihad al-Bina' (Holy Struggle Construction Foundation), which built a total of 10,528 schools, homes, shops, hospitals, infirmaries, mosques, cultural centres, and agricultural cooperatives between 1988 and 2002, and the Mu'assasat al-Jarha (Foundation for the Wounded), which provided 11,062 war medical emergency services, health services, social services, and educational services between 1990 and 2001 (Hamzeh 2004, 50–51, 53). Hizbullah's Islamic Health Unit provides health care to more than 400,000 beneficiaries yearly through a variety of the unit's hospitals, dispensaries, mobile dispensaries, dental clinics, and civil defence centres (54). Between 1996 and 2001, its Education Unit dispensed more than 21 billion Lebanese liras (averaging CA$20,150,029 at the time) on financial aid and scholarships (55). This list of services is by no means exhaustive.

Although there are glaring exceptions, such as Hizbullah, many Islamist movements have provided these services with limited or no state or international donor funding—having both a greater degree of financial independence from the state and a higher degree of institutional and project sustainability than most non-Islamist civil society organizations.[17] In Egypt, for example, a 1994 World Bank study notes that religious welfare NGOs are far more independent of state aid and other grants than other NGOs. Activity fees make up approximately 52 percent, donations 34 percent, and state and foreign aid approximately 20 percent. In contrast, in secular social welfare NGOs, 22 percent, 24 percent, and 20 percent of total revenues came from activity fees, donations, and state and foreign aid respectively; in community development associations, 31 percent, 15 percent, and 34 percent of total revenues came from activity fees, donations, and state and foreign aid respectively. Religions welfare NGOs, of which Islamic welfare NGOs are the majority, are the most successful at raising funds and donations locally (Clark 2000, 168; 2004, 60).

The grassroots support that NGOs rightfully have garnered from their social welfare activities has served them well politically. Despite electoral systems designed to keep their numbers low, Islamist candidates score successfully in elections at all levels of society—clubs, university councils, professional associations, and national and municipal elections (Gause 2005, 2006). Islamist popularity is most highly witnessed in the streets. Islamist movements through-out the region are able to mobilize large numbers of supporters to their streets, far outstripping the mobilization capacity of any other civil society sector.

Increasingly, Islamists in Jordan, Egypt, and Yemen and other authoritarian regimes, are using professional associations, parliaments, and the streets as podiums from which they criticize authoritarian practices of their respective governments. Most importantly, they are pressuring for reform together with elements of secular civil society. More and more examples of cross-partisan activism are taking place in the region, ranging from tactical cooperation on an issue-by-issue basis to a more sustained strategic cooperation with the creation of "coordinating bodies" to deal with issues as they arise. These initiatives and bodies are seen in Egypt, Yemen, Jordan, Lebanon, and, to a lesser extent, Morocco. What brings these diverse groups together in the cases of Egypt, Jordan, Morocco, and Yemen in particular is their increasing realization of shared interests in confronting authoritarianism and in doing so jointly.

In Egypt, leftists, Islamists, and all political stripes participated in demonstrations and rallies against the Iraq War, culminating in a massive demonstration in Cairo in March 2003. Ongoing efforts of political movements and parties to create a united front against the regime continued building as the 2005 parliamentary elections approached. Before the election, al-Wasat (a centrist Islamist party, itself a coalition of different political ideologies), Kifaya (also a cross-partisan party), al-Karama (a breakaway group from the Nasserites), and several nationalist opposition parties announced the formation of the United National Front for Change (UNFC), pledging to coordinate the selection of parliamentary candidates to run against Hosni Mubarek's National Democratic Party (NDP) in the 2005 elections (Schwedler and Clark 2006, 10–11). While the Muslim Brotherhood did not join the UNFC, it upheld its promise to coordinate its activities with the UNFC in specific districts and case by case (Shehata forthcoming).

In Jordan, under the leadership of the Islamists, 13 opposition parties meet regularly, often weekly, under the umbrella of the Higher Committee for the Coordination of National Opposition Parties. The committee includes the IAF, the Jordanian Communist Party, and several leftist and nationalist parties and has been meeting since the mid 1990s to address issues of common concern. While this cooperation does not translate into a bloc in parliament or into a united list during elections, it has resulted in numerous joint memos to the prime minister and king on issues of national concerns, particularly foreign affairs, and the hammering out of a unified position on electoral reform (Schwedler and Clark 2006, 11; Clark 2006).

In Yemen, the Yemeni Congregation for Reform (the Islamic Islah Party) has forged an alliance with the Yemen Socialist Party to act as counterweight to the increasingly authoritarian ruling party and regime. Although the alliance got off to a troubled start with the assassination of Jarallah Umar, a prominent socialist leader, at the party's annual conference in 2002, the two parties managed to form a tactical joint meeting group for the 2003 elections. The Yemeni Congregation for Reform promised to withhold running candidates in 30 districts where the Yemen Socialist Party's prospects were better, and the Yemen Socialist Party agreed not to campaign in 130 constituencies where the Yemeni Congregation for Reform stood a good chance. The coalition continues to last (Schwedler and Clark 2006, 11).

In Morocco, there are also instances of informal cooperation on specific issues areas or themes between Islamists and other opposition groups. Furthermore there has been formal cooperation among Islamist associations and human rights groups on issues ranging from freedom of speech to the end of torture and the legal protection for political prisoners (Cavatorta 2006, 218).

These encounters or "coincidence of interests" are important (Cavatorta 2006, 217). As Jillian Schwedler states, they "bode very well for the question of tolerance, live-and-let live cooperation—what we would like to see if we're going to build a democratic society" (Ottaway et al. 2005, 6). Indeed, Carrie Rosefsky Wickham (2004) and Francesco Cavatorta argue that it is through these instances of cross-ideological cooperation that political learning takes place. Wickham's research on the Wasat party in Egypt indicates that cross-ideological cooperation has lead to Islamist moderation, specifically a greater commitment to democratic principles. Experience with the "Other" has led to changes in core beliefs and values.

Other scholars are less optimistic about democratic learning as a result of cross-ideological cooperation (Clark 2006; Schwedler and Clark 2006; Schwedler forthcoming). Schwedler, for example, argues that the type of cooperation discussed above could in fact create divergent learning experiences and shifts in worldviews (Schwedler 2006; Clark 2006, 542). In other words, the learning experience could reinforce or harden core differences. Michaelle Browers (2007) notes, as reflected in the examples above, that it is often political exclusion more than inclusion from formal politics that brings various political actors with divergent views into contact with one another (see also Clark 2007b). However, Schwedler agrees with Wickham and others that Islamists, such as in Jordan, have embraced a growing number of democratic concepts. Similarly Shadi Hamid (2005, 11) states that whereas the IAF made only one reference to democracy in its 1993 electoral program, in 2003 it made no fewer than five references. It also referred to "alternation of power" and "the people are the source of authority" for the first time in 2003. Both Hamid and Schwedler note that the IAF increasingly justifies its actions based on secular rationale and argues for increasing democratic space, expanding political liberties, applying the constitution, fighting corruption, and responding to the needs of the citizens (Schwedler 2006).

As Schwedler (forthcoming) observes, questions about the effects of including and excluding Islamists have moved to the centre of debates about Islamist groups. Scholars are increasingly debating the conditions or mechanisms under which Islamists can and do moderate their view and democratize. She argues that Islamists are moderating their views and that the context in which they operate and their encounters with the state and with other political parties are crucial to the potential process of moderation. Her research demonstrates that institutional changes such as political liberalization force Islamists to justify new strategies, such as forming a political party. Islamists efforts to justify these new strategies to members and supporters ultimately create new opportunities for future strategic changes that used to be unimaginable. Each ideological justification allows for (and may even demand) the justification of even more unimaginable choices (Schwedler 2006; Clark 2006, 541–42).

Similarly, Burhanettin Duran and Engin Yildirim (2005) note that in Turkey the Islamist trade union Hak-İş has not only come to embrace democratic concepts over time but is also playing a role in forcing a democratization of the Islamist movement as a whole. As they delineate, the transformation of Hak-İş began when it tried to encourage relations with European and international labour organizations and was originally rejected due to its lack of a clear position on secularism and democracy (235).[18] This began a fairly rapid process of change that demonstrates that

> whether Islamist politics … foster democratic consolidation and a strong civil society depends less on Islamic political principles and culture than on the relationship between Islamist elites and institutions and on strategic decisions made by Islamist political leaders to deal with the political, economic and social problems of Turkish political life. By focusing primarily on cultural explanations of Islamist attitudes to democracy and civil society, existing studies have ignored the implications of economic structure, political institutions, and labour issues in the transformation of Islamism and its incorporation into the political process. (Duran and Yildirim 2005, 231)[19]

These pressures to revise their discourse and activities may also come from within Islamist movements and parties. While civil society organizations in general in the region fair poorly in terms of internal democratic procedures, Islamist movements and parties such as the Muslim Brotherhood in Jordan, the Islah Party in Yemen, and even Hamas in the Palestinian territories allow a considerable role in decision making to ordinary members (Mishal and Sela 2000). Both the Muslim Brotherhood and the Islah Party have regular conferences for their entire memberships and clear and transparent elections that result in high voter turnout and significant turnover in leadership. In both cases, prominent founding members, representing both "reformist" and "hard line" tendencies within the two parties, are no longer in positions of decision making. These parties have furthermore managed to transfer power regularly without losing members and splintering into different parties.

As Cavatorta (2006) argues, Islamists respond not only to their external environments but also their to internal environments and accordingly revise their positions. He cites the example of the Moroccan Jamiat al-Adl wal-Ihsan (Justice and Spirituality Group) and the issue of the revisions to the family code law. The amendments to the law were aimed at granting women legal equality and touched upon a variety of issues such as divorce rights. The Jamiat al-Adl wal-Ihsan originally opposed the law and later took what Cavatorta refers to as a U-turn in its position regarding the law. While a variety of domestic factors played a role determining the movement's change in attitude, Cavatorta argues that the organization changed its opposition to family code law in part due to pressure from within from female members (215–16). As he explains: "This does not necessarily mean that the association is indeed a shining example of internal democracy, but it points to the fact involvement of members may be greater than expected and that the Islamist ideology is flexible when the political rewards are high" (216). Quite simply, Islamists are not rigidly wedded to any or one presumed ideological stance. Rather, as all social actors they adapt to their internal and external environments and this ultimately has an impact on the organizations, members, and ideology.[20]

The debate regarding if and how Islamists can become democrats remains unresolved. Indeed, as long as elections are not free and fair in the region it is extremely difficult to know what Islamists will do once they come to power and if they will continue to retain their popularity and legitimacy. However, basing Canadian foreign policy on unproven assumptions about Islamist intentions appears unsound at best. In reference to the defence of the ban on women wearing headscarves in Turkish universities, Haldun Gülalp (2005) argues that it is based on the argument that if Islamists came to power they would surely impose an Islamic dress code that would make the headscarf (or the veil) mandatory. As he persuasively states, this may or may not be true; however, "an undesirable possibility in an uncertain future cannot reasonably be made to explain the mirror image of the same undesirable act at the present" (365). The same applies to the refusal to speak to the region's dominant actors, the Islamists. An increasing number of scholars in the field call for Islamist groups to be examined in light of other religious parties and groups and note, as Ottaway (2005a, 168) states, that it took decades for Christian democratic parties in Europe to really develop their identity and overcome the opposition of the Catholic establishment and the suspicion of other political parties. In the meantime, a growing number of Islamist movements are embracing democratic concepts and, most importantly, are at the forefront of movements to resist and eliminate authoritarianism. This, along with their broad-based popularity, should make us think: by excluding moderate Islamists, Canada may be ignoring the region's greatest democratic impulse, no matter how undemocratic it may appear.

Conclusions

As stated above, the debate over whether inclusion leads to moderation remains unresolved. Nonetheless, a growing number of academics and policy makers alike are calling for the need to engage with Islamists.[21] That Islamists vary greatly in their religious interpretations, strategies, and tactics, including whether they use or support violence, provides little comfort. No scholar claims that Islamists' commitment to democracy is clear, that none of their members support or engage in militant tactics, or that they are definitively not using democracy as a means to power only then to do away with it. The strongest argument for Canada to engage with Islamists lies in the fact that by not engaging with them merely makes Canada hypocritical and undermines its programs, credibility, and values and potentially the meaning of democracy itself.

This chapter does not argue that Islamists are, or will become, liberal democrats. Rather, it argues that if one of the objectives of democracy promotion is a pluralist political order, then one must include those one does not like, particularly when they are elected by a broad spectrum of people in the region to positions of political power. Including those who are not liked does not entail accepting or supporting all their actions, nor does it necessarily mean maintaining contact at all costs. But it does mean that they are not rejected as soon as or because they are democratically elected. The region's Islamists represent the most legitimate and popular sector of civil society and as such need to be included in any of Canada's efforts to promote democracy. Excluding the most popular voice in the region undermines both Canada's programs and its credibility. Furthermore, given the anti-westernism in the region today and the heightened sensitivity to western interference, dealing with hand-picked civil society organizations to the exclusion of Islamist ones may serve to further lessen the popular legitimacy of the very groups with which Canada works. The final argument is that civil society activism is context-dependent. Islamist movements respond to the environments in which they operate. If Islamist civil society organizations are to moderate and embrace democratic concepts and principles, they will only do so in interaction with their environment, not as a result of their exclusion from it.

If Canada is unwilling or unable to talk to Islamists, it must reconsider its foreign policy focus on democracy promotion. Canadian policy makers would not be remiss in not wanting Islamists to come to power. As Gregory Gause (2005, 2006) has stated, even if Islamists were to adjust their views regarding democratic rights and freedoms, they would most likely form governments that would be less receptive to western policies in the region and less willing to cooperate with western governments than are the current authoritarian leaders. Public support for Islamists comes in part as a result of their stance against the West. While the Arab public supports democracy, polls show it holds negative views of the U.S. and, by extension, western governments that support American policies such as the war on terror (Gause 2005). As Gause (2005) states, if Arab governments were democratically elected and more representative of public opinion, they would be more anti-American. It would not be in Islamist parties' interests, as political organizations, at least in the short run, to cooperate with western governments.

If Canadian interests weigh against including Islamists, then the government of Canada should reconsider, if not democracy promotion as a foreign policy objective, then the nature of its projects that promote democracy. A focus on political liberalization as opposed to elections would be but one example (Gause 2005). Ultimately, Canada's diverse efforts at democracy promotion must become more consistent. This includes consistency across policy-making levels, including diplomatic policy regarding the severing of ties with Hamas and Hizbullah, on the one hand, and civil society projects at the grassroots, on the other. It also requires consistency in terms of with whom Canada engages in dialogue. Pluralism requires that one deal with all actors. Furthermore, Canada requires consistency in terms of its values. If Canada considers itself as having pluralist and democratic values, it must respect the rights and will of others. Being consistent is as much about Canada as them. Finally, on a pragmatic level, inconsistency breeds hypocrisy and undermines pro-democracy groups in the region and, potentially, fuels the flames of terrorists' anger.

Notes

1 The author would like to acknowledge the much appreciated help of all the contributors to the volume, particularly Bessma Momani, Rex Brynen, and Paul Kingston, in the writing of this chapter.

2 The Canadian government did not issue its position on the unity government dividing responsibilities between Hamas and Fatah, which was not formed until 2007.

3 In 2002, Canada followed the U.S. lead and added Hizbullah to its list of terrorist organizations, an act that raises some of the same issues.

4 This definition and its discussion are based on Clark (2007a, 46).

5 The Democracy Council is co-chaired by DFAIT and the Canadian International Development Agency (CIDA) and was established as an "informal channel" to bring relevant Canadian institutions, such as the Centre for International Governance Innovation (CIGI), into the policy-making process through sharing information and practices regarding the developing world.

6 While in 2005/06 only 4.6 percent of CIDA expenditures were directed at the Middle East, this percentage amounts to approximately $129 million and cannot be dismissed as a negligible amount (CIDA 2007a).

7 Jordan's one-person-one-vote electoral laws favour pro-regime tribal candidates at the expense of political parties by forcing voters to choose between loyalties:

voters feel obliged to choose "those they know" over ideology. Similarly, the electoral districts are biased toward rural areas where pro-regime tribal candidates are located, at the expense of urban areas where the Muslim Brotherhood's Islamic Action Front and other political parties have their bases. For example, one seat is granted per 6,000 voters in rural Kerek while one seat per 52,255 voters is designated in the city of Amman (Faisal and Urbina 2003).

8 For a discussion of the U.S. loss of credibility as a democracy promoter, see Ottaway (2005b).

9 Approximately six of Jordan's twelve professional associations are very political active in confronting the state.

10 Anonymous interview, September 30, 2003, Amman, Jordan.

11 Anonymous interview, June 8, 2006, Amman, Jordan.

12 As Hawthorn (2005, 85–86) states, at the far margins of the Islamic sector are radical clandestine Islamist movements, such as Egyptian Islamic Jihad and al Qaeda, which strictly employ terrorism and indoctrination to achieve their goals.

13 The Muslim Brotherhood in Jordan was established in 1945 and began engaging in educational and charity activities and, after 1948, politically oriented activities. Based on its success, it created the ICCS in 1963 to deal specifically with its growing charity activities.

14 *Al-Hayat*, July 4, 2006 (in Arabic).

15 *Al-Arab Al-Youm*, July 1, 2006 (in Arabic). During this time period, 1 JD was approximately CA$1.72, £0.73, €1.04 or US$1.41.

16 *Al-Arab Al-Youm*, July 1, 2006 (in Arabic).

17 Islamic charities also have benefited from remittances and donations from locals now living in the wealthy Gulf region. Countries in the region heavily regulated foreign donations, including those from the Gulf governments. As a result, most Islamic charities, with notable exceptions, rely on far less official Arab foreign aid than many critics assume.

18 Similarly, Ziya Öniş and E. Fuat Keyman (2003, 99) argue that Turkey's Islamist Justice and Development Party (AKP) is democratizing under pressure from the European Union in its bid to have Turkey accepted into the EU.

19 See also Berna Turam (2004), who argues that the key to understanding the relationship between Islam and civil society is the state. Islamist groups' relations with the state vary from contestation to negotiation to cooperation. These interactions play an important role in determining civil and uncivil outcomes in the Muslim world.

20 Ayşe Buğra (2002), in her comparative study of the labour union Hak-İş and the Association of Independent Industrialists and Businessmen in Turkey found similar results. Both of these two organizations derive strength from political Islam and are similarly critical of the state, yet the social projects they support are extremely different. Looking specifically at the role of class, Buğra argues that "the nature of social projects designed around religious themes is significantly shaped by different life experiences that reflect class positions" (187). In other words, Islamist groups cannot be understood or judged by ideology alone.

21 This opinion is shared by many policy makers in the U.S., bringing its policies more in line with the Europeans. Most recently, the *New York Sun* reported that the Bush

administration is weighing the prospects of reaching out to the Muslim Brotherhood (Lake 2007). On June 20, 2007, the U.S. State Department's Bureau of Intelligence and Research hosted a meeting with other representatives of the intelligence community to discuss formal channels to the Muslim Brotherhood. This
follows a reception at the residence of the American ambassador in Egypt where
congressional leaders met with some representatives of the Egyptian Muslim
Brotherhood. The U.S. National Security Council and the State Department have
met indirectly with members of Syria's banned Muslim Brotherhood. And in Iraq
members of the Muslim Brotherhood participate in the coalition government. This
policy could include encouraging pro-western wings Islamist movements. See
also the *World Tribune.*

References

Abdelrahman, Maha. 2004. *Civil Society Exposed: The Politics of NGOs in Egypt.*
London: Taurus Academic Studies.

al-Atiyat, Ibtesam. 2003. *The Women's Movement in Jordan.* Berlin: Friedrich
Ebert Stiftung.

Browers, Michaelle. 2007. "Origins and Architects of Yemen's Joint Meeting Parties," *International Journal of Middle East Studies* 39(4). In press.

Brumberg, Daniel. 2003. "The Trap of Liberalized Autocracy." In *Islam and
Democracy in the Middle East,* ed. Larry Diamond, Marc F. Plattner, and
Daniel Brumberg, 35–47. Baltimore: Johns Hopkins University Press.

Buğra, Ayşe. 2002. "Labour, Capital, and Religion: Harmony and Conflict among
the Constituency of Political Islam in Turkey." *Middle East Studies* 38(2):
187–204.

Cavatorta, Francesco. 2006. "Civil Society, Islamism, and Democratisation: The
Case of Morocco." *Journal of Modern African Studies* 44(2): 203–22.

Canadian International Development Agency. 2006. "Update: Canadian Aid Programs in the West Bank and Gaza." April 1. www.acdi-cida.gc.ca/CIDA
WEB/acdicida.nsf/En/JOS-42618224-U8U (August 2007).

———. 2007a. "CIDA in Brief." www.acdi-cida.gc.ca/CIDAWEB/acdicida.nsf/En/
JUD-829101441-JQC#4 (August 2007).

———. 2007b. "Office for Democratic Governance." www.acdi-cida.gc.ca/
CIDAWEB/acdicida.nsf/En/NIC-54102116-JUN (August 2007).

Clark, Janine A. 2000. "The Economic and Political Impact of Economic Restruc-
turing on NGO-State Relations in Egypt." In *Economic Liberalization, Democratization, and Civil Society in the Developing World,* ed. Remonda
Bensabat Kleinberg and Janine A. Clark, 157–79. New York: St. Martin's
Press.

———. 2004. *Islam, Social Welfare, and the Middle Class: Networks, Activism,
and Charity in Egypt, Yemen, and Jordan.* Bloomington: Indiana University Press.

———. 2003. "'Honor Crimes' and the International Spotlight in Jordan" *Middle East Report* 229 (Winter): 38–41.

————. 2006. "The Conditions of Islamist Moderation: Unpacking Cross-Ideological Cooperation in Jordan." *International Journal of Middle East Studies* 38(4): 539–60.

————. 2007a. "Jordan." In *Islamist Opposition Parties and the Potential for EU Engagement*, ed. Toby Archer and Heidi Huuhtanen, 43–56. Helsinki: Finnish Institute of International Affairs.

————. 2007b. *Threats, Goals, and Resources: Islamist Coalition-Building in Jordan*. Unpublished paper.

Department of Foreign Affairs and International Trade. 2007. "A Uniquely Canadian Approach to Democracy Promotion." Ottawa. geo.international.gc.ca/cip-pic/library/democratie-en.aspx (August 2007).

Duran, Burhanettin, and Engin Yildirim. 2005. "Islamism, Trade Unionism, and Civil Society: The Case of Hak-İş Labour Confederation in Turkey." *Middle Eastern Studies* 41(2): 227–47.

Eickelman, Dale F. 2002. "Bin Laden, the Arab 'Street,' and the Middle East's Democracy Deficit." *Current History* 101(651): 36–39.

Faisal, Toujan, and Ian Urbina. 2003. "Jordan's Troubling Detour." *Los Angeles Times* July. www.merip.org/newspaper_opeds/jor_oped070603.html (August 2007).

Gause, F. Gregory. 2006. "Beware of What You Wish For." *Foreign Affairs* (February 8) www.foreignaffairs.org/20060208faupdate85177/f-gregory-gause-iii/beware-of-what-you-wish-for.html (August 2007).

————. 2005. "Can Democracy Stop Terrorism?" *Foreign Affairs* 84(5). www.foreignaffairs.org/20050901faessay84506/f-gregory-gause-iii/can-democracy-stop-terrorism.html (August 2007).

Gülalp, Haldun. 2005. "Enlightenment by Fiat: Secularization and Democracy in Turkey." *Middle Eastern Studies* 41(3): 351–72.

Hamid, Shadi. 2005. "New Democrats? The Political Evolution of Jordan's Islamists." Paper presented at the annual conference of the Centre for the Study of Islam and Democracy, Washington, DC, April 22–23. www.islam-democracy.org/documents/pdf/6th_Annual_Conference-ShadiAHamid.pdf (August 2007).

Hamzeh, Ahmad Nizar. 2004. *In the Path of Hizbullah*. Syracuse: Syracuse University Press.

Hawthorn, Amy. 2005. "Is Civil Society the Answer?" In *Uncharted Journey: Promoting Democracy in the Middle East*, ed. Thomas Carothers and Marina Ottaway, 81–114. Washington, DC: Carnegie Endowment for International Peace.

International Crisis Group. 2005. "Understanding Islamism." Middle East/North African Report No. 37, March 2. Brussels. www.crisisgroup.org/home/index.cfm?id=3300&l=1 (August 2007).

Kassim, Hisham, ed. 2006. *Directory of Civil Society Organizations in Jordan 2006*. Amman: al-Urdun al-Jadid Research Center and the Friedrich Ebert Stiftung.

Kassis, Mudar. 2001. "Civil Society Organizations and Transition to Democracy in Palestine." *International Journal of Voluntary and Nonprofit Organizations* 12(1): 35–48.

Lake, Eli. 2007. "Bush Weighs Reaching Out to 'Brothers.'" *New York Sun*, June 20.

MacKay, Peter. 2007. "How Canada Can Make a Difference in the Middle East." *National Post*, January 31, A16.

Mishal, Shaul, and Avraham Sela. 2000. *The Palestinian Hamas: Vision, Violence, and Coexistence.* New York: Columbia University Press.

Öniş, Ziya, and E. Fuat Keyman. 2003. "Turkey at the Polls: A New Path Emerges." *Journal of Democracy* 14(2): 95–107.

Ottaway, Marina. 2005a. "The Missing Constituency for Democratic Reform." In *Uncharted Journey: Promoting Democracy in the Middle East,* ed. Thomas Carothers and Marina Ottaway, 151–72. Washington, DC: Carnegie Endowment for International Peace.

———. 2005b. "The Problem of Credibility." In *Uncharted Journey: Promoting Democracy in the Middle East*, ed. Thomas Carothers and Marina Ottaway, 173–92. Washington, DC: Carnegie Endowment for International Peace.

Ottaway, Marina S., Jillian Schwedler, Shibley Telhami, and Saad Eddin Ibrahim. 2005. "Democracy: Rising Tide or Mirage? *Middle East Policy* 12(2): 1–27.

Schwedler, Jillian. 2006. *Faith in Moderation: Islamist Parties in Jordan and Yemen.* New York: Cambridge University Press.

———. Forthcoming. "Rethinking Moderation: Islamist Cooperation with Ideological Rivals." Cited with permission from author.

Schwedler, Jillian, and Janine A. Clark. 2006. "Islamist-Leftist Cooperation in the Arab World." *ISIM Review* 18: 10–11.

Standing Senate Committee of Foreign Affairs. 2007. Proceedings of the Standing Senate Committee on Foreign Affairs and International Trade. Issue 12, February 21. www.parl.gc.ca/39/1/parlbus/commbus/senate/com-e/fore-e/12ev-e.htm?Language=E&Parl=39&Ses=1&comm_id=8 (August 2007).

Shehata, Dina. Forthcoming. "Opposition Movements in Egypt." Washington, DC: United States Institute for Peace. Cited with permission from author.

Turam, Berna. 2004. "The Politics of Engagement between Islam and the Secular State: Ambivalences of 'Civil Society.'" *British Journal of Sociology* 55 (2): 259–81.

Wickham, Carrie Rosefsky. 2004. "The Path to Moderation: Strategy and Learning in the Formation of Egypt's Wasat Party." *Comparative Politics* 36(2): 205–28.

World Tribune. 2007. "U.S. Approves Contacts with Muslim Brotherhood: 'Region Is Going Islam.'" June 28. www.worldtribune.com/worldtribune/WTARC/2007/ss_egypt_06_27.asp (August 2007).

Promoting Civil Society Advocacy in the Middle East and at Home: Non-Governmental Organizations, the Canadian International Development Agency, and the Middle East Working Group, 1991–2001

If the Canadian government has doubts about governments [in the Middle East], then it should support NGOs to work with NGOs.
—Saad Eddin Ibrahim

Established in 1968, the Canadian International Development Agency (CIDA) aims to combat poverty, promote human rights, and enhance sustainable development in the developing world. Over the past 20 years alone, CIDA has disbursed more than $1.7 billion to support a variety of programs in the Middle East (see tables 7–1 and 7–2). In the 1980s and '90s, nongovernmental organizations (NGOs) began to emerge as more significant players in Canadian foreign and development policy. Hitherto at the margins of policy making in CIDA and the Department of Foreign Affairs and International Trade (DFAIT), development NGOs in Canada not only began to increase in number but also began to organize themselves into broader coalitions, oriented toward issues and toward regional concerns, that acted as channels for Canadian development assistance; they also served as forums for policy advocacy within Canadian and, later, international foreign policy making circles (Van Rooy 2001).[1] Indeed, between 1984 and 1990, more than a dozen NGO coalitions had emerged, supported by the NGO Division of CIDA's Partnership Branch and registered with the Canadian Council for International Cooperation (CCIC).[2] The latter is, itself, a coalition of Canadian voluntary sector organizations whose mandate, in partnership with civil society organizations in the South, includes working toward sustainable human development, poverty alleviation, and social justice around the globe, monitoring federal policies on foreign affairs, and engaging Canadians in a collective search for development alternatives. One area where there was a noticeable absence of NGO collective representation in Canada, however, was with respect to the Middle East. This chapter describes and analyzes an attempt by a grouping of Canadian NGOs to rectify this absence through the creation of the Middle East Working Group (MEWG) in the wake of the first Gulf War in 1991.

TABLE 7–I

Canadian International Development Agency Expenditures on
Projects in North Africa and the Middle East

Year	Total Disbursement
1989/0	$62,034,060.49
1990/1	$98,129,561.02
1991/2	$97,450,789.37
1992/3	$68,823,167.25
1993/4	$59,869,054.82
1994/5	$74,722,671.09
1995/6	$64,246,742.51
1996/7	$69,803,381.51
1997/8	$67,258,536.01
1998/9	$63,353,879.98
1999/0	$77,696,306.69
2000/1	$75,605,721.06
2001/2	$81,829,764.98
2002/3	$93,209,781.09
2003/4	$207,436,381.73
2004/5	$142,936,496.04
2005/6	$133,870,306.74
2006/7	$153,245,406.83
2007/8	$19,708,203.54

Source: Data provided by the CIDA library to the editors.

The initiative raises important questions about both the implementation and the formulation of Canadian foreign policy in the Middle East. First, should the Canadian government actively promote politicized movements for change abroad that work toward its broader foreign policy goals? At question here are actors within the NGO networks of civil society of the Middle East, some of which engage on more politically contentious advocacy politics. In general, civil society is defined as the realm of associations that lie between the state, the market, and the individual. In recognition of the diversity of actors— and interests—that can be found within this realm, scholars have moved away from making any definitive theoretical assumptions about the link between civil society and democratization, preferring to discuss it as a concept whose significance is defined by the context within which it operates. Indeed, rather than treating it in a unified manner, civil society is now recognized to be a more

TABLE 7–2

A Snapshot of the Canadian International Development Agency's Social Assistance to the Middle East

Women's Initiatives Fund, 1990–2001

The Canadian International Development Agency (CIDA) provided $8.5 million toward this project with the aim of improving the economic conditions of women in Egypt by promoting the participation of women in business. The project involved increasing access for women to microcredit and small business loans and by providing support and training.

McGill Middle East Program in Civil Society and Peace Building, 1998–2008

CIDA has committed $10.5 million to the McGill University Office of International Research to carry out this project. Fellowships have been granted to Israeli, Palestinian, and Jordanian students who first complete a Master in Social Work at McGill and then return to work in one of five practice centres run by the program in the region's most needy communities. More than 75,000 families are helped each year by the centers.

Networking for Peace, 1999–2006

CIDA provided $3 million to the Networking for Peace project, which "supports a series of small projects that encourage dialogue and regional co-operation within an expanded network of civil society organizations." The project helps civil society groups who wish to engage in effective dialogue initiatives "gain access to expertise and other resources that will help them design and implement constructive and effective dialogue and conflict management processes in various areas related to peace. A special emphasis is placed on projects that promote the active participation of women, youth and refugees." Palestinian NGOs were a specific focus.

The Scholarship Fund for Palestinian Refugee Women, 2000–2011

CIDA has committed $1.5 million to the International Development Research Centre (IDRC) to help Palestinian women refugees in Lebanon obtain university degrees and develop professional skills in areas such as business, engineering, and science. "It is expected that these women will become income-earners and play an increased leadership role in the Palestinian community alongside their male colleagues. They will contribute to the development of the community's capacity to manage and sustain itself culturally, psychologically and economically, enabling them to become major contributors and stakeholders in development."

United Nations Development Group Trust Fund, 2004–2010

CIDA has committed $70 million to the United Nations Development Group (UNDG) Iraq Trust Fund, which forms part of the International Reconstruction Fund Facility for Iraq (IRFFI). The IRFFI solicits donations for use in reconstruction, investment, technical, and developmental activities in Iraq. The UNDG Iraq Trust Fund aids in "technical assistance and capacity building across the following areas: human development and social justice; delivery of essential services, particularly in the area of health; the empowerment of civil society and local communities, water resources and food security; infrastructure rehabilitation; the protection and reintegration of vulnerable groups; the promotion of human rights and the rule of law; private sector development and employment generation, with due regard to gender equality and environmental protection and management."

Civil Society Capacity Building Fund, 2004–2007

CIDA provided more than $10 million to this fund, which supports Canadian non-governmental organizations (NGOs) in helping to establish a strong civil society in Iraq to help in the rebuilding of the country's social and economic foundation, and to promote good governance, democracy, peace, and tolerance.

International Mission for Iraqi Elections, 2005–2006

CIDA provided $7 million toward a project, led by a steering committee of independent chief electoral officers and commissioners, to "provide the Independent Electoral Commission for Iraq (IECI), political entities, civil society, Iraqi voters, and the international community with neutral and impartial assessments, evaluations, and observations on the Iraqi electoral process intended to support the building of democratic institutions in that country."

Water Demand Initiative, 2005–2010

CIDA has committed $2 million to the IDRC to execute this project, which involves research, field activities, and knowledge networking with the goal of "enhancing water-use efficiency, equity and sustainability in the countries of the Middle East and North Africa." Middle Eastern countries and regions benefiting from this initiative include Algeria, Egypt, Iraq, Jordan, Lebanon, Morocco, the West Bank and Gaza, Tunisia, Sudan, Syria, Turkey, and Yemen.

Support to Primary Schooling: STEPS II, 2005–2010

CIDA has committed $15 million to Agriteam Canada Consulting Ltd. to help improve the quality of primary schooling in Egypt. The project involves working with the Ministry of Education in Egypt to help develop its capacity to train educators, manage the school system, and "sustain the country's national standards of education."

Humanitarian Aid in Lebanon: International Committee of the Red Cross Appeal 2006–2007

In response to the 2006 conflict between Israel and Hizbullah, the International Committee of the Red Cross (ICRC) issued an appeal for aid to Lebanese citizens. CIDA responded with a total of $3.5 million to assist the ICRC in humanitarian relief efforts. The ICRC's activity in Lebanon involves "assisting the civilian population by providing them with water, food and medication. The ICRC is also restoring power and raising landmine awareness in the villages."

Special Gaza Refugees Support Program, 2006–2007

CIDA provided a $12 million grant to United Nations Relief and Works Agency for Palestine Refugees in the Near East (UNRWA) "to generate immediate improvements in refugees' lives in Gaza following the Israeli withdrawal in the autumn of 2005." This project provided aid in areas such as employment and shelter rehabilitation.

---

* All information was obtained from either the Canadian International Development Agency website www.acdi-cida.gc.ca or provided by the CIDA library upon request.

disaggregated entity, often made up of competing world views, actors, and networks that are empowered on a differential basis depending upon their connections with more underlying sources of socioeconomic and political power (Burnell and Calvert 2004; Kaviraj and Khilnani 2001; Hall 1995). To speak of promoting civil society, therefore, actually requires a political choice about which actors and networks one wants to strengthen. Canadian foreign policy makers, for example, have been active in supporting civil society actors that ostensibly worked in the name of sustainable development, liberal democracy, and peace, and have excluded the emerging Islamist actors and movements that were beginning to make their presence felt within the region (see Chapter 6). Yet, even within the realm of these more limited and "sanitized" possibilities that by and large consist of western-oriented NGOs, western donors have shied away from these political choices (see Jenkins 2001, 261). The example of CIDA's NGO Division and the MEWG suggests that although supporting more service-oriented NGOs can bring positive social impacts, engagement with more politicized actors within the region's NGO networks—if chosen wisely—can also bear important political fruit.

The second and related question concerns the issue of partnerships with NGOs at home and abroad and the challenges that partnership arrangements pose for the determination of broader Canadian foreign policy-making goals. NGOs and NGO coalitions, for example, often have a dual mandate: promoting the activities of overseas NGO partners in their own countries with the help of the Canadian government and acting as an advocate for the collective interests of these overseas partners within Canada. If successful at balancing this dual mandate, coalitions can add a powerful voice to the policy-making process, even if their views diverge from those of prevailing Canadian foreign policy. While the willingness on the part of the Canadian government to engage with such coalitions can facilitate policy advocacy success, the key factor remains the strength of the collectivities themselves. The MEWG, working in the highly politicized Middle East, especially with the deterioration of the peace process as the 1990s progressed, was unsuccessful in achieving this balancing act. Plagued by internal dissent about what its own collective interests were, it was unable to sustain itself as a coherent development arm of Canadian foreign policy, let alone a useful channel through which the voices of its partners in the region could be heard at home, and it ultimately fell by the wayside.

What follows is a social history of the MEWG initiative based upon records from its members as well as interviews of those connected to it. It begins with some background to the origins of the MEWG itself, establishing both why the initiative was launched and what its goals and initial successes were. The chapter will then examine the experience of the CIDA's NGO Division, in part through the MEWG, to promote civil society networks in the region, focusing in particular on Palestine and Lebanon, at a time that was felt to be a critical juncture in the region's history, especially with respect to the emergence of opportunities for political liberalization and democratization. The third section of the chapter will then provide an account of the advocacy efforts of the MEWG within Canada, efforts that sparked opposition from within Canadian foreign and development policy-making circles and, eventually, contributed to the demise of the MEWG's more formal relationship with the Canadian Government.

The Promising Origins of the NGO Middle East Working Group

The early 1990s was a time of great optimism in the Middle East. Iraq under Saddam Hussein had just been expelled from Kuwait, the product of the coming together of a global coalition of forces that included the participation of some Arab states—including Syria—and that was sanctioned by the United Nations Security Council (UNSC) in what was one of its first acts of collective security in the post–Cold War era. Simultaneous—and related to this—was the ending of the long and devastating civil war in Lebanon as a result of a robust Syrian military intervention, one tacitly agreed to by the United States and Israel as a quid pro quo for Syria's involvement in the multilateral coalition against Iraq. Moreover, in order to take advantage of the regional opportunities afforded by the end of the Cold War and the chastening of Iraq's Baathist regime, the first Bush administration initiated a diplomatic offensive designed to reach a comprehensive peace agreement between Israel and the Arab states, one that resulted in the launching of a multilateral peace process at Madrid in 1991.

Paralleling these changes at the regional and geo-strategic level in the Middle East were the emergence of hopeful signs of socioeconomic and political reform within the various states of the region—ones that suggested that the region was entering a critical juncture potentially favourable to the weakening of previously entrenched authoritarian state structures. Moreover, and most crucial to the civil society focus of discussion in this chapter, the region was also beginning to experience a significant growth in associational life—characterized not only by the revival of existing unions, syndicates, and social welfare associations but also by the growth of new forms of association life that consisted both of Islamist associations on the one hand and, on the other, the locally based NGOs, often closely associated with emerging developmental agendas in the West. It is the growth of these latter forms of associations that provides the particular context for this chapter.

In order to take advantage of this emerging state of flux, two interrelated strategic initiatives emerged within Canada. First, driven by a strong desire after the first Gulf War in 1991 both to strengthen existing partnerships with civil society actors in the Middle East as well as to develop new ones, a loose network of Canadian NGOs, most of which had longstanding experience in the Middle East, came together under the auspices of the CCIC and sent a delegation to the region in January of 1992, visiting Lebanon, Jordan, the occupied territories, and Iraq. Their main conclusion was that local NGOs and NGO networks in the region could play a key role in promoting peace, reconciliation, and political reform. As a way to start the process, they recommended the establishment of a Middle East/Canada Partnership Fund, to be financed by CIDA and administered by Canadian NGOs along the lines of some of the "delegative" coalition funding mechanisms that had been created in the 1980s.[3] The purpose of this fund was to support the consolidation of indigenous NGO and NGO networks in the region as well as to promote and coordinate local Canadian NGO efforts aimed at information sharing, development education, policy work, and advocacy on behalf of their partners within the region.

This emerging Canadian NGO initiative in the Middle East caught the eye of and gained the support of CIDA's NGO Division. Through a special initiatives fund, it had the means to support the initiative financially; it had already accumulated a significant degree of experience working with other regional coalitions in Canada, and the initiative itself provided CIDA with an opportunity to develop a more significant program in a region where it had traditionally had little substantive involvement. Indeed, it was also clear from the very beginning of the initiative that the NGO Division saw the MEWG as part of a broader strategy of civil society promotion within the Middle East as a whole at a critical moment in its political future (Cook 2007).

The first act of CIDA and this emerging NGO coalition, now called the Middle East Working Group, was the organization of a workshop in Ottawa in June 1993 called "Reconstruction, Rehabilitation, and Reconciliation in the Middle East: The View from Civil Society." NGO partners were invited from four countries and territories in the region (Lebanon, Egypt, Jordan, and the occupied territories) and the topics spanned four sectors of development activity (human rights, women, education and training, and the environment). All in all, there were more than 20 Middle East delegates, many of whom represented national NGO coordinating committees, in addition to more than 100 delegates from prospective Canadian NGO partners. One of the early discussions revolved around the question of how civil society partners would be defined and, with some dissent over the blanket vilification of Islamist actors, there was a working consensus that the group was most comfortable working with the more secularly oriented NGOs in the region that spoke the liberal democratic language of sustainable development and democracy. As one panelist at the Ottawa workshop argued, the MEWG initiative should be focused on "modern, professional, development NGOs," ones that would enlarge "the space of autonomy for the benefit of individuals without discrimination based upon color, ethnic identity, gender, or religion" (MEWG 1993, 10). Hence, not only was the CIDA/MEWG initiative designed to fight the forces of "despotism," but many also saw it as being designed to stave off the rising Islamist movements in the region. As Saad Eddin Ibrahim dramatically articulated in his introductory remarks, which captured much of the prevailing sentiment of the time, "there is a real race between the organs of civil society, on the one hand, and religious fanatics and despotic regimes on the other.... The only way to fight [these forces] is through the strengthening of the organs of civil society" (2).[4]

The workshop reached a number of conclusions: that NGOs could be key "agents of change"; that local NGOs are "severely constrained" in their efforts to mobilize at the grassroots and promote social change by their lack of capacity with respect to strategic planning, program management, and evaluation; that the capacities of NGOs in the region were further compromised by the fragmentation and lack of coordination at national and regional levels; and that these capacities could be enhanced both by direct Canadian assistance as well as by an improvement in the coordination of the activities among Canadian NGO themselves. The overarching (and somewhat self-serving) conclusion of the workshop was that the fledgling MEWG could play a helpful role in strengthening the capacities of civil societies in the region and that, therefore, every effort should be made to promote its continuation, consolidation, and expansion.

The MEWG's steering committee now kicked into action. First, it took a decision to remain a loose network, rather than a more formal incorporated coalition, with one NGO—interchangeably the YMCA and the Mennonite Central Committee (MCC)—acting as a lead agency or secretariat. It then put out a call for membership that netted about 20 NGOs, within which there was a core group.[5] With its institutional structure in place, the MEWG then got to work over the next year laying the ground work for more substantial regional programming. It prepared a concept paper for CIDA, justifying its request for funding by arguing that the region was "not a blank page" with respect to Canadian NGO involvement and that the work of the MEWG members in the region already represented "a substantial portion of Canadian-NGO supported work in the region."[6] Moreover, as a result of its developing efforts to rationalize Canadian NGO activity in the region, discussions about the concept paper stressed that the strategic advantage of the MEWG would be its ability to "make our resources (as well as those of CIDA) work harder."[7] In addition, a financial allocation mechanism was established within which decisions about project funding would be decided, first, by an internal vetting process within the MEWG itself and, ultimately, by a joint allocations committee made up of representatives from CIDA, DFAIT, and the MEWG (and chaired by the NGO Division)—a process that the MEWG described hopefully as "a new model of CIDA-NGO relations."[8] Finally, by the end of 1994, the approval process for what was now being called the "Linkage Program" was under way, and by mid 1995, the MEWG had seen flow through its NGO members approximately $500,000 in new funding for capacity building among NGOs in the region. Combined with the NGO Division's own initiatives within the region outside of the direct framework of the MEWG, the net result was an increase in the early 1990s in both the impact and profile of Canada within the emerging civil society communities of the Middle East.[9] Given Ibrahim's remark at the conclusion of the Ottawa workshop that the measure of the MEWG's success would be its ability to deliver "concrete do-able things," it appeared that Canada's civil society initiative in the post–Gulf War Middle East was off to a promising start.[10]

The Non-Governmental Organization Division and the Promotion of Civil Society Networks in the Middle East in the 1990s

However promising the MEWG beginning, the strategic thinking behind CIDA's support of this initiative did not only relate to the provision of increased social development assistance to the region—much of which went to enhance the service delivery capacities of selected NGOs. Rather, CIDA's NGO Division had grander designs, one of the principal ones being to support the development of a series of national and regional NGO networks that included the MEWG in Canada, helping to put them in a position to act as important mechanisms for social mobilization and political accountability at a critical juncture in the region's history. The head of the NGO Division, for example, made a point of distinguishing the approach of this initiative from those prevailing within circles of the U.S. Agency for International Development (USAID) at the time and that eschewed support for political organizations in favour of autonomous elements within civil society (Cook 2007).[11] He further spoke of it in terms of its compatibility with Canadian post-colonial values of anti-racism, equity, and social justice and suggested that, while a regional initiative, it was also clear that the Palestinian issue was implicitly "at the core of it." Hence, it would also be correct to say that the NGO Division's approach to promoting civil society in the region had an underlying political edge to it, in keeping with the social justice focus of many of its Canadian NGO partners.[12]

Most of Canada's support for NGO networks in the Middle East in the 1990s was concentrated in Lebanon and Palestine.[13] Both were political arenas in which NGOs were well established and had played prominent roles in contexts characterized by the absence of a functioning state, collapsed in the case of Lebanon and non-existent in the case of Palestine.[14] Indeed, it was in the Palestinian arena that Canada made its most important contribution to the development of civil society networks in the region in the 1990s, one that came in the form of support for the emerging Palestinian NGO Network (PNGO). Palestinian NGOs had performed a critical role in the occupied territories after 1967 in terms of delivery of essential social services, especially given both the absence of a state and the lack of Israeli investment in a social welfare infrastructure. By the time of the signing of the Oslo Accords in 1993, it was estimated that there existed a "vibrant and diverse" array of over 1,200 Palestinian NGOs employing more than 20,000 people (Brynen 2000, 49; Sullivan 1996). With the emergence of the peace process, and, in particular, the Oslo process that foreshadowed the creation of a Palestinian state, Palestinian NGOs now faced an existential crisis brought on both by the diversion of foreign funding away from them toward the new Palestinian Authority as well as by fears that the Palestinian Authority would seek to establish hegemony over the NGO sector and monopolize political life, fears that were further exacerbated by the fact that many within Palestinian NGO circles were aligned with leftist Palestinian factions that had emerged as some of the fiercest critics of the Oslo process. As representatives of the PNGO argued, "Palestinian NGOs find themselves in a historical juncture where they feel they have to strengthen the civil nature of Palestinian society... because they perceive it to be threatened" (Brynen 2000, 50, 188; Centre d'études arabes sur le développement 1995, 10).[15]

It was in this context that Palestinian NGOs decided to strengthen their position through the consolidation of a more unified territory-wide NGO network. With support from CIDA by way of its Montreal-based Canadian NGO partner Centre d'études arabes sur le développement (CEAD) in 1994, PNGO was able to consolidate its membership with more than 40 Palestinian NGOs, many of which were large with dynamic and professional leadership. By holding workshops and dialogues at the sectoral and territory-wide level, it started the process of establishing itself as the bona fide interlocutor and intermediary with and between the NGO community at large, the Palestinian Authority, and the numerous external agencies (Sullivan 1996, 97; CEAD 1995, 4).[16] Although it did not represent all NGOs in Palestine, PNGO nonetheless emerged as an effective defender of the rights of NGOs and associations within the Palestinian context as the 1990s wore on, resisting attempts by the Palestinian Authority to enact "repressive" laws regulating affairs of NGOs in the territories and contributing to the passage by the Palestinian Legislative Council in 1998 of an NGO law that was described as being "extremely liberal in the Arab context"

(Hammami 2000, 18).[17] Despite successful backtracking by Yasser Arafat, the entire episode over the NGO law was described by a critical observer of the Palestinian NGO scene as being "a victory for the NGOs and perhaps a larger symbol of what active and well organized lobbies can accomplish within the constraints of PA [Palestinian Authority] rule" (19).

Less successful were CIDA's efforts to support civil society networking in Lebanon, efforts that one member of the MEWG described unflatteringly as "meddling."[18] As in Palestine, NGOs had performed important functions during the long 15-year civil war and in the early postwar period, it is estimated that their numbers exceeded 3,000 by 1996.[19] However, the situation in Lebanon was more complicated than that of Palestine because of the prior existence of two national NGO networks—the Lebanese National Forum and le Collectif— both of which had emerged in the latter stages of the civil war and each of which was associated with a distinct membership and set of foreign and domestic donors. Complicating the situation even further was the emergence of a Palestinian NGO network in Lebanon in the postwar period.[20] Various attempts were made by CIDA's NGO Division to rationalize these networks by bringing them together—efforts that entangled CIDA officials and NGOs within the MEWG in the highly competitive and politicized world of Lebanese NGOs. Similar to Palestine, for example, NGOs in Lebanon experienced dramatic falls in assistance from foreign donors and were trying to reposition themselves as development as opposed to emergency relief organizations. Hence, the competition for scarce foreign resources was fierce and this competition was underpinned by significant political differences between the two NGO networks—the Lebanese National Forum headed by the skilfully entrepreneurial, if not aggressive, YMCA of Lebanon, which acted as the lead agency for what were largely sectarian social welfare organizations closely linked to the various religious communities, and le Collectif, with a more diverse membership of both sectarian and non-sectarian NGOs and whose core group were more interested in working toward a non-sectarian path forward for the country.[21]

When CIDA arrived on the scene, the two main Lebanese networks were beginning to try to bridge their differences and, in the wake of the Israeli incursions into Lebanon in 1993, had actually collaborated on joint relief operations. CIDA officials, however, made attempts to push these efforts further along, to manage and promote greater unity within Lebanese civil society. For example, both groups were invited to represent Lebanon at the MEWG's inaugural workshop in Ottawa in 1993; after a series of false starts, CIDA also funded an NGO management training program in which members from all three networks participated; and, in the mid 1990s, in its most interesting initiative, CIDA supported the creation of a Lebanese parliamentary centre—in effect, a new independent NGO—designed to act both as a forum for civil society networking as well as a go-between aimed at strengthening consultations between the parliament of Lebanon, its committees, and Lebanese NGOs as a whole; the head of CIDA's NGO Division spoke of the initiative as being a genuine attempt "to pull together the political class and civil society in Lebanon into a more coherent piece" (Cook 2007).

However, the goals of this project were never fulfilled. They were stalled by the difficulty of finding common ground between Lebanese deputies, unwilling to allow for the creation of a lobbying forum for NGOs through which they could criticize parliamentary activities, and NGOs themselves, many of which were unwilling to risk jeopardizing their own private access to the corridors of political power in Lebanon for a more collective civil society voice. Referring to the process as being a "delicate one that had to take into account many different interests," the implementing Canadian agency, the Parliamentary Centre, tried to bridge these differences by formulating a mandate for the independent centre that rejected an NGO-oriented watchdog model and promoted instead a more limited and politically neutral one with the goal simply to use the centre to establish "a point of contact between Parliament and civil society" in order to begin the process of building trust. However, even this institutional model failed to materialize and the initiative was reduced to an office within and, hence, controlled by the Lebanese parliament (Parliamentary Centre 1998).

What are the lessons from these two country experiences in civil society promotion? First, many NGOs lack strong broad-based social roots in the societies in which they operate; in the words of Eva Bellin, they are not "robust" (Fares Center for Eastern Mediterranean Studies 2006, 23). They face "legitimacy questions," especially if perceived to be promoting western values at the expense of local ones (see Chapter 6). Moreover, many NGOs have also become highly professionalized organizations, pulled more in the direction of and, hence, more accountable to, their foreign donors than to their local constituencies. While they may prove to be effective and accountable partners in the delivery of foreign aid programs and, hence, desirable from the administrative perspective of the donor as was the case with the YMCA of Lebanon, they are less likely to be in the vanguard of civil society advocacy campaigning. Indeed, in Lebanon, it was clear that the kind of socially rooted civil society networks willing to push for greater social and political accountability were emerging in more informal ways elsewhere in the country—part of a new generation of activists working on more particular issues such as the environment, disability, and a remarkably successful campaign for the holding of municipal elections in the country in 1998 (Kingston 2001, 2000; Karam 2004). However, even in the case of Palestinian NGOs that originally grew out of the solidarity and self-help imperatives of the occupation, Hammami (1995, 58) argues that "little by little, NGOs became distanced from the wider community of which they had once formed an organic part. They came to see themselves as devel-

opment professionals, rather than as catalysts of community political organization and mobilization."[22]

Moreover, even the most socially rooted of NGO activists and movements
are highly susceptible to dynamics of fragmentation. In part, this fragmentation is related to competition for domestic and foreign donor capital. However,
the main reason for the highly fragmented nature of civil society networks is
their vulnerability—due to their lack of robustness—to the co-opting dynamics of those in "political society," ones that often leave them powerless in the
face of efforts to stymie their autonomy and activism. Even in Palestine, where
NGOs were quite politically active and exhibited, in the words of Hammami
(2000, 27), "tremendous political skills," they nonetheless proved unable to prevent the Palestinian Authority from instituting its own version of the NGO law.
These weaknesses were even more visible in the Lebanese context, where
forces within "political society"—be they related to clan, sect, or class—proved
extremely effective in penetrating or thwarting the mobilizing efforts of civil
society actors at the national level, the failure of the relatively innocuous
Lebanese parliamentary centre to take root being a prime example. In short,
because of the powerful hierarchical dynamics of politics in the region, political connections often prove more important to protect than social solidarities,
a dynamic that problematizes goals of promoting strong, autonomous, and
united civil society networks.

Finally, it is doubtful that NGOs and other associations within civil society
will ever be at the vanguard of social and political change in the region and,
as Bellin argues, it is "absurd" to think that they could ever play this role
(Fares Center for Eastern Mediterranean Studies 2006, 24). She goes on to
argue, however, that civil society can help to push forward political reform once
a democratic opening has emerged. The key here, she adds, is for civil society to continue to develop to such an extent that when a political opening does
arrive, it will be ready "to swoop in." Hence, the goal of promoting civil society in the Middle East remains a vital and important one. Where CIDA and
much of the West miscalculated, however, was in first thinking that the early
1990s did represent that historical opening for political change in the region—
something that, in hindsight, it clearly did not—and, subsequently, in overestimating the political (as opposed to technical) capacity of NGOs and civil
society actors to be in the forefront of efforts to take advantage of it.

Supporting Civil Society at Home? Advocacy Politics, the Palestinian Refugee Question, and the Demise of the Middle East Working Group

Early on in the deliberations over the formation of the MEWG, it was clear
that, for the NGOs involved, effecting improvements in policy advocacy in
Canada on the Middle East was one of its most important goals; the MEWG had

to be something more than just a mechanism for funding.[23] However, much of the MEWG's time in its formative stage was taken up preparing the "Linkage Program" for CIDA, a task that had clearly deflected the MEWG's attention away from its broader development as an NGO coalition. At its annual meeting in February 1995, therefore, it was decided that the MEWG should not only continue to make efforts to "deepen the progress that MEWG has made with CIDA" but to also "look for ways both to increase advocacy work and share the concerns of many MEWG members about the nature of the peace process."[24] It is on this issue of the unfolding peace process, in particular the Oslo process, that MEWG discussions about advocacy increasingly focused and, as shall become evident, ultimately led to the MEWG's demise as a government-supported NGO coalition.

One of the key issues for many members of the MEWG was the plight of the Palestinian refugees, both from a social perspective as well as from a political perspective, and the dire circumstances of Palestinian refugees in Lebanon was highlighted as being of particular concern by all involved. It was the issue of the right of return for Palestinian refugees, however, ignored by both the Oslo peace process and the previous but ongoing multilateral peace process, that increasingly began to preoccupy the deliberations of the MEWG. With Canada being given gavel-holder responsibility for the Refugee Working Group (RWG) of the multilateral peace process in 1992, some MEWG members together with their NGO partners in the field hoped that the MEWG could provide them with some degree of access to the process as it unfolded.

Initially, DFAIT officials were also interested in using Canadian NGOs as mechanisms for pursuing Canada's responsibilities associated with the RWG, especially with regard to the delivery of social assistance to Palestinian refugee camps in Lebanon. Indeed, it was the assistant deputy minister responsible for the Middle East in DFAIT and the first gavel holder of the RWG, Marc Perron, who initially approached CIDA about the possibility of using Canadian NGOs in this manner. CIDA, in turn, suggested that the NGOs in the MEWG might be just the channel that DFAIT officials were looking for, especially if linkages could be established with the newly formed Palestinian NGO Forum in Lebanon (Cook 2007).[25] Moreover, members of the MEWG were also enthusiastic about becoming more involved in this issue. The YWCA agreed to act as the funding channel, delivering an initial $250,000 package of social assistance to Palestinian refugees in Lebanon in 1994; and the MEWG as a whole began to formulate proposals designed both to raise awareness about the plight of Palestinian refugees within Canada and to develop a coordinated strategy to deliver projects to improve the conditions under which the Palestinian refugees lived.[26] All agreed that a good way to start this process was to organize a second MEWG workshop on the issue for the summer of 1995.

Here, however, the consensus ended. A core group within the MEWG, many of whom had been involved with the North American Coordinating Committee for the United Nations NGO Forum on Palestine, wanted to take their involvement in the Palestinian refugee issue to the political level. There was great concern, for example, that the issue of Palestinian refugees outside the occupied territories was being ignored, a concern exacerbated by the moving of the offices of United Nations Relief and Works Agency for Palestine Refugees in the Near East (UNRWA) from Geneva to Gaza. To start the ball rolling, CEAD along with its partner PNGO decided to host its own conference—supported by CIDA—on Palestinian refugees in March of 1995 in Amman. One of the main purposes of the conference was to begin the process of giving the refugees "a voice in the dynamic transitions overtaking the region."[27] A memo from PNGO to the MEWG stressed that no lasting peace in our troubled region is possible "without the people directly affected being invested in the process." From this launching pad, CEAD envisioned a progressively more intensive lobbying campaign that would make subsequent stops in Ottawa and New York at the UN. Instrumental in this campaign would be the three emerging NGO networks—the PNGO, the Palestinian NGO Forum in Lebanon, and the MEWG in Canada—all of which could create "a unified NGO front actively pursuing the goal of a just solution to the Palestinian refugee problem. It is with one voice, made louder by our unity, that we should call for the implementation of UN resolutions 181 to 799 ... all of which are ignored by Israel. It is only through a coordinated strategy that we can effectively face and surmount the challenges that confront us today."[28] With respect to the proposed workshop in Ottawa, for example, CEAD spoke about "rocking the boat" in Canada, especially with respect to politicians and the Canadian public and suggested that the conference needed to be "confrontational" but "in a civilized way," all of which would help to push forward the Canadian government's position, one that it stressed was not "adequate."[29]

This proposal sparked considerable and, at times, vitriolic, debate within the membership of the MEWG, debate that raised larger questions about whether the MEWG actually had enough common ground—a "central idea" as one MEWG member put it—on which it could establish a viable collective.[30] Some NGO representatives were worried, for example, that the focus of the MEWG was becoming too narrow; after all, as one member argued, "we are a 'Middle East' Working Group, not a 'Palestinian' Working Group."[31] Other members felt that a better strategic direction for the MEWG would be to focus on the broader and less immediately political task of public education in Canada. A third voice in the MEWG strongly argued that, while working on behalf of Palestinian refugees should be an important part of its work, the MEWG's time and money would be better spent on humanitarian work: "we believe that the interest of the Palestinian refugees would be far better served if the money used to host repetitive workshops discussing their fate would be used for sustainable efforts in improving their days, if not their lives."[32] Further complicating the internal dynamics in the MEWG were some underlying political—not to speak of institutional and personal—differences between the Palestinian-oriented members of the MEWG with regard to support for the peace process, some with stronger ties to Fatah (and therefore the Palestinian Authority), others with stronger partnership ties to the Palestinian oppositional left. Stressed an NGO representative more sympathetic to the former camp, by becoming involved in advocacy against the peace process, the MEWG will find itself aligned with "people like [Libya's Muammar] Ghaddafy."[33]

While the NGO Division was not opposed to the some of the MEWG's lobbying on the Palestinian refugee issue, DFAIT officials were incensed that CIDA would fund a conference that, in essence, would advocate against the activities of the Canadian representatives associated with the RWG and they sent a strong request to the NGO Division to pull the funding for a conference on this issue.[34] A workshop with a more general theme—"Canada and the Middle East: Developing an NGO Vision"—was eventually held in October 1995 in Ottawa. However, the controversy over the underlying purpose of the MEWG continued, cutting "right to the heart of the future of the MEWG as a network."[35] In terms of political advocacy, it was stressed that there was a tradition in Canada of NGO coalitions intervening, sometimes successfully, in cases where human rights were being systematically violated, as was argued was the case with Palestinian refugees. Moreover, it was also clear that humanitarian and development work had to be put within a political framework, something that they argued was already recognized by the NGO Division itself. Finally, with respect to the Palestinian refugee issue, the proponents of the advocacy mandate for the MEWG emphasized that a well-orchestrated campaign on behalf of Palestinian refugees was not only technically and politically feasible, especially if Palestinian leadership could be won over to it, but was also a moral imperative:

> Ignoring this issue would be in our minds a grave mistake that would be severely criticized by our Palestinian partners and by Canadians still concerned with social justice and human rights. It will also question our ability to function as a group committed to social justice and democracy and undermine our credibility as an autonomous network capable of influencing our government's policies to address Palestinian's concerns with self-determination, the rights of return, development, and peace.[36]

Countering these arguments, however, were those on the development side of the debate. It was argued that the MEWG should focus on humanitarian activities, stressing that the bulk of any funds should be spent on projects whose direct beneficiaries are the individuals and the communities that need them (refugees, women, the disabled, etc.). At the moment, however, "it seems that in, our attempt to stand in solidarity with our partners, we are circumnavigating our real targeted beneficiary."[37] Moreover, in a realistic appraisal of NGO capacities in the region and in Canada, they stressed that "NGOs cannot solve the political problems of the refugees (right of return, right of work, right of property in host countries, etc.) but we can lobby our government … on a limited basis in assisting to solve some of the immediate grave problems they are facing."

The divisions within the MEWG only deepened with the deterioration of the Oslo peace process as a result of the growing influence of radicals on both sides of the "green line"—symbolized by the assassination of Israeli prime minister Yitzhak Rabin on the one hand and the growth of Palestinian suicide bombing in Israel on the other. The differences between the members widened, and the voices of those in the MEWG interested in using the coalition as a vehicle for policy advocacy became much stronger. Not wanting to see the collapse of the MEWG, CIDA's NGO Division encouraged the coalition to bridge their differences by focusing on the formulation of a new "linkage program" proposal that requested both an increased budget for development and capacity-building projects as well as seed money for the creation of a more substantial secretariat with a half-time coordinator who could lay the ground work for the MEWG to act "with greater legitimacy in its advocacy work and an ability to speak more forcefully from the convictions of the collective on matters related to the Middle East."[38]

However, the writing was on the wall for the MEWG and, in the end, its funding proposal was never approved. DFAIT and the RWG team had clearly lost any interest in the initiative they might have had. Instead, they began to explore the use of more discrete channels through the International Development Research Centre (IDRC), funded by the joint CIDA/DFAIT Peacebuilding Fund, as a way of engaging with Palestinian refugees, civil society actors in the region, and academics. This relatively successful approach gave way to what was coined the "Ottawa Process," much to the chagrin of the NGO Division in CIDA, which it was argued "seemed to view the entire project as an invasion of their area of responsibility" (Brynen et al. 2003, 13).[39] The proposal also ran into more concerted opposition from within CIDA, which was facing serious budget cuts as it was—cuts that had led to the end of program funding for other NGO coalitions including the CCIC—and whose bilateral division concerned with the Middle East had always given much more weight to government to government assistance, especially with regard to the Palestinian Authority, which was an issue that had been a constant source of tension between it and the NGO Division.[40] More generally, in keeping with the recommendations of the various foreign and development policy reviews of the time, there seems to have been an effort in the 1990s to more tightly coordinate foreign and development policy making, a process that also began to result in a drift of resources away from CIDA toward DFAIT. In the Canadian NGO world, this led to concerns in the 1990s that CIDA was moving away from "responsive" and toward more "directive" programming in which NGO activities would have to contribute to "the general strategic framework for the region in which they are being carried out" (Morrison 1998, 336; see also Draimin and Tomlinson 1998). In an interesting set of reflections after the fact, Norman Cook (2007) of the NGO Division lamented this loss of "policy development space."[41]

However, the main reasons for the demise of the MEWG in the mid 1990s relate to the inability of the MEWG members themselves to develop a consensus or a central idea on which to focus their activities. Debates about advocacy versus development, Palestine versus the rest of the Middle East, supporting civil society networks versus a broader array of non-aligned NGOs in the region combined with the bitter personal differences and histories among some of the core members and organizations of the MEWG to create an atmosphere of acrimony within the MEWG that many within the coalition could simply not understand.[42] In the first few years as a result of the relative optimism of the early post–Gulf War period and the presence of development finance from CIDA, the MEWG achieved a momentary sense of purpose. With the deterioration in the regional climate, especially within the Palestinian arena, and the increasing concerns about the future of the MEWG's relationship with CIDA, which was negatively clarified at the beginning of 1997, the future of the MEWG was now in doubt. Even those most committed to the idea of the MEWG such as the MCC's Bill Janzen expressed strong hesitations as to its actual usefulness—hindered as it was "by the dangling CIDA carrot and also by the difficult dynamics among MEWG members."[43] In a thoughtful reflection on whether the initiative was worth continuing, Janzen argued that

> in one sense, the MEWG is not important. But, to let it die would seem to reflect badly on Canadian NGOs. I think we should have a body where we can come together and think about Middle East concerns, where we talk about our perception of the issues and, perhaps do some things together. I think we would have a weaker hand with the Canadian Foreign Affairs Department if we allowed it to die.... But how do we keep MEWG alive and useful? I am not sure.[44]

In the end, most of the membership of the MEWG fell away. Left was a core group of NGOs, all of which were much more firmly committed to establishing the MEWG as a forum for policy advocacy within Canada that targeted, in particular, the question of Palestine. However, repeated requests from the more streamlined MEWG for seed money for conferences failed and its own attempts to lobby within CIDA for a resurrection of the MEWG initiative, proved unsuccessful.[45] Meanwhile, the NGO Division continued its own civil society promotion activities with individual NGOs.[46] There was a brief and intense revival of advocacy activity in the early 2000s, brought on both by a collapse of the peace process after the outbreak of the second intifada in the occupied territories as well as by a more open attitude toward consultation with Canadian civil society groups on the part of those involved with the peace process within DFAIT.[47] Indeed, this resulted in a series of meaningful and much more focused policy dialogues on the question of where to go with the peace process between NGO members of the MEWG and officials from DFAIT and CIDA, which Janzen later described as the MEWG's "highpoint."[48] By this point, however, the MEWG was simply one of many voices to which DFAIT listened and, while its members had considerable experience in the region gained through longstanding regional partnerships, DFAIT considered their views about what the parameters for "peace with justice" should look like to be too challenging from the domestic political perspective to have much mileage within foreign policy making circles (Janzen 2007).[49] Moreover, further muffling their voice was the lack of the kind of constituency base that would have given it greater political weight. It is not surprising, therefore, that as the MEWG initiative died away, pioneering though it may have been as a Canadian lobby group on behalf of Middle Eastern and especially Palestinian interests when it was created, other more politically significant constituency-based forums and venues have emerged to take its place. These have revolved around a nascent working group within a new ecumenical human rights coalition (KAIROS) and a growing array of associations lobbying on behalf of the Arab and Muslim communities within Canada, as well as the already well-established lobbying organizations that have long been working on behalf of Israel. Amidst these larger constituency-based players, Canadian NGOs working in the Middle East—even if they could reorganize themselves into a more effective, cohesive, and sustainable group—are now a relatively insignificant political lobby.

Conclusions

Canadian NGOs and CIDA's NGO Division showed great initiative in jumping on the apparent political opportunities emerging in the Middle East of the early 1990s to promote civil society in the region. Given the growth in associational life, hopeful (if nascent) signs that progress might be possible with respect to peace between Israel and its Arab neighbours, and murmurings of a regional trend toward political liberalization in the air, the time seemed right to work at establishing stronger partnerships between civil society actors in Canada and their counterparts in the region. Establishing a partnership with an emerging NGO coalition as a means to implement and represent Canada's new civil society promotion policy in the region also seemed a logical way to proceed, both because it promised a more integrated approach to the initiative and because its national scope might allow Canada to "fly its flag." Finally, members of the MEWG also hoped that its establishment would facilitate the work of individual Canadian NGOs in advocacy and public education work on a region that was little understood by the Canadian public. All associated with the MEWG continue to think that, at least in theory, it was a useful experiment and they see its passing with some lamenting over lost opportunities.

The initiative did have some positive impacts, especially for individual organizations that would never have received needed social and development assistance had the MEWG initiative not emerged. In that sense, CIDA's policy was most beneficial for particular and strategically targeted civil society organizations in the region, and this kind of CIDA work deserves to receive continued, if not increased, support as it will help to lay the ground work for these organizations to "swoop in" and assist (although not lead) in political reform efforts in the various countries of the region in the event of the emergence of genuine political opportunities.[50] CIDA's initiative also had more limited success in promoting more politicized civil society networks in the region but this success depended upon its ability to identify, with the crucial assistance of Canadian NGO partners, networks that had substantial social—often middle class—roots in the country. While it worked well in Palestine, in Lebanon these more important civil society networks were missed and this had much to do with the weak presence that Canada had on the ground in the early postwar period, which made it difficult to sort through the complex political dynamics in that country. Furthermore, targeting and supporting even the more politicized NGOs and civil society networks in the region, while useful in the promotion of particular development and advocacy goals, will not transform them into critically important strategic players within the broader civil societies of the region. These roles are reserved for political parties, the most powerful of which are often associated with Islamist social movements. Hence, in terms of its relationship to broader goals of democracy promotion, there are inherent, built-in, limits to the impact that a policy of civil society promotion can have.

Finally, what of the role that Canadian NGOs—and their partners—can play in the formulation of broader Canadian foreign policy goals? This is a much more difficult question to answer and, in many ways, goes to the heart of the MEWG's own *problématique*. Clearly, there exists a considerable amount of longstanding, on-the-ground experience within the Canadian NGO community involved with the Middle East. These are voices that should be heard and, if possible, collectively expressed. CIDA's NGO Division, implicitly supportive of the political vision of many—but not all—of the more advocacy-oriented NGOs in the MEWG, tried to create this collective voice by funding them. But, as has been the experience of others, "consortiums and coalitions that come together simply because government funds were being offered [do] not last."[51] The MEWG, therefore, was never able to achieve a consensus on its dual mandate or, in other words, on the balance that needed to be struck between its role as a development arm of the Canadian government and its interest in acting as a base from which to lobby on broader issues of Canadian foreign policy related to Middle East issues. Interesting in this regard is the temporary revival of the MEWG in early 2000 as a more focused and coherent advocacy coalition but now one at an arm's length from the Canadian government. Here, we witnessed the coming together of the two essential ingredients needed to facilitate serious policy dialogue: the emergence of an autonomous and collective voice grounded in a strong consensus about the message that wants to be communicated and the active and genuine commitment on the part of the Canadian government to facilitating, listening to, and deliberating with the variety of voices that come to the table, something that is not always present, as the MEWG's experience in the 1990s suggests. In that sense, just as the Canadian government works to promote serious policy dialogue within the Middle East among civil society actors and the states of the region, so too must it continue to recognize the crucial role that it needs to play in promoting genuine—and broad-based—policy dialogue on its Middle East foreign policy at home.

Notes

1   Van Rooy (2001, 254, 257) described traditional Canadian foreign policy culture as being "unconvinced" of the value of non-governmental inclusion with DFAIT, especially prior to the Axworthy era, being "a closed shop."

2   In 2005 CIDA's NGO Division was changed to the Voluntary Sector Program.

3   A delegative funding mechanism is one in which the coalition assumes responsibility for making funding allocation decisions.

4   Ibrahim's comments about fanatics sparked much debate, both because of its essentialist stereotyping and because it ignored the fact that these organizations were much more deeply rooted in contemporary Arab society than the more secular and professional-oriented NGOs. As a delegate from Yemen asked, what does it mean to support this western notion of civil society in societies characterized by the absence of a functioning market economy and in which significant proportions of the population were illiterate? Isn't this simply ignoring "local realities" (MEWG 1993, 21)?

5   Some of the more active MEWG members were the YMCA, the MCC, Centre d'études arabes pour le développement (CEAD), Human Concern International, Medical Aid for Palestine (MAP), Canadian Council of Churches, Near East Cultural and Education Foundation (NECEF), Canadian Public Health Association, Canadian Auto Workers, Canadian Labour Congress, Carrefour des Cèdres, Comité européen pour la défense des réfugiés et immigrés (CEDRI), the Association of Universities and Colleges of Canada (AUCC), and the Association of Community Colleges of Canada (ACCC).

6   MEWG, "Concept Paper," draft, June 16, 1994.

7   MEWG, "Concept Paper," draft, October 4, 1993.

8   MEWG to Norman Cook, memo, February 9, 1995.

9 Most of the projects were in Lebanon (training for handicapped youth, vocational training programs for tailors, computer training, support for NGO networking, support for Palestinian refugees) and the Palestinian territories (support for the renewal of trade unions, NGO networking, a variety of income generation and micro-credit projects, land reclamation, a hospital management project, support for elementary home care physiotherapy, a conflict resolution centre, and support for Palestinian women refugees), plus support for the Gaza Human Rights Center and the Gaza Red Crescent Society. There were also projects in Jordan (Mukhibeh Community Housing, support for preparation for a Beijing UN Conference, a rainkeep project), Yemen (feasibility study of NGOs), and Algeria (support for female journalists), as well as Syria (l'Arche), despite the ban on funding to that country.

10 Ibrahim, director of the Ibn Khaldoun Center for Development Studies in Cairo, has been one the region's main champions of civil society (MEWG 1993, 99).

11 Rob Jenkins (2001, 260–64) has also argued that USAID's approach to civil society promotion with its emphasis on "public-spirited watchdogs quarantined from political society" is "excessively cautious" and "jeopardizes the healthy development of 'political society.'"

12 Indeed, it was also clear that the NGO Division had particularly strong ties with a few NGO personnel within the MEWG, such as Pierre Beaudet of CEAD, Bill Janzen of the MCC, and Jim Graff of NECEF, both of whom were politically active with respect to the Palestinian issue and had played leading roles within the North American Coordinating Committee (NACC) for the United Nations NGO Forum on Palestine.

13 Some financial and logistical support was also provided to an emerging NGO network in Yemen and Morocco's "Espace associatif" during this time period.

14 It is interesting to note that the NGO communities within Lebanon and Palestine, along with those of Morocco, are considered today to be among the most active in the region (see Hawthorne 2005, 88).

15 Brynen (2000) estimates, for example, that the Palestinian NGO sector experienced a reduction in annual foreign aid flows from a high point of $200 million in the early 1990s to somewhere between US$60 million and US$90 million later in that same decade.

16 Among the initial practical accomplishments of PNGO, all of which were facilitated by CIDA financial support, was the commissioning of a study by three Palestinian lawyers (Usama Halabi, Raja Shehadeh, and Raji Sourani) that compared state legislation concerning NGOs in various countries, assistance in support for the establishment of BARAKA, a Palestinian-led email, conferencing, and communication system, and various other policy papers and PNGO newsletters.

17 There was significant discussion within the MEWG, for example, that the PNGO initiative excluded many other "non-aligned" Palestinian NGOs that were not affiliated with leftist factions.

18 Interview with MEWG member, June 5, 2007.

19 For an account of NGO activities in wartime, see Slaiby 1993.

20 As is discussed later, this Palestinian NGO Forum in Lebanon became of interest to officials in DFAIT who were now responsible for the Refugee Working Group (RWG) that the multilateral peace talks had asked Canada to chair. They saw this

network as a potentially useful channel for delivering social assistance to Palestinian refugee within the camps in Lebanon where social conditions were considered appalling.

21 For more background information on the formation of these two NGO networks, see Kingston (forthcoming).

22 Asef Bayat (2002, 18) reached a similar conclusion in his survey of social activism in the Middle East, arguing that "what NGO activism means in reality is the activism of NGO leaders, not that of the millions of targeted people. These NGOs serve more their employees than the political beneficiaries."

23 Minutes of the MEWG Steering Committee, February 10, 1994.

24 Internal MEWG correspondence, April 20, 1995.

25 See also internal MEWG correspondence, January 16, 1995.

26 MEWG draft proposal, March 6, 1995.

27 PNGO to the MEWG, June 7, 1995.

28 Draft proposal by CEAD and MEWG draft proposal, March 6, 1995.

29 Minutes of MEWG meeting, March 3, 1995. See also "The Peace Process and Palestinian Refugees," draft proposal, CEAD and MAP, undated.

30 MCC to the Canadian Council of Churches, November 27, 1995.

31 Notes from MEWG meeting, July 21, 1995.

32 Internal MEWG correspondence, February 28, 1995.

33 Internal MEWG correspondence, November 27, 1995.

34 Internal MEWG memo, February 8, 1996.

35 Internal MEWG correspondence, February 6, 1996.

36 Internal MEWG correspondence, February 6, 1996.

37 "Notes for Consideration on the MEWG Vision," December 4, 1995.

38 Internal MEWG correspondence, June 6, 1996. The MEWG's proposal to CIDA— "Canada and the Middle East: A Strategic Partnership"—called for an increased budget of $700,000 with priority given to five areas: strengthening civil society and democratic development, increasing the capacity of NGOs working with Palestinian refugees, strengthening cross-sectarian NGO networks and social service delivery mechanisms in Lebanon, promoting public education efforts on the Middle East in Canada, and providing support for a half-time MEWG coordinator.

39 When the MEWG approached CIDA and DFAIT again for a much smaller sum of money to assist them in hosting a conference on "The Middle East in Crisis" in early 1998, which would have included some highly respected critics of the peace process such as Sara Roy, Yusuf Sayigh, and Atif Kabursi, the proposal was again turned down on the basis that it was clearly "political," the agenda "too biased," and the proposed resource people "one-sided" (memo to MEWG board, October 29, 1997). Revealing the extent of the MEWG's fall from policy grace, it was suggested that "some junior DFAIT staff put their veto" to the proposal.

40 Norman Cook (2007) has suggested that the opposition of CIDA's bilateral division had always been a significant impediment to the MEWG initiative, although it seems that NGO Division also faced increasing challenges in the 1990s from within its own Partnership Branch, the director general of which at one point spoke about "working towards a cultural shift in the NGO Division to prevent experiences like [the MEWG's]" (internal MEWG memo, January 15, 1997). Cook added that this was

part of a broader attempt by bilateralists within CIDA to put NGO work into a neo-country focus.

41 With respect to the MEWG initiative in the early 1990s, for example, Cook (2007) praised his team within the NGO Division (which included Jonathan Laine, who later went on to become the Canadian representative to the Palestinian Authority in Ramallah) as well as the support he initially received from the director general of the Partnership Branch, stating that "we certainly had more policy space [then] and we used it to the maximum."

42 For example, Janet Sutherland (2007), the representative on the MEWG for the YMCA, remarked that while other coalitions that she had been apart of had experienced serious political disputes, only the MEWG failed to ever transcend them. Bill Janzen (2007) of the MCC likewise remarked that he would come home from some of the more contentious MEWG meetings "not wanting to go back again."

43 Internal MCC memo, December 12, 1996.

44 Bill Janzen to the Canadian Council of Churches, November 27, 1995.

45 See Consultancy Report (1999), in which it was recommended that "CIDA should support the reorganization of the Middle East Working Group (MEWG) including the active participation of Middle East partners, both financial and with a meaningful role in the planning, implementation and evaluation of CIDA's strategies and programs with civil society organizations in the Middle East."

46 Alternatives (formally CEAD), for example, would later receive a $10 million three-year program grant in 2004 to administer a "Civil Society Capacity Building Fund" targeting Iraq.

47 The key to this renewed relationship with DFAIT officials was the appointment of Michael Molloy to head the peace process desk (the day the second intifada began). Molloy was committed to wide consultations with all concerned with Middle East policy, both within government and within Canadian civil society, and his efforts were greatly appreciated by all associated with the MEWG at this time—even if these consultations failed to effect the kind of changes in Canadian government policy toward a "peace with justice" for which members of the MEWG were pushing.

48 The first dialogue organized by the MEWG was entitled "Beyond the Crisis in Palestine: An NGO Stocktaking Workshop," on February 6, 2001. The second dialogue was on April 23, 2001, and was based on a discussion paper prepared by the MEWG entitled "A Call for Canadian Initiatives on the Middle East." The dialogues were considered to be so successful that the head of the NGO Division hoped that they might lead to CIDA and DFAIT reconsidering a more comprehensive revival of MEWG initiative. "Think big" was the advice to the MEWG in recommending that they submit a new funding proposal to CIDA.

49 While the MEWG made numerous recommendations—many of which requested that Canada respond to the immediate social and economic needs of the Palestinians and the refugees—the focus of the MEWG discussion paper was on the need for Canada to engage actively and politically with efforts to end the Israeli occupation of the West Bank and Gaza. While recognizing that "some Israeli fears are understandable and should be taken into account" and while "pleased that Canada recognizes the illegality of the occupation," the document went on to argue that "we

have been troubled by references on the part of the government to accepting 'whatever the two parties agree on.' Since the Palestinians are the weaker party, they will be disadvantaged in bilateral negotiations. Their rights have been sacrificed for too long. Substantial measures to correct the injustices on the basis of international law are urgently needed" (MEWG 2001, 4).

50 Current CIDA civil society initiatives in the region include $10 million for a Civil Society Capacity Building Project in Iraq administered by Alternatives (formerly CEAD), Networking for Peace ($3 million), McGill University's Program in Civil Society and Peacebuilding (over $10 million), in addition to the various Canada Funds administered by Canadian embassies in the region that can provide important seed money for small NGO and civil society initiatives. For an analysis of some of the work of various funds in the region, see Jacobi (2000).

51 See also Africa Canada Forum (2000).

References

Africa Canada Forum. 2000. "Africa Canada Forum—Report." Report on the symposium of May 28–31. www.ccic.ca/e/archives/acf_2000_05–31 _lac_mcdonald_report.pdf (August 2007).

Bayat, Asef. 2002. "Activism and Social Development in the Middle East." *International Journal of Middle East Studies* 34(1): 18.

Brynen, Rex. 2000. *A Very Political Economy: Peacebuilding and Foreign Aid in the West Bank and Gaza.* Washington, DC: United States Institute for Peace.

Brynen, Rex, Eileen Alma, Joel Peters, Roula al-Rifai, and Jill Tansley. 2003. "The Ottawa Process: An Examination of Canada's Track Two Involvement in the Palestinian Refugee Issue." Paper presented at the Stocktaking Conference on Palestinian Refugee Research, Ottawa, June 17–20. www.idrc .ca/uploads/user-/10576789140Session_3_BRYNEN_OTTAWA_PROCESS _PAPER.doc (August 2007).

Burnell, Peter, and Peter Calvert, eds. 2004. *Civil Society in Democratization.* London: Frank Cass.

Centre d'études arabes sur le développement. 1995. "Strengthening the NGO Movement in the West Bank and Gaza." May. Montreal.

Consultancy Report. 1996. "An Assessment of CIDA's Program with Civil Society Organizations in the Middle East." Prepared for the Priorities and Special Initiatives Directorate, Canadian Partnership Branch, Canadian International Development Agency, June.

Cook, Norman. 2007. Interview by author. June 6, Ottawa. Written notes.

Draimin, Tim, and Brian Tomlinson. 1998. "Is There a Future for Canadian Aid in the Twenty-First Century?" In *Canada Among Nations: Leadership and Dialogue,* ed. Fen Osler Hampson and Maureen Molot, 143–68. Ottawa: Carleton University Press.

Fares Center for Eastern Mediterranean Studies. 2006. "Democratizating the Middle East?" Occasional Paper No. 2. Tufts University. farescenter.tufts.edu/conferences/2007Paper2-Democratizing.pdf (August 2007). 2006.

Hall, John, ed. 1995. *Civil Society: Theory, History, Comparison*. Cambridge: Polity Press.

Hammami, Rema. 1995. "NGOs: The Professionalisation of Politics." *Race and Class* 37(2): 51–63.

———. 2000. "Palestinian NGOs Since Oslo: From NGO Politics to Social Movements?" *Middle East Report* 214: 18.

Hawthorne, Amy. 2005. "Is Civil Society the Answer?" In *Uncharted Journey: Promoting Democracy in the Middle East*, ed. Thomas Carothers and Marina Ottoway. Washington, DC: Carnegie Endowment for International Peace.

Jacobi, Tami Amanda. 2000. "Canadian Peacebuilding in the Middle East: Case Study of the Canada Fund in Israel/Palestine and Jordan." Ottawa: Canadian Centre for Foreign Policy Development.

Janzen, Bill. 2007. Interview by author. June 6, Ottawa. Written notes.

Jenkins, Rob. 2001. "Mistaking 'Governance' for 'Politics': Foreign Aid, Democracy, and the Construction of Civil Society." In *Civil Society: History and Possibilities*, ed. Sudipta Kaviraj and Sunil Khilnani, 250–68. Cambridge: Cambridge University Press.

Karam, Karam. 2004. "Revendiquer, mobiliser, participer: les associations civiles dans le Liban de l'après-guerre." Doctoral thesis, Université de Provence, Aix-Marseille.

Kaviraj, Sudipta, and Sunil Khilnani, eds. 2001. *Civil Society: History and Possibilities*. Cambridge: Cambridge University Press.

Kingston, Paul. 2001. "Patrons, Clients, and Civil Society: Environmental Politics in Postwar Lebanon." *Arab Studies Quarterly* 23(1): 55–72.

———. 2000. "Understanding Governance in Lebanon: The Case of Disability Policy-Making." Governance and Civil Society Project, Institute of Development Studies, Sussex University.

———. Forthcoming. "Advocacy Politics, NGOs, and Associational Networks in Postwar Lebanon" (manuscript in progress).

Middle East Working Group. 1993. "Reconstruction, Rehabilitation and Reconciliation in the Middle East: The View From Civil Society." Workshop Report. Ottawa, June 21–22.

———. 2001. "A Call for Canadian Initiatives on the Middle East." Discussion paper prepared for meeting on April 23, Ottawa.

Morrison, David. 1998. *Aid and Ebb Tide: A History of CIDA and Canadian Development Assistance.* Waterloo: Wilfrid Laurier University Press.

Parliamentary Centre. 1998. "Report to the Advisory Council of the Canada-Lebanon Policy Dialogue on the Second Policy Workshop, July 8–9, 1998." Ottawa.

Slaiby, Ghassan. 1993. "Les actions collectives de résistance civile à la guerre." In *Le Liban aujourd'hui*, ed. Fadia Kiwan, 119–36. Centre d'études et de recherches sur le Moyen-Orient contemporain: Paris.

Sullivan, Denis. 1996. "NGOs in Palestine: Agents of Development and Foundation of Civil Society." *Journal of Palestine Studies* 25(3): 93–100.

Sutherland, Janet. 2007. Interview by author. June 5, Ottawa. Written notes.

Van Rooy, Alison. 2001. "Civil Society and the Axworthy Touch." In *Canada among Nations: The Axworthy Legacy*, ed. Fen Osler Hampson and Maureen Molot, 253–69. Ottawa: Carleton University Press.

The International Development Research Centre and the Middle East: Issues and Research[1]

The International Development Research Centre (IDRC) is a rarity in global development organizations: it funds southern researchers in order to build research capacity in the developing world. The IDRC has been active in the Middle East for more than 30 years and has funded development research on a myriad of topics, including civil society, gender, agriculture, water, governance, and small and medium-sized enterprises. The idea of creating an organization like the IDRC was conceived in the late 1960s by Prime Minister Lester Pearson and by the head of the newly established Canadian International Development Agency (CIDA), Maurice Strong. On the eve of Canada's centennial celebrations in 1967, Pearson addressed the Canadian Political Science Association on the imperative of extending the benefits of "modern existence" to the world community. He stated that after two decades of "trial and error in the field of international development" the world needed an institution that "could act as an internationally recognized focal point" for research on international development (Pearson 1967, 6). In 1970, the act of Parliament that created the IDRC set a clear direction for the new organization. According to the IDRC Act, the organization was to "initiate, encourage, support and conduct research into the problems of the developing regions of the world and into the means for applying and adapting scientific, technical and other knowledge to the economic and social advancement of those regions." With its creation, the IDRC became the first institution in the world with "research for development" as its sole mandate. Lauded by many for giving the organization the independence, breadth, and depth of focus that are behind the IDRC's success, the act was a sign of the times and a logical outcome of the evolution of Canada's foreign assistance programming.

The IDRC's defining characteristic is to provide a framework within which southern researchers determine the projects critical to progress, as southern researchers define and perceive it. Furthermore, as its strategic plan notes, the IDRC (2005, 5-1) "manages to successfully pursue two seemingly contradictory objectives—'investing ahead of the curve' while remaining a 'listening organization.'" Partly as a result of striving to achieve these goals, the IDRC has garnered a remarkably positive reputation in those countries in which it has worked.[2] At the same time, the IDRC is little known in Canada, a point raised as a missed opportunity by IDRC (see MacLeod and Spiegel 2003, 11). The IDRC leverages relatively modest amounts of financial resources and yet it both has an impact on the ground and provides the Canadian government with evidence-based foreign policy advice. It is argued that the IDRC succeeds in making a little money go a long way in building a positive Canadian reputation abroad and in achieving Canadian foreign policy goals. Despite the difficulty of operating in the Middle East, the IDRC has created a perceptible but, more importantly, welcome Canadian presence in the region.

This chapter focuses on the IDRC's work in the Middle East and how its involvement has helped to build its reputation abroad and at home and to bring credit to Canada in the process. The IDRC provides assistance in several ways: by funding researchers from developing countries to solve and address problems they identify as crucial to their communities, by funding projects that result from direct exchanges between the IDRC and developing country institutions, and by providing expert advice to those researchers, as well as helping to build local capacity in developing countries generally, to research and innovate (IDRC 2007). The IDRC supports bottom-up, indigenous development research programs and the Middle East has received funding since the Centre's inception (see Table 8-1).

The IDRC's establishment by the Canadian government, only two years after the creation of CIDA, acknowledged the need for a development assistance organization with a distinct mandate, objectives, and modus operandi to support research and research capacity. In dealing with the funding of science

TABLE 8-1

Estimated Spending on Middle East and North Africa Programmes by the
International Development Research Centre

Year	Amount
1990–94	17,178,319
1995–98	11,164,602
1999–02	13,010,576
2003–05	16,518,275
2006–07	11,687,275

Source: Data Provided by the IDRC.

and technology, and the "knowledge business," agility and flexibility are imperatives given the long-term and risky nature of research, and the international
(i.e., non-bilateral) character of knowledge where cross-cutting linkages play
such a vital role. The 1970 *IDRC Act* passed by Parliament sketched the path
forward; as a Crown corporation, the IDRC operates at arm's length from the
government under direction of a board of governors that is responsible for
guiding its overall direction and ensuring its effectiveness and accountability.
Variously described as an expression not an instrument of Canadian foreign policy or as a member of the Canadian foreign policy family, the IDRC has a complex relation to the government: its budget comes mostly from the same international assistance envelope that funds all other official aid (such as CIDA and
international financial institutions), and its governors are named by the government (often proposed by the board), and it reports to Parliament through the
minister of foreign affairs. In particular cases, as one illustrated below on the
issue of Palestinian refugees, the IDRC has worked more closely than usual
with government ministries on a specific foreign policy question. More often,
its relative autonomy in support of research for development is taken itself as
a reflection of the open, non-directive way in which Canada wishes to deal with
developing countries.

The IDRC's distance from the Canadian government allows it to fund research
that the government does not have an immediate interest in or to fund research
in countries and at times when Canada, for political reasons, prefers to maintain its distance. For example, throughout the 1970s the IDRC worked with
dissidents opposed to their military dictatorships in the southern cone of South
America, while Ottawa maintained diplomatic relations with the same military
regimes. Similarly, the IDRC remained active in South Africa during the fight
against apartheid in the early 1990s, despite Canada's official policy banning
most contact with the country. In the Middle East the IDRC has also supported
individuals who have been marginalized, or worse, by the authorities in their
country. A good example is Egyptian academic Saad Eddin Ibrahim who was
jailed, in part, because he accepted "unauthorized funding" for his research.
The funding in question was not from the IDRC, but the IDRC did continue to
support Ibrahim even after it became clear that the Egyptian government did
not approve of his research. Unlike in South Africa and South America where
fundamental changes in government provided new opportunities, in the Middle East individuals such as Ibrahim await a similar political opening. And,
when it happens, IDRC-supported researchers will be ready to take on the challenges that will arise. Keeping the IDRC at arm's length from international and
domestic political currents benefits both the IDRC and the Canadian government.

Particularly since the 1990s, the IDRC has had "a renewed commitment by
senior management to ensuring that the IDRC-supported research had some
influence on public policies, and the corresponding development of new mech-

anisms to foster such linkages. Yet many of the challenges entailed in fostering research for policy change, anticipated and intensely debated in earlier
times, still endure" (Gonsalves and Baranyi 2003, 1). The IDRC has maintained
that it supports southern researchers in order to make an impact in their respective societies, but that this support must be "at the initiative of decision-makers and others in those countries" (4). Working toward bottom-up inspired
social change has been a recurrent theme in IDRC involvement in the Middle
East.

The International Development Research Centre in the Middle East

The IDRC first established a presence in the Middle East in 1974, locating its
regional office in Beirut on the outskirts of a Palestinian refugee camp.[3] Establishing itself near a poor refugee camp as opposed to the comfortable and
westernized surroundings of Beirut's core gave the IDRC a certain credibility
that helped its initial work (Pfeiffer 2006). As the Lebanese civil war began that
same year, however, the IDRC office was obliged to move away from the camp,
relocating to the comparatively calm surroundings of Cairo. The IDRC's exit
from Lebanon was dramatic: the last employee rode to Beirut's airport on the
floor of a taxi as gunfire raged overhead (Pfeiffer 2006). This anecdote reflects
some of the challenges facing the IDRC, which operates during unsettled times
and in less hospitable parts around the world, the very regions that need the
IDRC's attention.

The IDRC concentrates its very limited resources of approximately $150
million annually on funding applied research "that both generate[s] knowledge
and influence[s] policy."[4] The IDRC also emphasizes themes and networks
and, unlike CIDA, does not provide country programming and funding. The
IDRC uses networks of local researchers as an effective way to respond to the
research needs of the Middle East. Over time, this development approach has
been reflected in areas such as governance, demilitarization, and the political
economy of peacebuilding throughout the region. As Eglal Rached, the IDRC's
Cairo regional director, has noted, the IDRC's development approach follows
best practices in development research:

> Development research witnessed in the past decades an important shift…
> from the traditional, positivist, scientific paradigm, which arose to bring
> certainty and verifiability to natural science research questions, to post-pos-
> itivism which recognizes and tries to address the complex human and social
> problems often embedded in natural resource degradation issues. Participa-
> tory action research situates itself firmly in the latter. One of the main dif-
> ferences between the two research paradigms is that, while the first tends to
> be linear, starting with a hypothesis and proceeding to a conclusion, partic-

ipatory action research proceeds through repeated cycles in which the researchers and the community start with the identification of major issues, concerns and problems, initiate research, originate action, learn about this action and proceed to a new research and action cycle. The process is continuous. (Rached 2006, ix)

Again, the IDRC has emphasized bottom-up, participatory research at times when top-down, foreign-imposed modernization ideas were fashionable.

To respond to bottom-up research needs, the IDRC has, at times, used a less official and more flexible approach toward funding research. A rigid adherence to rules and procedures could have prevented assistance to beneficial projects. To illustrate, in the late 1990s, joint Israeli-Palestinian research was conducted on a shared aquifer. The IDRC funded the Palestinian component while the program officer involved, David Brooks, convinced the Andrea and Charles Bronfman Philanthropies, the semi-independent Israeli arm of the Montreal-based Andrea and Charles Bronfman Foundation, to fund the Israeli component. This worked well technically, but its greater significance was political: a joint Israeli-Palestinian exercise resulted in valuable work being done on a critical and highly political commodity.

The IDRC's Middle East Special Initiatives comprise three Middle East–focused, externally funded programs: the Expert and Advisory Services Fund (EASF), the Scholarship Fund for Palestinian Refugee Women in Lebanon, and the Middle East Good Governance Fund. These are discussed in turn.

The Expert and Advisory Services Fund

The EASF is one of the few areas in which the IDRC actively and explicitly supports the pursuit of Canadian foreign policy objectives. In 1992, the EASF was established with funding from CIDA after the IDRC was approached to manage a mechanism that could support Canada's role in the Middle East peace process: Canada's position as gavel holder of the Refugee Working Group (RWG). The EASF, thus, has focused on researching solutions to the Palestinian refugee question, which dates from 1948 (for a history of the issues, see Chapter 5). It supports a negotiation process based on evidence provided by research into specific problems and this, in turn, supports Canadian foreign policy on the Palestinian refugee issue. The EASF has been an early example of a cross-government programming initiative, involving two government departments and a Crown corporation: the Department of Foreign Affairs and International Trade (DFAIT), CIDA, and the IDRC. The IDRC's initial task was to engage experts to investigate issues raised, for both the EASF and for any other of the four working groups on water, the environment, regional economic development, and arms control and regional security.[5]

CIDA funded the EASF, despite problems reconciling its role in official development assistance (ODA) with support to research backing up a foreign policy initiative led by DFAIT. Some observers have viewed this reluctance as an instance of the inflexible nature of CIDA, regarded as being a general weakness. As one DFAIT official familiar with the EASF noted, "[CIDA was] very good at knowing what it did not do, but not so good at knowing [what it did]."[6] Despite difficulties in working with different organizational mandates and achieving a shared perspective and approach, the CIDA-IDRC-DFAIT relationship delivered valuable support to a key foreign policy issue. The IDRC invested heavily in the EASF and in the region more generally. The IDRC participated as a mediator between researchers in the EASF and played "a crucial role," according to an interviewed official.

The EASF became an important instrument for contributing research, dialogue, and networking on the Palestinian refugee issue. When the peace negotiations between Israelis and Palestinians hit an impasse in 1997, the Canadian government—through the IDRC—acted once again. Through the IDRC, DFAIT initiated "Track II Diplomacy," helping to foster on-the-ground, people-to-people exchanges. Specifically, the IDRC supported activities aimed at facilitating Israeli-Palestinian dialogue, knowledge generation, and analysis of key aspects of the refugee problem. It also supported research focused on the questions of repatriation and absorption of refugees into a future Palestinian state, compensation to Palestinian refugees as part of a comprehensive solution, and gauging and engaging stakeholders' opinions on the refugee issue.

These issues were selected based on the gaps identified during official bilateral negotiations in the Middle East peace process. The IDRC had organized two major stocktaking conferences, in 1997 and 2003, on the Palestinian refugee question. The findings of the conferences were further used to help support the Palestinian Authority's Refugee Coordination Group, a 2001 coordinating body created by Palestinian prime minister Mahmoud Abbas. The group comprised four primary Palestinian components working on the refugee file: the Ministry of Planning, the Ministry of Foreign Affairs, the Department of Refugee Affairs, and the Negotiation Affairs Department. The objective was to contribute to a more effective Palestinian negotiation position in final status talks with Israel and to assist the Palestinian Authority in effectively undertaking and planning implementation of solutions to the Palestinian refugee issue. A secretariat was created to manage existing knowledge on refugee issues, facilitate coordination among key stakeholders, liaise with donors, and facilitate future studies. The project was completed in 2005 and not renewed after the 2006 Hamas electoral victory. It had allowed the partners to provide better coordination, but also illustrated the difficulty of collaboration on the refugee issue in the absence of a viable peace process. More recently, the IDRC has also focused on the issues of Palestinian refugees in Lebanon as well.

The contribution of the EASF and the IDRC to the refugee file has been substantial, both through formal project support and through the networks, informal dialogues, and quiet linkages that IDRC work has fostered. The IDRC's support to the work of a core group of Palestinian and Israeli officials during the Oslo process led to the production of ideas that influenced the positions of both parties in final status negotiations in 2000–01. IDRC-supported work on refugee compensation not only shaped past negotiations, but has also continued to create an array of research that would likely inform any future negotiations on the topic. Over the years, the IDRC's support of research on refugee compensation and on refugee absorption has also helped break many taboos on these sensitive issues. The essence of the EASF's work and findings is that it has a "long shelf-life." Canada's minister of foreign affairs has recently confirmed the priority accorded to the Palestinian refugee issue. At a recent meeting of the Refugee Coordination Forum, a new donor group led by Canada, this continued commitment was highlighted. In light of the stalemate in the peace process, the volatility of the region, and the shifting political dynamics, the IDRC's consistent, methodical focus on core policy issues is important to any negotiated solution in the future.

The Scholarship Fund for Palestinian Refugee Women

In the late 1990s, a number of international donors, notably Canada, Qatar, the United States, Spain, France, and the Organization of the Petroleum Exporting Countries (OPEC), requested that the IDRC manage the Scholarship Fund for Palestinian Refugee Women, which supports undergraduate university studies by Palestinian women from refugee camps in Lebanon. This project responds to a Canadian-led international mission's finding and report that young people, particularly women in Palestinian refugee camps in Lebanon, had little access to post-secondary education. Given the severe poverty faced by many Palestinian refugees in Lebanon, Palestinian high school graduates found it too expensive to continue their studies; women were at a particular disadvantage. The project supported refugee women registered with the United Nations Relief and Works Agency for Palestine Refugees in the Near East (UNRWA) or the Lebanese Directorate of Refugee Affairs, with particular focus on those whose economic circumstances would preclude them from continuing their studies. As comptroller and manager of the fund, the IDRC was given a new and unfamiliar role. International donors, however, appreciated the past efforts of the IDRC and wanted its direct involvement (Salameh and Al-Shonar 2007). Elements of the project have been emulated in programs funded by international donors, such as the European Commission and Japan (El Rifai 2007).

IDRC's management of the scholarship fund was facilitated by its selection of UNRWA as the local administrator. To ensure local participation, the Palestinian community was also closely involved in its administration, including an advisory committee of four Palestinian education experts and three UNRWA staff. With the help of the local administrator and committee members, the IDRC facilitated major decisions concerning the administration of the fund, including the setting of selection criteria and the annual selection of scholarship recipients.

The Middle East Good Governance Fund

The Middle East Good Governance Fund (MEGGF) is a four-year IDRC initiative established in 2004. It investigates the important question of what role, if any, Islamic parties and civil society can play in national development, democratization, and the realization of social and economic development (for a debate on some of the issues, see Chapter 6). The MEGGF is a regional fund established at the IDRC with funding from CIDA's Iraq Task Force and in cooperation with DFAIT.[7]

The MEGGF's working definition of good governance is the promotion of free and democratic space that allows civil society organizations and political movements to take part in decision-making processes, and that allows the media to hold an independent position in disseminating information and fostering public discussions. The MEGGF focuses on three themes: the impact of the integration of Islamist political parties in political systems on governance processes, the role and impact of Islamic social movements on governance processes, and the political role of local and predominantly conservative tribes. As with most IDRC-funded research, the MEGGF is driven by local needs and seeks to feed into a subject matter of great concern to local researchers, policy makers, and the international community at large.

The emergence of Islamist political parties is an important political development in the region. Islamist parties have won democratic elections and formed government in the West Bank and Gaza (Hamas) and in neighbouring Turkey (the Justice and Development Party). Islamists are also members of the government in Iraq, members of the parliamentary opposition in Morocco (the Justice and Development Party [AKP]), and unofficial members of the congress in Egypt (the Muslim Brotherhood) and Yemen (Yemeni Alliance for Reform—the Islah Party). The rise of Islamist forces in the Middle East is also forcing secular movements to reassess their approach to social, political, and economic development and to devise strategies to deal with them. To this end, the MEGGF supports research that assesses where Islamic movements, through their political and social structures, stand on key issues such as the rule of law, gender equality, and democratic governance, and how, if at all, their integration into the political process has affected their agendas on these matters. Simply put, will Islamist political parties that ascend to power through democratic processes respect liberal values? The IDRC is helping to fund innovative, bottom-up research that addresses this key question.

The EASF, the scholarship fund, and the MEGGF have a number of common features: they owe their existence directly to Canadian foreign policy initiatives (the EASF and the scholarship fund) and suggestions from the government (the MEGGF); they are directed by mechanisms that include representatives from CIDA, DFAIT, and the IDRC that play a major role in setting general directions and in approving individual projects; and they are funded predominantly from outside the IDRC, with CIDA as the main source of support. What can be learned about the IDRC from these programs? First, the IDRC manages all three as special initiatives to differentiate them from programs funded from its core budget and, second, all three appear to have benefited, in varying degrees, from the IDRC's comparative advantages of being at arm's length from the government and, in particular, from DFAIT.

West Bank researchers, interviewed by the authors, appreciated the IDRC's arm's-length relationship from the Canadian government. For example, Mudar Kassis (2007), the former head of the Institute of Law at Birzeit University, spoke highly of the IDRC's role in the region. The IDRC is perceived among many Birzeit researchers as one of the more progressive western organizations that exhibit a significant degree of understanding of the needs of researchers. Kassis did, however, note that Ottawa has recently insisted that any IDRC aid recipients in the Middle East sign a disclaimer that they have not had links with terrorist organizations such as Hamas. With Hamas being a prominent presence in Palestinian society and government, it has been very difficult to respect this "no-link policy" in practice. The IDRC's arm's-length relationship to the Canadian government, it was believed, would be useful when locals perceived Canadian policy in the region to be less favourable. For example, Kassis suggests that local Palestinian perceptions of Canada have changed recently. Whereas Canada had been perceived as more neutral in the region, it is now perceived as tilting closer to Israel and the United States. Canada's recent voting pattern at the United Nations, for example, was cited as evidence of a change in policy. The head of the Applied Research Institute of Jerusalem (ARIJ), Jad Isaac, is also an IDRC recipient who expressed concern with changes to Canadian policy with regard to the Israeli-Palestinian conflict. Isaac claims that the IDRC can take significant credit for ARIJ's international and positive reputation. Like Kassis, Isaac also appreciates the IDRC's distance from the Canadian government. The IDRC should, he believes, remain as an international development research centre and not become an extension of Canadian foreign policy. For Isaac the world "would have been a worse place" without the IDRC functioning as it has (Isaac 2007). While these personal interviews by no means constitute a comprehensive survey of IDRC grant recipients in the region, they are evidence of the benefits from having the IDRC operate at arm's length at times when Canadian foreign policy in the region is not regarded favourably.

The International Development Research Centre's Innovation at Work in the Middle East

While the IDRC supports research efforts to improve sociopolitical conditions, it is also active on research topics that range from water studies in Egypt and Yemen to gender relations in Syria and Algeria. This section turns to these important issues, which further exemplify the IDRC's support for local researchers' innovative ways to solving problems.

ARIJ focuses its research in the areas of Palestinian society, economy, natural resources management, water, and governance. The IDRC was one of the first international donors to support its research agenda. The ARIJ recognized that Palestinians needed a database to record water levels, environmental findings, and other concerns. With IDRC funding, ARIJ developed data baselines using technology, such as Geographic Information Systems, in which Canadians had expertise. ARIJ further examined the pace of Palestinian urbanization in the West Bank and Gaza, the Israeli confiscation of land in the West Bank and Gaza, the layout of Israeli settler road systems, the Israeli construction of a separation barrier in the West Bank, and a myriad of other issues. Digitizing ARIJ's findings and placing them on its website has been a successful way to disseminate its research. In 1996, there were approximately 200,000 visits to its website; in 2006, there were more than 6 million. ARIJ's successes have been due in part to IDRC funding.

The IDRC has also helped fund Egyptian projects examining ways to manage water resources that support reclaimed land in its deserts. Farafra is an oasis in the Sahara about 650 kilometres northwest of Cairo. Its source of water is the large Nubian Sandstone Aquifer, which stretches under Chad, Libya, eastern Egypt and the Sudan. At present, Egypt has about 8 million acres of cultivated land, with approximately 20 percent of that being reclaimed desert. Egyptian farmers use six million cubic metres of water per year from the aquifer; but, the Egyptian government needs to increase this to about 2 billion cubic metres to support future development plans (Tutweiler 2007). However, there are a number of concerns if the desert becomes waterlogged and the affect this would have on the aquifer's water levels. Moreover, tapping into water that underlies five countries can affect international relations, and any race to use the water can heighten political tensions. The IDRC has funded the Community-Based Integrated Water Management in Farafra Oasis to address some of these concerns, using a regional network of researchers.

Richard Tutweiler (2007), the executive director of the Desert Development Center located at the American University in Cairo, which is the lead agency in the project, has noted that the IDRC brings new ideas and ways of looking at problems. For more than 20 years, the IDRC has supported research on water rights and climate change well before it became fashionable in popular discourse. The IDRC example has also helped encourage other international agencies to devote resources to this area. Moreover, the IDRC's activities gave the program added credibility; as Tutweiler points out, without IDRC involvement and the professional concept notes and proposals, it could have been difficult to raise the interest of other donors.

At Cairo University's Toxicology Centre, the IDRC funds helped train medical students in Egypt and the wider Arab world to treat illness stemming from exposure to pesticides. The Toxicology Centre was first realized after an IDRC grant supported its founder, Mahmoud Amr, to study the medical effects of pesticide use and to bring regional and international attention to the ill effects of improper pesticide use to the hinterland. Prior to establishing the centre, Amr had not written a research proposal, despite having published 45 papers in academic journals on the results of his research. Amr's proposal to the IDRC received a modest amount of $250,000 over four years beginning in 1989. The IDRC funding made the Toxicology Centre possible; without the initial seed money it would not have gotten started (Amr 2007). Today the centre has 2,000 trained graduates and another 135 medical students undergoing training in laboratories. It has treated more than 10,000 Egyptian victims of poisoning (about one third of whom having been exposed to pesticides). It is the only toxicology laboratory in the Middle East and North Africa. The Egyptian minister of higher education was in the first cohort of students who graduated from the program in 1990, and there are 15 professors from that cohort at faculties of medicine throughout the Arab world.

In the early 1990s the IDRC encouraged a number of women in the women's studies department at Birzeit University in the occupied territories to write an ambitious research proposal focusing on women in Palestinian society, with the help of Rita Giacaman (2007), a Palestinian researcher in the West Bank who has a long history with the IDRC. The IDRC funded the project, which included a gender review of feminist literature from which the group produced a number of working papers on various issues. After helping the researchers contact feminist scholars in the West, the group received a grant from the United Nations Development Programme (UNDP). The research continued with the establishment of a gender unit in the Palestinian Bureau of Statistics. In the days following the 1993 Oslo Accords, Birzeit's women's studies department "had high hopes" that it would make a substantial contribution to Palestinian society (Kuttab, Jad, and Lightstone 2007). However, the advance of knowledge depended on the level and intensity of the always-latent regional conflict, and as the conflict escalated, the focus on gender issues declined proportionately. The research group turned its attention to modes of Palestinian survival and changing family dynamics; this was also partly funded by the IDRC. The research group complained, however, that many Palestinians perceive that women's issues are secondary to securing economic and political justice. The research group is now struggling to prevent the marginalization of women from public discourse by striving to keep the West Bank and Gaza a progressive society for girls and young women (Kuttab, Jad, and Lightstone 2007).

Women's issues have also been a focus in other parts of the Middle East, centring on protecting biodiversity, defending land tenancy rights, training women agriculturalists, and promoting positive gender relationships. If, for example, women had secure access to land, how would it contribute to biodiversity? The IDRC has funded research in this area and worked with investigators to help them develop a proposal. Based on preliminary work in Egyptian and Tunisian villages, investigators found that unless underprivileged women inherited land, they tended to have limited access. With the help of international donors a "new land village" was developed on reclaimed land and at least 20 percent of this land reserved for women. The project was further developed to examine the effects of using commercial hybrid seeds in lieu of local varieties on biodiversity. The findings of the study suggested that gender indeed had an effect on seed selection; the women in the study were more interested in seed collection and storage than men.

Cairo's Gender and Economic Research and Policy Analysis (GERPA), funded by the IDRC, also promotes policy-relevant research work on women in the Middle East. GERPA has researched the connection between women and the size of economic firms in four Middle Eastern countries. Then executive director Heba Handoussa (2007) said that the IDRC "held their hand" by hosting research application seminars and generally providing encouragement. Seven donors, including the Ford Foundation, the Arab Fund for Economic and Social Development, the UNDP, and the European Union, eventually contributed funds to the GERBA project, but the IDRC was the largest contributor. Handoussa noted that IDRC funding was an important signal to other donors that the project was sound because of the IDRC's international reputation for excellence.

Similarly, the IDRC has funded a project that examines the role of small and medium-sized enterprises in the Egyptian economy. The Small and Medium Enterprises Policy Development project (SMEPOL) was undertaken in collaboration and with funding from CIDA and the Egypt's Ministry of Finance. The objective of SMEPOL was to improve the policy environment for small, usually individually or family-owned enterprises (Court and Osborne 2006, 1). The socioeconomic benefit of engaging small and medium-sized firms in developing economies is an underappreciated policy area, but has an enormous effect on many poor people's lives (see Environmental Quality International 2005, 1). According to the International Finance Corporation, there were 2.5 million such firms (of which 2.4 million were microenterprises with one to four employees) and they accounted for approximately 90 percent of the non-agricultural private sector, 75 percent of the total labour force in the private sector, and 75 percent of the value added in Egypt. Egypt's Prime Minister Ahmed Nazif (2005) has noted that the SMEPOL helped shift national policy directions to "address ways and means of developing the capacities of SMES."

The IDRC has also supported Egypt's Population Council to examine the socioeconomic condition facing men aged 15 to 29 who are frequently identified as "angry young men" (Assad 2007). Due to socioeconomic hardships in the Middle East, a large group of men is only partly successful at making the transition from school to the labour force. The labour market is restricted and they fail to find jobs, consequently defer marriage, and continue to live with their parents. The "youth" of these men is extended, so their participation as full citizens is postponed. It is argued that this delay is impeding men from taking up the responsibilities of citizenship and that this can have profound social and political effects. The IDRC has contributed substantially to providing the Population Council with the tools with which to measure the extent of this socioeconomic problem. An important 2006 Egyptian labour force survey relied on the IDRC-funded work. As the survey revealed, between 1998 and 2006, the Egyptian labour force had nearly doubled. The Population Council has been instrumental to further studies carried out by the Egyptian national council for women, the national council for childhood and motherhood, and the national council for youth; their impact on social studies in Egypt is a clear indication of the IDRC's impact.

Conclusion

IDRC program officers have identified numerous fields of research (or researchers) that show great promise and have worked with them to build their capacity. It is in this way that the IDRC (2005, 5-1) listens "to visionary researchers and practitioners in developing countries," and assists in funding their proposed work. Frequently, the IDRC's funding is leveraged by researchers to bring in other, and often larger, donors. The research findings might then go on to achieve international significance, but the IDRC can be lost in the background. Some might say the IDRC has frequently been the victim of its own success and policies; it is often not present for the photo op when ministers and researchers share the stage. Its critical role in taking risks to support an unknown scientist in the early days of the research agenda, however, is not forgotten by the researchers who were helped.

Ottawa should continue to invest and expand in research undertaken by people in the developing world, because they have a more intimate and nuanced understanding of the challenges they face. Given the IDRC's positive role in the Middle East, Canadian foreign policy should take more advantage of the IDRC's regional presence and develop models of cooperation that build on its success. The IDRC has been active and on the front line in the Middle East for decades, funding hundreds of research projects, largely unknown to Canadians. Similarly, many Canadians would not know that the IDRC has acted as a facilitator of research efforts that affect the lives of people in the region, such as the effects of environmental degradation or water scarcity. Many Canadians would also not know that Canada has a remarkable reputation in many parts of the region because of IDRC activities. Nor would many know that it has funded dynamic work that has had a direct impact on policy in those countries. Often, the capacity building that the IDRC has funded in the Middle East has been cutting edge and innovative, and the IDRC remains active in terms of determining future trends in the developing world, and funding research programs that anticipate the problems of tomorrow.

IDRC-supported research has proved to be of significant importance to states and their policy processes in areas such as agriculture, small-scale private enterprise, gender, and other social issues. According to those interviewed for this chapter, the IDRC is perceived by many researchers in the region to function at arm's length from the main lines of Canadian foreign policy while still operating within parameters laid down by Ottawa. Despite the fact that the IDRC's budget is modest it has contributed substantially to many southern societies, including in the Middle East.

Notes

1 The authors gratefully acknowledge helpful comments from Tim Dottridge and Roula El-Rifai.

2 For example, the IDRC has funded people who have later become presidents and prime ministers. Nelson Mandela was very well aware of IDRC activity in South Africa in the years before 1993, and sent an angry letter to Prime Minister Jean Chrétien when the IDRC's South African office was closed for budgetary reasons in 2002. When it arrived, a program officer suggested that "Nelson Mandela knew the IDRC intimately while Chrétien did not even know [it] existed" (Pfeiffer 2006). While that statement was not true, it does convey and underlying sentiment often expressed by IDRC personnel. As well, Ricardo Lagos, a former president of Chile, had been a recipient of IDRC funding during the 1980s as was Brazil's Fernando Henrique Cardoso in the 1970s.

3 The IDRC maintains a series of six regional offices to complement head office in Ottawa. These are in Cairo, Dakar, Montevideo, Nairobi, New Delhi, and Singapore. The Beirut office was moved to Cairo in the mid 1970s.

4 David Brooks, "Summary Trip Report," IDRC Archives, April 24, 2000. As the Corporate Strategy and Program Framework document points out, the IDRC (2005, 5–2) "will continue to place a value on linking research to policy formulation *and implementation*. The Centre's consultations, particularly in the regions, highlighted the need to focus more carefully on policy *implementation* rather than just policy *formulation*. This was brought out consistently through discussions on why exist-

ing policies, rules, and regulations are not enforced, how corruption undermines their intent, and why technocratic approaches to solving a problem will not work without a sound understanding of the institutional context in which they are applied. As the Centre's extensive study on the influence of IDRC-supported research on public policy showed, the links between research and policy are complex, nuanced, and seldom linear."

5 In this regard, the IDRC's reputation was such that if, for example, the Japanese, who chaired the water resources group, needed an expert to address certain questions, they would ask it to find that person for them. Clearly, all countries involved in the Middle East peace process knew the IDRC to be an extremely well-connected impartial arbiter in the region (anonymous interview).

6 Anonymous interview.

7 In 2004, as a follow-up, IDRC was approached by the Iraq Task Force for possible collaboration on research on democratic development in the Middle East to be funded from "regional mitigation funds" within the overall support for Iraq. CIDA expressed an interest in copying the governance structure of the EASF, which is managed by IDRC with direct involvement of CIDA and DFAIT. This research has evolved into a program focusing on Islamist political parties and civil society, and their effects on governance and democratic development.

References

Amr, Mahmoud. 2007. Interview by authors. February 19, Cairo. Written notes.

Assad, Raqui. 2007. Interview by authors. March 1, Cairo. Written notes.

Court, Julius and David Osborne. 2006. "Independent Evaluation of the SMEPOL Project: Impact, Lessons, and Options for Replication." Overseas Development Institute. www.odi.org.uk/RAPID/Projects/RAP0018/docs/SMEPOL_Report_Final.pdf (August 2007).

El Rifai, Roula. 2007. Interview by authors. June 27. Written notes.

Environmental Quality International. 2005. "Profile of M/SMES in Egypt: Update Report." Egypt: Environmental Quality International.

Giacaman, Rita. 2007. Interview by authors, February 24, Ramallah. Written notes.

Gonsalves, Tahira, and Stephen Baranyi. 2003. "Research for Policy Influence: A History of IDRC Intent." Ottawa: International Development Research Centre. idrinfo.idrc.ca/archive/corpdocs/119955/History_of_Intent.pdf (August 2007).

Handoussa, Heba. 2007. Interview by authors. February 28, Cairo. Written notes.

International Development Research Council. 2005. Corporate Strategy and Program Framework, 2005–2010. Ottawa. www.idrc.ca/uploads/user-S/11250758901CSPF_2005_e.pdf (August 2007).

———. 2007. "About IDRC." www.idrc.ca/en/ev-8513-201-1-DO_TOPIC.html (August 2007).

International Finance Corporation. 2004. "The SME Landscape in Egypt." Washington, DC: World Bank Group (April).

Isaac, Jad. 2007. Interview by authors. February 26, Bethlehem. Written notes.

Kassis, Mudar. 2007. Interview by authors. February 26, Ramallah. Written notes.

Kuttab, Eileen, Islah Jad, and Penny Lightstone. 2007. Interview by authors. February 24, Ramallah. Written notes.

MacLeod, Stuart, and Jerry Spiegel. 2003. "Research for Human Development Evolution in the Canadian Research Sector." Ottawa: International Development Research Centre. www.idrc.ca/en/ev-44358-201-1-DO_TOPIC .html (August 2007).

Nazif, Ahmed. 2005. "Enhancing Competitiveness for SMEs in Egypt." Cairo: Ministry of Finance. www.sme.gov.eg/English/main_english.htm (August 2007).

Pearson, Lester. 1976. "Notes for the Prime Minister's Remarks to the Canadian Political Science Association Banquet." Carleton University, Ottawa, June 8. idrinfo.idrc.ca/archive/corpdocs/010474/Pears05.pdf (August 2007).

Pfeiffer, Jim. 2006. Interview by authors, April 16. Written notes.

Rached, Eglal. 2006. "Foreword." In *Research for Development in the Dry Arab Region: The Cactus Flower*, ed. Shadi Hamadeh, Mona Haidar, and Rami Zurayk, ix–xi. Ottawa: International Development Research Centre.

Salameh, Saji, and Osama Al-Shonar. 2007. Interview by authors. February 25. Written notes.

Tutweiler, Richard. 2007. Interview by authors. March 1, Cairo. Written notes.

Canada's Economic Interests
in the Middle East[1]

Canada–Middle East economic relations have clearly not been a top priority for Canada and are never going to be under any reasonable scenario. Still, Canadian business activity in the Middle East has produced very worthwhile benefits to Canada's economy and to our trading partners. This chapter argues that there are significant potential benefits still to be had in promoting stronger Canada–Middle East relations, particularly with respect to the countries of the rapidly growing Gulf Cooperation Council (GCC). To enjoy these benefits, however, there is a need for enhanced political engagement in the region, as well as a commitment on the part of the Canadian government to forge stronger economic ties, formal and informal, with selected Middle Eastern countries. Canada has developed a number of formal links with the Middle East, most notably a free trade agreement with Israel, and a number of bilateral tax agreements, but there is room to secure further formal links to the region and to foster trade more generally. These formal and informal relationships, accompanied by enhanced strategic governmental contacts and more savvy efforts by Canadian businesses, would likely be rewarded by substantially higher levels of business activity, particularly with the Gulf States.[2]

Canada–Middle East Trading Patterns: Room for Improvement

With the Middle East representing approximately only 1 percent of Canada's imports and exports, should Canadian officials be investing time and strategic efforts to furthering economic ties with the region? Indeed they should, as the Middle East carries the potential of being a significant economic partner.

While the Middle East might appear to be marginally important to Canada's economy, especially compared to the United States, closer examination reveals that Canada's overall trade with the region is perhaps of greater importance than initial assumptions suggest. For example, Canada's exports to the GCC are comparable to Canada's exports to India and greater than exports to Brazil or Russia. Specifically, the GCC ranks as equivalent to Canada's 15th export destination; in comparison, India ranks 14th, Brazil ranks 17th, and Russia ranks 20th (see Table 9-1). Canada's business community and trade bureaucrats would be remiss to suggest that Brazil, Russia, or India were insignificant trading partners. Moreover, trade with the Middle East is growing at a steady, healthy rate. Accordingly, the Middle East, and the GCC specifically, have been overlooked by Canada's trade officials.

Over the past 15 years, the Middle East has attracted minimal Canadian export and import trade and investment. Canadian export of goods to the region, totalling approximately $3.1 billion, account for only 0.71 percent of Canada's total exports (see Table 9-2). Canadian imports from the region, although double the size of exports ($4.8 billion in 2006) are also minor. Imports from the Middle East surpassed 1 percent of total Canadian imports in 2005 and now represent 1.21 percent of total imports (see Table 9-3).[3] The GCC—a customs union of six Persian Gulf oil-producing states in the process of creating a common currency—has been a particularly important trading partner. While two-way trade between the GCC and Canada declined significantly in the 1980s and '90s, it has recently skyrocketed (see Figure 9-1). Saudi Arabia, Iraq, and Israel have consistently been the most important import partners in the region. Main import products from these countries are oil and

Table 9-1
Canada's Top Export Partners in 2006

	Exports in 2006 (CA$ millions)	Rank in 2006	Share of Total Exports
United States	359,258	1	81.6%
United Kingdom	10,133	2	2.3%
Japan	9,416	3	2.1%
China	7,661	4	1.7%
Mexico	4,385	5	1.0%
India	1,677	14	0.4%
Gulf Cooperation Council	1,613	15	0.4%
Brazil	1,338	17	0.3%
Russia	870	20	0.2%
Total Canadian Exports	439,500		

Note: Gulf Cooperation Council = Bahrain, Kuwait, Oman, Qatar, Saudi Arabia, and the United Arab Emirates.
Source: Adapted from Department of Foreign Affairs and International Trade 2007a.

Table 9–2

Canada's Exports to the Middle East, Selected Years, CA$ millions

	1995	1997	1999	2001	2003	2005	2006	Average Rank over 10 Years
Bahrain	17.6	10.8	12.6	13.6	17.2	28.1	31.1	14
Egypt	153.4	185.7	188.2	221.5	232.0	314.3	411.8	5
Iran	430.5	728.2	540.4	496.7	235.1	274.3	309.0	2
Iraq	0.2	1.2	33.1	6.7	5.4	75.9	144.1	10
Israel	237.4	252.1	298.2	351.3	246.3	431.2	445.7	4
Jordan	12.5	14.7	19.6	33.6	30.8	122.5	56.3	9
Kuwait	64.8	55.4	38.3	62.3	82.3	118.1	90.2	6
Lebanon	57.1	62.8	46.0	32.3	31.1	49.8	60.2	7
Oman	24.3	14.8	11.6	19.3	49.2	22.7	55.9	12
Qatar	11.5	16.3	11.2	26.0	36.7	85.7	104.9	8
Saudi Arabia	521.1	557.7	296.9	339.7	469.0	439.2	543.6	1
Syria	21.7	24.3	21.2	16.6	20.6	66.8	48.3	11
United Arab Emirates	200.9	260.4	181.1	208.8	343.0	587.7	787.3	3
Yemen	19.0	10.1	24.4	36.0	34.0	46.7	27.6	13
Subtotal	1,772.1	2,194.5	1,722.8	1,864.3	1,832.7	2,663.1	3,115.9	
Total Canadian Exports	262,266.6	298,072.0	355,420.3	404,085.0	381,071.4	436,225.9	439,500.4	
Share of Total Canadian Exports	0.68%	0.74%	0.48%	0.46%	0.48%	0.61%	0.71%	

Source: Based on information obtained from the Department of Foreign Affairs and International Trade.

Table 9–3
Canada's Imports from the Middle East, Selected Years, CA$ millions

	1995	1997	1999	2001	2003	2005	2006	Average Rank over 10 Years
Bahrain	1.47	2.39	5.10	11.82	11.24	7.61	101.95	10
Egypt	18.84	29.02	40.07	42.08	116.20	142.04	140.15	5
Iran	121.74	506.01	111.54	44.60	63.24	44.47	44.50	4
Iraq	0.07	132.51	163.62	874.06	1,126.30	1,206.43	1,667.88	2
Israel	240.84	314.77	442.69	622.27	620.17	811.26	872.63	3
Jordan	1.16	0.89	0.99	3.92	5.78	8.75	14.58	12
Kuwait	0.04	1.97	3.10	18.86	51.33	60.41	63.78	8
Lebanon	4.28	5.67	15.33	8.21	9.76	10.85	11.70	11
Oman	1.00	0.84	1.59	2.70	7.00	4.66	6.13	14
Qatar	0.51	37.84	6.11	14.33	7.67	46.14	52.17	9
Saudi Arabia	501.83	647.78	429.46	800.44	919.28	1,701.35	1,706.15	1
Syria	27.31	1.37	2.44	61.49	96.93	21.77	25.29	7
United Arab Emirates	5.99	13.65	29.01	72.19	30.22	66.27	93.93	6
Yemen	0.06	28.92	0.26	0.13	0.20	0.19	0.23	13
Subtotal	925.1	1,723.6	1,251.3	2,577.1	3,065.3	4,132.2	4,801.1	
Total Canadian Imports	225,552.9	272,946.3	320,408.7	343,110.5	336,141.3	380,809.6	396,442.9	
Share of Total Canadian Imports	0.41%	0.63%	0.39%	0.75%	0.91%	1.09%	1.21%	

Source: Based on information obtained from the Department of Foreign Affairs and International Trade.

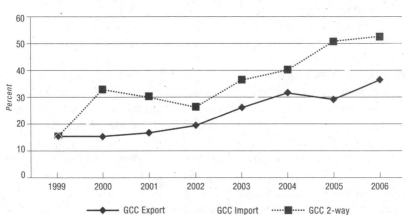

FIGURE 9–1

Gulf Cooperation Council's Share of Canada's Trade, 1999–2006

◆ GCC Export   ■ GCC Import   ▪▪▪■▪▪▪ GCC 2-way

Note: Gulf Cooperation Council (GCC) = Bahrain, Kuwait, Oman, Qatar, Saudi Arabia, and the United Arab Emirates.
Source: Based on data obtained from International Trade Canada.

oil products, electrical machinery, precious stones, and pharmaceuticals. On the export side, the United Arab Emirates (UAE), Saudi Arabia, Iran, and, recently, Israel are the main markets for Canadian products, especially vehicles, aircraft products, machinery, cereals, metals, and wood and paper.

While data on service trade are not readily available, some reports estimate it to be in the hundreds of millions of dollars (Veilleux 2004, 21). Unofficial estimates, according to a number of interviews with former officials of the Department of Foreign Affairs and International Trade (DFAIT), suggest that export of Canadian services to the region could be equivalent to that of exports of goods. Based on interviews with officials of Export Development Canada (EDC), EDC unofficially estimates that services could represent 40 percent of overall trade in exports.

In recent years, Canada's exports to the Middle East have been growing rapidly. In 2005 alone, there was a 25 percent increase in exports to the region. Yearly growth rates of Canadian trade with the Middle East were unstable prior to 2003; however, this rate of growth followed the general trend of Canadian exports overall over the past 15 years. Remarkably, Canadian exports to the GCC have risen by 192 percent since 1999 (see Figure 9–1); in comparison, Canadian exports to China have risen by 188 percent. EDC estimates that Canadian exports to the GCC, specifically, are expected to double by 2013. Similarly, Canadian imports from the Middle East have increased by more than 300 percent since 1990, mostly as a result of energy imports. Until 1999, Canada had enjoyed a consistent trade surplus with the Middle East, but subsequently

Canada's trade deficit with the region has increased more than threefold to $1.5 billion. Canada's growing trade deficit with the Middle East is mainly attributed to rising oil prices.

An examination of the impressive growth in imports and exports to the Middle East suggests that Canada should be interested in forging stronger ties to the region. Notwithstanding political instability in the Middle East, the revenues generated by oil and gas trade as well as the resulting accumulation of wealth and growing middle class, especially in the oil-rich economies of the GCC, open up a number of opportunities for exporters. Countries in the Middle East are among the fastest growing economies in the world. Over the past ten years, growth rates in the Middle East's gross domestic product (GDP) have grown an average of 4.2 percent per annum. Some GCC countries have shown outstanding GDP growth rates, comparable to China and exceeding India and other emerging market economies (see Table 9–4). Qatar's GDP, for example, has grown at 9.4 percent per annum over the past 10 years (Metz and Van Ark 2007, 10). The GCC's foreign reserves have also been accumulating significantly over a number of years (currently at US$1.6 trillion, compared to China's US$1.1 trillion), mainly due to increases in oil revenues. These petrodollars need to be recycled or spent and Canada can be considered a safe destination for Gulf investments. It is important to highlight that the Middle East, especially the GCC as the main economic force in the wider region, has demonstrated that it is indeed an important driver of the global economy. The Middle East's GDP growth rate is double that of the member countries of the Organisation for Economic Co-operation and Development (OECD) and significantly higher than the world average (5.4 percent, 2.5 percent, and 3.2 percent respectively in 2006) (World Bank 2006, 4).

Canada has a trading presence in the Middle East and most notably in the GCC. However, Canada could vastly improve its economic relationship with the region. A comparison of Canada's trade performance with the GCC to other industrialized countries illustrates this point. Canada's exports to the GCC average only 11 percent of those of other OECD members. In other words, for every dollar exported to the GCC by France, Germany, or Italy, for example, Canada exports only 11 cents. In comparison, Canada captures nearly half (46 percent) of the average OECD member's trade with China and India (Lingenfelter, Azzam, and Mann 2005, 1). Thus, while Canada is a strong exporter to China and India, the GCC market is being overlooked.

Another indicative measure of Canadian trade potential in the Middle East is to examine Australia's trade activity in the region. Australia has a similar economy to that of Canada (Ciuriak and Kinjo 2005). By way of example, both countries rank similarly in net exports in most product categories, with the exception of transport equipment and wood products where Canada is one of the top five exporters and Australia is a large importer of both (International

TABLE 9–4
Gross Domestic Product Growth Rates of the Middle East and
Brazil, Russia, India, and China

	1995	1998	2001	2004	2005	Average 1995–2005
Gulf Cooperation Council						4.0
Bahrain	3.9	4.8	4.6	5.4	6.9	4.9
Kuwait	4.9	3.7	0.7	6.2	8.5	4.4
Oman	5.0	2.6	7.4	3.1	—	3.5
Qatar	—	—	—	20.8	6.1	9.4
Saudi Arabia	0.2	2.8	0.5	5.3	6.6	3.0
United Arab Emirates	7.9	4.3	8.0	9.7	8.5	6.8
Other Middle East						4.3
Iran	2.7	2.7	3.7	5.1	4.4	4.6
Iraq	—	34.8	−6.6	46.5	—	6.6
Jordan	6.2	3.0	5.3	8.4	7.3	4.8
Lebanon	6.5	3.0	4.5	6.3	1.0	3.4
Syria	5.8	6.3	5.2	3.9	5.1	3.4
Yemen	11.6	6.5	4.6	2.5	2.6	5.1
Egypt	4.5	4.0	3.5	4.2	4.9	4.5
Israel	6.7	3.7	−0.3	4.4	5.2	3.6
Other Economies						
India	7.6	6.0	5.2	8.3	9.2	6.5
China	10.9	7.8	8.3	10.1	10.2	9.3
Brazil	4.2	0.1	1.3	4.9	2.3	2.4
Russia	−4.1	−5.3	5.1	7.1	6.4	3.2

Note: Aggregates for the Gulf Cooperation Council and the other Middle East countries are quoted in Metz and Van Ark (2007, table 1, 10).
Source: World Development Indicators Online, World Bank.

Trade Centre 2007). Canada also has a clear advantage over Australia in terms of product diversification in fresh and processed food and chemicals (International Trade Centre 2007). However, despite the similarities in export performance and competitiveness, Australia has consistently enjoyed a trade surplus with the Middle East, whereas Canada's trade deficit with the region is increasing (see Figure 9–2). Australia is negotiating a free trade agreement with the UAE and has been in free trade discussions with the GCC, for example. Australia appears to have put more effort into fostering strong trade ties with

FIGURE 9-2

Canada and Australia Trade Balance with Middle East and
the Gulf Cooperation Council, 2000-2005 US$ millions

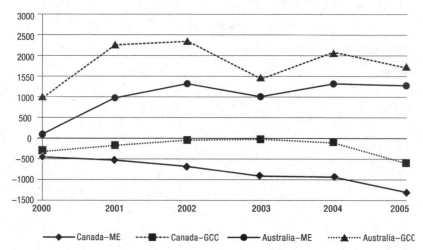

Notes: Gulf Cooperation Council (GCC) = Bahrain, Kuwait, Oman, Qatar, Saudi Arabia, and the
United Arab Emirates. Middle East (ME) = GCC, Egypt, Iran, Iraq, Israel, Jordan, Lebanon, Syria, and
Yemen.
Source: United Nations Commodity Trade Statistics Database (COMTRADE).

the Middle East, particularly with the GCC. The impression of Canadian government officials formerly stationed in the region is that Australia has made it
a formal policy commitment to bring senior government officials into the
region and to set up regional trade offices. The payoff has been extraordinary.
In the past five years, Australia has increased its exports to the GCC by more
than 500 percent (Subcommittee on International Trade, Trade Disputes, and
Investment of the Standing Committee on Foreign Affairs and International
Trade [SINT] 2005). In absolute terms, Australian exports to the Middle East
as a whole are almost double that of Canadian exports in recent years (compare Tables 9-2 and 9-5). It is suggested that Canada, put simply, has a lot of
room to grow in its trading relationship with the Middle East and, more specifically, the GCC.

Where does Canada have complementarity in trade of goods with the Middle East? What products can Canada provide the Middle East that are needed
throughout the region? According to the Trade Specialization Index, Canada
has a comparative advantage in almost all products with the exception of min-
eral products (GCC), chemicals (Egypt, Israel, Saudi Arabia, and Qatar), textiles (Israel, Egypt, Oman, and Bahrain), food (Israel and Egypt), precious
metals and stones (Israel and Egypt), and arms and ammunition (Israel).[4] It is
no surprise then that the sectoral mix of Canadian–Middle East trade is tilted

TABLE 9–5
Australia's Trade Balance with the Middle East, 2000–2005,
us$ millions

2000	Import	2,197
	Export	3,221
	Trade Balance	1,024
2001	Import	1,701
	Export	3,986
	Trade Balance	2,285
2002	Import	1,460
	Export	3,825
	Trade Balance	2,365
2003	Import	1,872
	Export	3,333
	Trade Balance	1,460
2004	Import	2,256
	Export	4,375
	Trade Balance	2,119
2005	Import	2,360
	Export	4,109
	Trade Balance	1,749

Note: Middle East: Bahrain, Egypt, Iran, Iraq, Israel, Jordan, Kuwait, Lebanon, Oman, Qatar, Saudi Arabia, Syria, United Arab Emirates, Yemen.
Source: United Nations Commodity Trade Statistics Database (COMTRADE).

in favour of exported machinery, wood, agriculture, aerospace, and automobile products, and in favour of imported natural resources and textiles (see Tables 9-6 and 9-7). Canada has complementary trade with the Middle East, but, more importantly, the potential for growth in noted sectors is also an important source of Canadian economic growth.

To begin, it is important to note that recent Canadian economic growth is increasingly generated by new sectors. In the late 1990s, Canada's economy was dominated by sectors such as high tech, auto manufacturing, and information and communication technologies. Since the beginning of the decade, however, these industries have slowed, while construction, resources, health, education, and related services are currently driving the Canadian economy (Cross 2006, 3.4). By way of example, yearly growth in construction in 2006 was 7.2 percent and oil and gas extraction 3.4 percent, while manufacturing and primary industries (agriculture, forestry, fishing, and hunting) experienced negative growth (Statistics Canada, various tables). An important factor in the weak performance of the manufacturing sector has been increased

TABLE 9–6

Sectoral Breakdown of Canada's Exports to the Middle East

	Aero-space	Commun-ications & Technology	Biotech/ Pharm-ceuticals	Natural Resources	Agri-culture	Heavy Machin-ery	Con-struction	Wood/ Paper Products	Energy	Textiles	Tourism	Profes-sional Services	Auto-mobile
Egypt	•	•		•	•	•		•				•	
Israel	•	•											
Jordan	•		•		•	•		•	•				•
Lebanon		•	•		•	•		•			•		•
Syria		•		•	•	•		•					
Saudi Arabia	•		•					•	•	•			•
United Arab Emirates	•			•	•	•			•				•
Iran					•			•					
Kuwait					•	•	•	•					•

Sources: Department of Foreign Affairs and International Trade (2007b), Canadian Trade Commissioner Service (2006, 2007).

Table 9–7

Sectoral Breakdown of Canada's Imports from the Middle East

	Communications & Technology	Biotech/ Pharmaceutical	Natural Resources	Agriculture	Heavy Machinery	Energy	Textiles	Automobile
Egypt			•	•		•	•	
Israel	•	•	•			•		
Jordan			•	•		•	•	•
Lebanon			•	•	•			
Syria			•	•			•	
Saudi Arabia	•	•						
United Arab Emirates	•	•					•	
Iran			•	•			•	
Kuwait			•				•	

Sources: Department of Foreign Affairs and International Trade (2007b), Canadian Trade Commissioner Service (2006, 2007).

competition from emerging countries (for example, China and India). This is especially visible in textiles, clothing, electrical equipment, leather products, and furniture (Industry Canada 2006, 15). On the other hand, computer and electronic products, wood, chemicals, and transportation equipment are currently the most successful manufacturing areas in Canada.

DFAIT (2005) has highlighted key market access priorities with countries in the Middle East. These specified sectors can be correlated to sectors where opportunities for growth and positive ripple effect on the Canadian economy have been suggested by other economic analyses. According to DFAIT, opportunities in the Middle East have been identified in the wood and pulp and paper sectors (Egypt and Syria), equipment and veterinary health products, transportation equipment and machinery, and aircrafts (Jordan), water (Jordan), energy (Syria), information technology and communications (Egypt and Syria), automobiles (Iran), and petrochemical (Egypt) industries. In high-tech products (such as computer, communications equipment), firms have already started diversifying their exports away from the declining United States and United Kingdom markets to more prospective emerging markets (EDC 2007, 61–62). Given the declining exports of Canadian forestry products to the U.S., expansion of trade with the Middle East is an option worth considering. In primary industries, despite overall negative growth, crop production drives economic activity due to the opening of new export markets for wheat and canola products (35). Canada sees trade opportunities in—and seeks further liberalization of bilateral trade in—canola oil (Israel, Iran, and Egypt), processed food (Jordan and Iran), dairy products (Jordan), live cattle (Iran) and beef and veal (UAE).

In services, the potential for growth seems to be located in professional, scientific, and technical services (currently growing at approximately 2.8 percent annually) and architectural and engineering services (3.3 percent) (Statistics Canada, various tables). Entertainment, recreation, and accommodation services have also recently experienced accelerated growth (between 3 percent and 5 percent annually). The overall export of Canadian services is not growing significantly at the moment; however, this is mainly a result of the strong Canadian dollar and declining demand in the United States. EDC (2007, 15) estimates that service exports to emerging markets will grow faster than to the U.S. (3 percent to 4 percent and 1 percent respectively).[5] In services, the potential for expansion has been noticed in education (Egypt and Saudi Arabia), consulting, training, software, and financial services (Syria), tourist services (UAE), infrastructure, construction, and engineering (Bahrain, Qatar, Saudi Arabia, and the UAE), and health care (Saudi Arabia) (DFAIT 2005, 136–51; Lingenfelter, Azzam, and Mann 2005).

EDC has also highlighted oil and gas, infrastructure, and environment as key sectors for strong Canadian investment and export potential. In this context, it seems that the market access priorities in the Middle East as identified by DFAIT follow domestic developments in various sectors of the economy. In addition, the fact that the oil-rich economies of the GCC are working toward higher economic diversification, using the oil revenues to increase spending on infrastructure, construction, other non-oil industries, real estate, tourism, and finance is a clear sign that Canada needs to look to the region for potential commercial opportunities.

While Canadian energy companies have traditionally established their presence in the Middle East and include, to name a few, Nexen, Petro-Canada, and BC Gas, companies from other sectors of the economy are becoming increasingly interested in the region. In aerospace, CAE, a Canadian manufacturer of flight simulators, has invested in a large flight training centre in Dubai; in infrastructure, SNC-Lavalin, Bombardier, and Gartner Lee are also well represented in the region. Canso and Cansult have provided engineering and project management expertise throughout the UAE on multi–million-dollar building initiatives. Canada is also increasingly active in providing educational services, such as the College of the North Atlantic–Qatar, and health training such as InterHealth and training of Saudi medical doctors in Canada. A number of Canadian retailers also figure prominently in the GCC, including Aldo, CinnZeo, La Vie en Rose, and Second Cup. The GCC stands out in the Middle East as a place where Canadian businesses can grow at remarkable rates.

Making the Case for Enhancing Canada–Middle East Economic Ties

Canada has a positive image in the Middle East. The importance of image cannot be overestimated. Canadian businesses are well liked by Middle Easterners, in part owing to the perceived impartiality of Canadian foreign policy in the region and in part owing to the likeability of Canadians. Former parliamentary secretary to the minister of international trade Mark Eyking has even suggested that Canada gained added respect in 2004 for the government's handling of the Iraq crisis (Buchanan 2005). Peter Ventin, vice-president of Cansult—one of the most profitable Canadian engineering firms working in the GCC—adds that Canadians have "got an incredible reputation…. Doors are open to us because we're a Canadian firm. That may not be the case if you're an American firm or a British firm, especially in light of the recent political environment in that part of the world" (SINT 2005). During the Middle East's unofficial consumer boycott of U.S. and UK goods in the region, a former Canadian trade representative noted that Canada was an unintended benefactor, with many Arab consumers switching to Canadian-made goods (Seguin 2007). Moreover, Canada is favoured in the region because it is seen as having "no preset agenda" and being a country of diversity and compromise and are therefore considered good business partners (Seguin 2007). Yet, as the president of the Canada-Arab Business Council (CABC) noted, there is a longstanding misperception that Canadian businesses do not perform well in the region (Mann 2007).

Canada's business community has often assumed that U.S. and UK businesses perform better in the Middle East because of their stronger political and historical ties to the region (Mann 2007). Canadian businesses are often surprised that the Middle East has a high income per capita and generally have a misperception that the region is unfriendly to foreign business (Seguin 2007). The CABC president, however, has commented that Gulf businesses noted their preference in dealing with Canadian companies, particularly as opposed to U.S. ones (Mann 2007). Canada, in some respects, has an edge over the United States.

Since 2005, the CABC has brought Canada's potential and growing level of trade with the GCC to the Canadian government's attention in a number of presentations to the Standing Committee on International Trade (CIIT). The Canadian government has also taken increased notice of the GCC market, in part owing to the attention raised by the CABC presentations (Mann 2007). In 2006, the government created a special committee to investigate potential opportunities for enhancing Canadian-GCC linkages. The most significant indication of this heightened interest came when Canada's trade minister David Emerson (2007) noted in a speech to the CABC that negotiations on a free trade agreement with the GCC might be launched. He stated that "bilateral trade agreements in key markets—markets like the Middle East and North Africa—will become a major priority for us in the near term."

There have been some synergies to push trade further with the Middle East. In 2005 Prime Minister Paul Martin addressed the CABC and stated: "Unfortunately, and I speak to government, I speak to the business community, and I speak to the ambassadors who are here, the simple fact of the matter is we have done little more than scratch the surface of the opportunities that are open to us in the Arab world." Trade Minister David Emerson made similar remarks in his 2007 address to the CABC:

> There's an awful lot of room for improvement; and just the few conversations I had coming in and meeting people [at the CABC annual meeting], I heard just enormous enthusiasm coming from people of just the highest calibre realizing that there is a window of opportunity here to deal with the Middle East in a way that would bring tremendous benefits to Canada and the region over the next couple of years. (Emerson 2007)

While commentators may have noted Canada's changed policy with respect to the Middle East under the Harper government, particularly with respect to Canada's United Nations voting record on issues concerning the Middle East, the CABC believes that this has not filtered negatively to the business community. While Middle Eastern diplomats have complained about Canada's UN voting during official visits intended to promote business ties with Canada, several individuals in government noted in personal interviews with the authors that this was not nearly as damaging to our reputation as critics have argued. Canada's ambassador to Saudi Arabia, Roderick Bell, reflected on this by saying:

> Some might say we're coasting on our reputation from the past. I personally think there is merit in that argument and that perhaps in recent years we haven't deserved the reputation we garnered in the past. Nonetheless, we still have it, more particularly since the events of 9/11. The Canadian position on Middle Eastern issues, and more particularly on Iraq, are extremely valued, and this is not just at the government level.... We really do have a special place in these Arab countries, but we don't exploit it as much as we should. (SINT 2005)

Without a comprehensive survey of Middle East business and government on perceptions of Canada, the effect of changes to Canada's Middle East policy under Prime Minister Harper cannot yet be measured. Nevertheless, there appears to be some goodwill banked in the Middle East that continues to serve Canadian businesses positively in the region. Moreover, regardless of which party is in government, both the Liberals and the Conservatives have expressed a strong will to promote Canadian business in, and exports to, the Middle East. The question becomes, then, if there is clear quantitative economic evidence supporting increased Canada–Middle East trade and the Middle East is eager for Canadian business, why has Canada underestimated trade with the Middle East and, specifically, the GCC?

Challenges to Enhancing Canadian Business Interests in the Middle East

This chapter uses 15 interviews with interested business leaders, stakeholders, parliamentarians, and past and present government bureaucrats to synthesize a number of factors that present challenges to enhancing business in the region. First, as the U.S. monopolizes Canada's official and business interests, there is a declining interest for much else. Why do Canadian trade officials not pursue trade in regions such as the Middle East? A number of interviewees noted that while there is interest in DFAIT and EDC to exploit new markets, the emphasis is more often placed on the better known emerging market economies called the BRICS: Brazil, Russia, India, and China. In a sense, Canada wears "blinders" when pursuing trade opportunities beyond the BRICS. Dwain Lingenfelter (2005), the vice president (international relations) of Nexen, says that "it's much more difficult to get ministers to lead trade missions to the Middle East than I think it is to India or Brazil or China. At least the record would show that there are many more ministers going to those countries than going to the Middle East. And so I think this is just one part of it, but I think we all have to do our part." This sentiment exists despite the EDCs observation, similarly echoed in many interviews, that it is relatively easier to conduct business in the Gulf than in India or China.

Second, part of the difficulty in selling the idea that the Middle East, and specifically the GCC, is worthy of business and bureaucratic interest is that the Middle East and GCC populations are relatively small (Mann 2007). Business and the bureaucracy are more impressed by and interested in exporting to larger consumer markets, such as India and China. It is simply more impressive to boast that Canada has secured stronger ties with a market of more than 1 billion than to boast ties with a Middle East market of 250 million or a GCC market of 35 million.

Third, there are strong perceived political risks associated with conducting business in the region. Undoubtedly, business has been dissuaded by the news headlines about Iraq, Lebanon, and Israel and Palestine. The CABC has painstakingly reminded Canada's business communities that, apart from several states, the region is relatively safe. Moreover, the region is relatively transparent and, compared to other emerging market economies, it is relatively "easy to do business" there. That said, some countries in the region make it difficult for business people to travel and visit the region. Saudi Arabia and Libya, in particular, have cumbersome visa application processes that make it a challenge for Canadian business people to travel to their countries.

Fourth, in conducting business in the GCC, cultural nuances need to be respected. Gulf states can be highly image conscious. There is a strong involvement of royal family members in key portfolios in Gulf governments. It is important for Canada to send senior ministers to the Gulf states, where their counterparts will often be members of the royal family (Ligenfelter, Azzam, and Mann 2005; Mann 2007). Ambassador Bell emphasizes the importance of this issue in promoting economic ties, saying that "culture values face-to-face contact, but believe me, Arab culture puts a premium on it. We need the Prime Minister there, we need ministers there, and we need MPs [ministers of Parliament] there" (Bell, quoted in SINT 2005). Canadian businesses involved in the region have picked up this theme. Paul Mariamo (quoted in CIIT 2007, 4), senior vice-president of SNC-Lavalin, states that "we would love to see our Prime Minister or minister there often, promoting our product. We can fight companies, but we cannot fight governments. We need you to fight the governments for us; we cannot do it ourselves." In other words, Canadian businesses need the political support of Canadian government officials to help promote strong bilateral economic relationships. Sending bureaucrats in lieu of ministers to important trade meetings in the GCC does not help trade negotiations with the region. This is something that the European Union has learned in its trade negotiations with the GCC (Saleh 1999).

Canadian businesses operating in the Gulf have asked for stronger involvement of Canadian MPs, but it seems difficult for MPs and politicians to travel without risking the potential criticism of the media. As Nexen's Lingenfelter (quoted in CIIT 2007, 8) commented, "no one wants to be on what might be determined as a political junket in the media. No one wants to be away when the House has a vote, but believe me, that's not helping us in the international work that we work in." Furthermore, in the current context of a Canadian minority government, it was noted that it has been difficult to arrange ministerial level trade negotiations in the Middle East because of the possible call for an election (Mann 2007). Canadian businesses operating in the Middle East have repeatedly stressed the need for stronger visibility of Canadian MPs and government members to help augment the stature of Canada's business community in the region (CIIT 2007). The CIIT's trade mission to the region in June 2007 was a promising step in the right direction.

Fifth, Canadian embassies need to be better represented in the Middle East. Canada's embassies serve a vital function in promoting bilateral economic relations. While Canada has embassies in many Middle East countries, there are a number of important posts remaining to fill. Qatar, Oman, Yemen, Bahrain, and Iraq are still waiting for a permanent Canadian mission. A number of these countries have actively sought a Canadian embassy to help foster stronger bilateral trade (Lingenfelter, Azzam, and Mann 2005). According to Lingenfelter, DFAIT has allocated a fixed budget to manage Canadian embassies and opening an embassy in a new post is rationalized only when there is a closing of another post (CIIT 2007, 11). While this is not effective government policy in any way, some argue that the government has failed to view embassies as investments in Canadian business and economic growth. Instead, it has rationalized embassies as a zero-sum cost (David Hutton, quoted in CIIT 2007, 50). A number of people interviewed for this chapter noted with frustration the closing of Canadian offices in Osaka and Fukuoka in Japan, Milan in Italy, and St. Petersburg in Russia, which are all key business markets abroad. The overarching problem, however, is the lack of DFAIT capacity in fulfilling competing and rising demands. Moreover, Canadian embassies in the Middle East are overwhelmed with offering visa and immigration services, making trade and investment promotion a relatively lower priority.

Finally, airline links between Canada and the Middle East, particularly the GCC, need to be improved significantly. Business travellers going to the Gulf, for example, must stop in Europe, adding significant costs in time and money. For a number of years, Canada had only three flights to the UAE via Brussels per week; in contrast, Australia had more than 60 flights a week to the country (Hutton, quoted in CIIT 2007, 5). Australian businesses also transit through the UAE to get to Europe, making business contact convenient even if incidental to Australian-European travel. This is an added advantage to Australian businesses. Providing Middle East and Gulf airlines with enhanced access to Canadian airports via landing rights, called open skies agreements, is a policy decision requiring the attention of the highest levels of government (5). Canadian businesses may likely start pressuring the Canadian government, as had been the case with businesses dealing with China, to increase air services to the Middle East as trade ties continue to strengthen.

In 2005, the UAE's Etihad Airlines started offering three direct flights between the region and Toronto and Emirates Airlines is scheduled to begin flying to Toronto in fall 2007. The Canadian government, however, has tried to protect Air Canada from Gulf competitors that can offer travellers, specifically those going to the Indian subcontinent, an alternate air route. Needless to say, however, business travel made cumbersome and difficult will deter bilateral trade and investment relations, and an integrated approach that considers industry, economic, and safety concerns needs to be considered.

Steps Forward in Strengthening Economic Ties

In April 2007, a *Maclean's* cover article entitled "Land of the Timid…Home of the Careful" essentially argued that Canadian businesses have an aversion to international branding and risk (Mandel-Campbell 2007). This is far from the truth for those Canadian companies trying to expand business opportunities in the Middle East. There are indeed real challenges to enhancing trade with the Middle East, particularly when the business community and public at large have a misconstrued image of the region. However, the Canadian government needs to enhance its political commitments to pursuing closer ties with the Middle East by initiating an integrated study of the issues that inhibit stronger economic ties.

Taking stock of Canada's formal arrangements and links with the Middle East reveals how Canada's institutional links with the region remain underdeveloped. Canada has only four free trade agreements in the world, only one of which is with a country in the region, Israel. Under the Mulroney government in the early 1990s, Israel had actively pursued closer economic ties with Canada and raised the idea of a bilateral free trade agreement. However, the Mulroney government was preoccupied with the Canada-U.S. free trade agreement and did not want to pursue yet another politically contentious bilateral trade agreement. Prime Minister Jean Chrétien raised the issue with Israeli prime minister Yitzhak Rabin when they met in 1994.

The main motivations for the Canada-Israel Free Trade Agreement (CIFTA) were to strengthen economic relations and create a framework for promoting investment and cooperation (DFAIT 1996).[6] Despite Chrétien's support for the idea, Canadian foreign affairs political officers remained wary, whereas trade officials in the same department argued that Canadian firms needed an free trade agreement with Israel to level the playing field with the EU and American competitors that enjoyed tariff-free access (the EU in 1975 and the U.S. in 1985 had both concluded free trade agreements with Israel) (Spector 1996; see also Andrew Moroz, quoted in Standing Senate Committee of Foreign Affairs 1996). In contrast, Canadian producers and industries, such as telecommunications, were paying tariffs of 10 percent to 25 percent to export into Israel. This discrepancy presented a considerable disadvantage to Canadian exporters. Additional free trade agreements in the region could help level the playing field abroad.

Analysts have recommended that DFAIT's attention would be better spent furthering multilateral trade agreements, instead of bilateral trade agreements (Goldfarb 2005). That said, multilateral trade talks, such as the Doha talks of the World Trade Organization (WTO), are not accelerating fast enough to meet the needs of the Canadian business community. Many countries, including our partners in the North American Free Trade Agreement (NAFTA), are ahead of the game in signing free trade agreements with important trading partners. Canada has tended to approach bilateral trade agreements with caution, ensuring that they are comprehensive and bullet-proof. In any case, the stretched capacity of DFAIT means that Canada cannot keep up with its competitors in trade negotiations.

In February 2007, the Harper government announced that it would make bilateral free trade agreements an important government policy by committing greater financial resources to trade negotiations. However, DFAIT cannot train individuals in complex trade negotiation fast enough to meet the demands of the business community. In June 2007 DFAIT concluded the agreement with the European Free Trade Association (EFTA) countries and is currently in negotiations with South Korea, Singapore, and four Central American states. Trade negotiations with Peru, Columbia, and the Caribbean Community and Common Market (CARICOM) are also on the horizon. DFAIT has argued that an agreement with Japan would be worthwhile as well. Simply put, the possibility of an advanced trade agreement being negotiated with the GCC anytime soon is unlikely. DFAIT has not yet begun a comprehensive exploration process with the region.

Although further bilateral free trade agreements with most countries in the wider Middle East are not recommended, the GCC is nonetheless a region worthy of Canadian attention. The U.S. has been pursuing multiple trade agreements throughout the Middle East with small, relatively less important economies in hopes of achieving peace in the region (Momani 2007). This is not an approach that Canada should replicate. While DFAIT has always maintained that the agreement served economic interests, Canada's motivations for negotiating CIFTA were also political and geopolitical. The same could be said for the potential trade negotiations with Jordan announced in the summer of 2007 by Stephen Harper (Prime Minister's Office 2007). At the Standing Senate Committee on Foreign Affairs on the eve of the CIFTA signing, Senator Pierre De Bané expressed scepticism that the creation of CIFTA was motivated on economic grounds:

> We all know the size of the trade between our country and Israel, and if we were interested in having a level playing field, I can give you a lot of other markets where we do not have a level playing field because of their agreements with the European Union. The reason here—everybody knows. As a Canadian, I applauded when that agreement in principle was announced, because it was our gift to that region—we wanted to encourage them in the peace process. This is it. You have your own point of view about what kind of spin to give to this, but let me tell you that it is essentially a political gesture on the part of Canada, and you cannot, with all due respect, hide it with an economic rationale. (De Bané, quoted in Standing Senate Committee on Foreign Affairs 1996)

Nevertheless, since the implementation of CIFTA, bilateral trade between Canada and Israel has more than doubled, from $567 million in 1997 to an all-time high of more than $1.2 billion in 2005 (DFAIT 1999, 2006, 27).[7] Free trade, as per CIFTA and many other American bilateral trade agreements with Middle East countries, is presumed to promote peace in the region and thereby to help to achieve geopolitical ends, rather than simply economic ones (Momani 2007).

Regardless of U.S. motivations to sign free trade agreements with Middle East partners, Canada clearly reacts to U.S. trade agreements with enhanced interest. Canadian businesses worry that they will shut out Canadian business. The U.S.-Moroccan FTA, for example, has generated worries in Canada's business community, particularly among wheat exporters. There is indeed some rationale in having a similar trade web within NAFTA. Similarly, once the GCC concludes its nearly completed trade agreement with the EU, Canadian businesses may put pressure on the Canadian government to level the playing field. The fact remains, however, that Canadian trade negotiators are stretched to the limit. The unprecedented amount of bilateral free trade negotiations recently undertaken by Canada indicates that the GCC cannot possibly be on the near horizon of the government's trade agenda. Moreover, due to DFAIT's limited resources and capabilities in negotiating trade agreements, there is a greater need for Canada to pursue a commercial rationale as opposed to a geopolitical one.

If Canadian trade officials are stretched to the limit, what can be done in the short term? For now, Canadian trade officials can negotiate additional foreign investment protection and promotion agreements (FIPAS). It has been suggested that a free trade agreement, for example, can require 30 highly trained DFAIT employees to negotiate and manage at any given time, whereas, a FIPA requires only six, with some cooperation from the Department of Finance. Canada has signed two FIPAS with Lebanon and Egypt in 1997 (in force 1999) and 1996 (in force 1997), respectively. The agreements contain provisions for the treatment of established investment, expropriation, transfer of funds and performance requirements, taxation measures, and dispute settlement, among others. FIPA negotiations with Jordan have just been completed (Prime Minister's Office 2007) and the groundwork has been laid for talks with Kuwait.

Double taxation agreements can also help to promote stronger Canada–Middle East business ties without committing a large amount of DFAIT resources. Cooperation on taxation agreements (also known as agreements on the avoidance of double taxation) have been signed with Israel, Jordan, Kuwait, Lebanon, Oman, and the UAE. An older agreement with Egypt (1983) is currently being renegotiated and talks with Iran are ongoing. In addition to formal government-to-government agreements, Canadian agencies have also expressed interest in deepening links to countries in the Middle East. EDC, for example, will open a regional office in Abu Dhabi in January 2008. This will be one of 11 regional offices placed in emerging market economies throughout the world. Strengthening EDC office resources in the Middle East would also be a useful policy.

Conclusion

Canada–Middle East economic relations are an under-appreciated dimension of Canadian trade and foreign policy. Beyond CIFTA, Canada has no other free trade agreement with the region, and only a small number of formal economic agreements—a shortcoming that needs to be addressed. An free trade agreement with the GCC would be beneficial and would be a welcomed signal for Canadian foreign investment, but DFAIT's limited capacity makes this proposal less likely in the short term. The challenges noted in advancing trade in the Middle East, and most importantly in the GCC, however, are political ones. Indeed, there is a real need for enhanced political commitment on the part of the Canadian government to help enhance Canadian business activity in the Middle East. Expanding embassy services to include more trade commissioners would similarly be valuable in many more Middle East postings. Finally, it is clear that there is a greater need for personal involvement of senior government members in Canada's trade policy with the Middle East. The prime minister, members of Parliament, and even Canadian senators could be useful in opening many doors to lucrative business opportunities that will effectively help Canada's economy grow and prosper, and improve relations between Canada and the Middle East generally.

Notes

1 The authors are grateful to Dan Ciuriak for his suggestions and comments on an earlier draft and to those interviewed in Ottawa.

2 For an interesting history of Canada-GCC relations, see Bookmiller (2006).

3 Unless otherwise noted, statistics quoted in the text are authors' calculations based on International Trade Canada data.

4 Using Statistics Canada data, the Trade Specialization Index is calculated (by sector) as a ratio of net exports (exports less imports) to total trade (exports plus imports). The index ranges from −1 when there are no exports, which reveals comparative disadvantage, to +1 when there are no imports, which reveals comparative advantage.

5 For more information on Canada's export potential in various sectors see EDC (2007).

6 The content of the CIFTA focuses on goods trade and the related elimination of tariffs. It also contains provisions on rules of origin, national treatment, and customs procedures. No commitments were included on trade in services, intellectual property, or investment. Tariffs on most industrial products were removed when the agreement came into force. The few remaining tariffs were phased out over the following three years (DFAIT 1996, Annex 2.1.1). The provisions of the CIFTA were expanded in 2003 to include approximately 80 percent of two-way trade in agricultural and food products (Agriculture and Agri-Food Canada 2003). The CIFTA also contains provisions on the establishment of the Canada-Israel Trade Commission,

which is a binding dispute settlement system that includes a panel of experts, and an enforcement mechanism.

7 In comparison, Canada's total trade increased by approximately 60 percent over the same period (DFAIT 1999, 2006).

References

Agriculture and Agri-Food Canada. 2003. Canada-Israel Free Trade Agreement (CIFTA): Update 2003. agr.gc.ca/itpd-dpci/english/trade_agr/cifta.htm (August 2007).

Bookmiller, Robert. 2006. *Discovering the Arabian Gulf: Canada's Evolving Ties with the GCC States*. Dubai: Gulf Research Center.

Buchanan, Terri-Sue. 2005. "The Gulf Cooperation Council: Refining Endless Growth." *ExportWise* (Spring). Ottawa: Export Development Canada. www.edc.ca/english/publications_9332.htm (August 2007).

Canadian Trade Commissioner Service. 2006. "Rendez Vous—Newsletter" (January/February 2006)—Middle East. www.infoexport.gc.ca/ie-en/Display-Document.jsp?did=62885 (August 2007).

———. 2007. Country profiles. www.infoexport.gc.ca (August 2007).

Ciuriak, Dan, and Shinji Kinjo. 2005. "Trade Specialization in the Gravity Model of International Trade." In *Trade Policy Research 2005*, ed. John M. Curtis and Dan Ciuriak, 189–98. Ottawa: Department of Foreign Affairs and International Trade. www.international.gc.ca/eet/research/TPR-2005/TPR -2005_Chapter_09_-_Ciuriak-Kinjo-TSI.pdf (August 2007).

Cross, Philip. 2006. "The Year in Review: The Revenge of the Old Economy." *Canadian Economic Observer* 19(4): 3.1–3.21. April www.statcan.ca/cgi -bin/downpub/listpub.cgi?catno=11–010-XIB2006004 (August 2007).

Department of Foreign Affairs and International Trade. 1996. "Free Trade Agreement Between the Government of Canada and the Government of the State of Israel." www.international.gc.ca/tna-nac/cifta-en.asp (August 2007).

———. 1999. "CIFTA—Two Years Later." Business Development Mission to the Middle East. www.tcm-mec.gc.ca/missions/middle-east/cifta-en.asp (August 2007).

———. 2005. "Opening Doors to the World: Canada's International Market Access Priorities 2005." www.international.gc.ca/tna-nac/2005/pdf/ITC _English_05.pdf (August 2007).

———. 2006. "Opening Doors to the World. Canada's International Market Access Priorities 2006." www.dfait-maeci.gc.ca/tna-nac/2006/pdf/ITC _06-en.pdf (August 2007).

———. 2007a. "Canada's Merchandise Exports." www.international.gc.ca/eet/ pdf/PFACT_Ann_Merch_Trade_2006_July_2007-en.pdf (August 2007).

———. 2007b. "Country and Regional Information." geo.international.gc.ca/cip -pic/geo/geographic_location-en.aspx (August 2007).

Emerson, David. 2007. "Notes for an Address by the Honourable David L. Emerson, Minister of International Trade and Minister for the Pacific Gateway and the Vancouver-Whistler Winter Olympics to the Canada-Arab Business Council's Conference on Canada and the Arab World," Gatineau, February 13. www.canada-arabbusiness.org/newsletter/101.doc (August 2007).

Export Development Canada (EDC) (2007). "Global Export Forecast: Adapting to the Evolving Trade Paradigm." Spring 2007. Ottawa.

Goldfarb, Danielle. 2005. "U.S. Bilateral Free Trade Accords: Why Canada Should Be Cautious About Going the Same Route." *Border Papers.* Toronto: CD Howe Institute.

Industry Canada. 2006. "Report on Canada's Industrial Performance." Micro-Economic Policy Analysis Branch, Industry Canada. strategis.ic.gc.ca/epic/site/eas-aes.nsf/vwapj/CIPQ406E.pdf/$FILE/CIPQ406E.pdf (August 2007).

International Trade Centre. 2007. Trade Performance Index. www.intracen.org/countries/toolpd05/tpi-2007–05.xls (August 2007).

Lingenfelter, Dwain, Mohamad Azzam, and Richard Mann. 2005. "Presentation to the Subcommittee on International Trade." February 21. Canada-Arab Business Council. www.canada-arabbusiness.org/eventfiles/80.pdf (August 2007).

Mann, Richard. 2007. Interview with Bessma Momani. June 18, Toronto.

Martin, Paul. (2005). "PM Martin's Speech at the Canada-Arab Business Council Dinner." Gatineau, November 21. www.canada-arabbusiness.org/eventfiles/111.pdf (August 2007).

Mandel-Campbell, Andrea. 2007. "Land of the Timid ... Home of the Careful." *Maclean's* April 16, 120(14): 32–35.

Metz, Andreas, and Bart Van Ark. 2007. "Growth in the Middle East Depends on Productivity." Executive Action Report, February. Series no. 227. New York: Conference Board.

Momani, Bessma. 2007. "A Middle East Free Trade Area: Economic Interdependence and Peace Considered." *World Economy* (forthcoming).

Prime Minister's Office. 2007. "Prime Minister Harper Concludes Successful Meetings with King Abdullah II of Jordan." July 13. news.gc.ca/web/view/en/index.jsp?articleid=341439& (August 2007).

Saleh, Niven. 1999. "The European Union and the Gulf Sates: A Growing Partnership." *Middle East Policy* 7(1): 50–71.

Seguin, Richard. 2007. Interview with Bessma Momani. June 25, Guelph.

Spector, Norman. 1996. "How Canada and Israel Signed Their Free-Trade Deal." *Globe and Mail*, August 16, A15.

Standing Senate Committee of Foreign Affairs. 1996. Proceedings of the Standing Senate Committee on Foreign Affairs. Issue 15, December 3. www.parl.gc.ca/35/2/parlbus/commbus/senate/Com-e/fore-e/15ev-e.htm?Language=E&Parl=35&Ses=2&comm_id=8 (August 2007).

Subcommittee on International Trade, Trade Disputes, and Investment of the Standing Committee on Foreign Affairs and International Trade. 2005. Evidence. 38th Parliament, Number 012. February 21. cmte.parl.gc.ca/cmte/CommitteePublication.aspx?SourceId=103470&Lang=1&PARLSES =381&JNT=0&COM=9099.

Standing Committee on International Trade. 2007. Evidence. 39th Parliament, Session 1, Number 050. February 27. cmte.parl.gc.ca/Content/HOC/Committee/391/CIIT/Evidence/EV2753158/CIITEV50-E.PDF (August 2007).

Veilleux, Patrice. 2004. "Canada's Commercial Relations with the Arab World." In "Canada and the Arab World: Challenges and Opportunities," 21–23. Proceedings of the 2004 National Foreign Policy Conference of the National Council on Canada-Arab Relations, Ottawa. www.nccar.ca/publications/ArabConference2004.pdf (August 2007).

World Bank. 2006. *Global Economic Prospects 2006: Economic Implications of Remittances and Migration*. Washington, DC: World Bank. go.worldbank .org/CGW1GG3AV1 (August 2007).

Canada's Jewish and Arab Communities and Canadian Foreign Policy[1]

There are multiple factors and considerations that determine a state's foreign policy, including global developments, geo-strategic location, individual leaders and their cognitive or emotional frameworks, public opinion, and the interests and efforts of domestic political actors. The relative weight of any factor varies across time and circumstance, but it has been argued that Canadian foreign policy is, in part, or should ideally be, determined by societal input; that is, Canadian international policy should be informed by the values, ideas, and preferences of Canadians themselves, rather than just determined by political leaders on the advice of a professional public service. If this is indeed the case, then we need to understand how and under what conditions societal groups affect or do not affect policy.

In the framework of Canadian policy toward the Middle East, and more particularly the Arab-Israeli conflict, the impact of domestic ethnic groups (specifically the Jewish and Arab communities) on policy making has become an issue of significant debate.[2] But the issue has been under-studied. This chapter raises questions about how Canadians view this process and lays the groundwork for a more rigorous investigation of the impact of organized domestic ethnic groups on the foreign policy-making process.

In particular, it raises questions about the accuracy and effectiveness of existing studies on the impact of Canadian Arab and, especially, Canadian Jewish groups on policy making. The chapter argues that such studies have several conceptual and empirical problems, including a lack of a rigorous theoretical framework, serious measurement problems, inadequate attention to situational variables, deficiency of evidence, and a paucity of sustained empirical analysis. Furthermore, they are almost all quite dated; many are the work of an earlier generation of scholars. These problems inhibit a useful understanding of the influence of ethnic groups on foreign policy making, which in turn hinders politicians and others from making optimally effective decisions representing the best interests of Canadians and reflecting their key values and beliefs.

The first section of this chapter focuses on the theoretical and empirical questions surrounding current studies on this topic, including a discussion of the general literature on interests groups and ethnic groups and their lobbying, and notes their limited applicability to the Canadian context. The second section develops an analysis of the theoretical and empirical problems inherent in the existing approaches to understanding ethnic group lobbying in Canada and suggests a new theoretical model that includes the interplay between domestic political competition and efforts by domestic groups to shape Canadian interests and identity along their preferred interests and identities. The next part deals with advocacy efforts by Jewish and Arab groups in Canada. This empirical supplement to the section on theory highlights the problems of evidence used by studies on ethnic group lobbying in Canada by examining the differences between the Jewish and Arab communities. The final section discusses some of the policy implications of our investigation.

Interest Groups, Ethnic Groups, and Lobbying

To understand when and how domestic ethnic groups are successful or not in influencing policy, one must account for the conditions under which the views of a group become attractive enough to policy makers to become translated into policy. There is a significant extant literature on interest groups, lobbying, and foreign policy (for one overview, see Haney and Vanderbush 1999). It has been found that interest groups engage in three broad types of activities to obtain their objectives (Dietrich 1999, 283). First, they try to frame an issue for policy makers so that it fits with their own narrative or interpretation of events. This can include mobilization of society and shaping of public opinion. They try to shape policy discussions along their preferred lines, and even put favourable policies on the agenda. Second, they provide information and analysis to legislators, particularly politicians, who usually cannot access this information on their own due to lack of time and resources. Third, they monitor government policy toward their areas of interest and, if a policy does not meet with their preferences, will engage in a process of trying to change policy, or limit the "damage" done to their objectives.

In this literature, politicians tend to be the key focus of interest group activity. The argument is that politicians wish to be elected or re-elected, and so will make policy that, in their consideration, best enhances their chances at electoral victory (see Bueno de Mesquita et al. 2003; Siverson 1998). For this to work, interest groups must be able to play a significant role in the electoral process. In the American system this is done partly through information campaigns, but primarily through campaign financing and other forms of direct support for politicians running for office (see, for example, Ansolabehere, Snyder and Tripathi 2002; Brunell 2005). This understanding is not so appropriate for Canada, however, since the nature of executive-legislature relations is very different. Canadian legislators are much more subject to party discipline in the parliamentary system; there is less emphasis on individual candidates in elections; and campaign contributions are distinctly limited by law.

A growing body of literature deals specifically with ethnic groups. Ethnic groups tend to maintain strong emotional, psychological, cultural, and material ties with "homeland" countries or states with a majority of their kin (see Smith 2000), which gives them a deep incentive to mobilize in order to shift policy along lines more favourable to their kin countries. Their political activity on such issues can be significant enough that they may even be considered a "third actor" apart from governments and domestic society as a whole in the foreign policy-making process (Shain 2002). But, as above, much of this literature focuses on the United States. That it would do so is natural: the American political system affords more access points for interests groups. In addition, because of America's superpower status, its foreign policies have a profound impact on what goes on in the international arena. Studying how U.S. foreign policy is made is therefore critical for understanding much of world politics.

Comparatively, Canada is neglected in the general study of ethnic groups and lobbying. Its Westminster-based system allows for fewer access points for lobbying. Furthermore, the Canadian public service is less partisan and therefore less susceptible to third-party influence, although within the government and bureaucracy there is said to be a perception that criticism of Israel could lead to charges of anti-Semitism, which in turn promotes self-censorship.[3] Finally, Canadian foreign policy is much less consequential in world politics, overall, and much more circumscribed. Communal groups in Canada are therefore structurally constrained in what they can push Canada to do. In the general literature on ethnic groups and foreign policy, then, there is less that is helpful to understanding the Canadian context.

Conceptual and Empirical Problems

While there have been numerous studies by Canadian scholars and observers on the impact of ethnic groups on Canadian foreign policy, they have generally been divorced from the larger questions and theories found in the general literature. In addition, most of these studies have focused on the role of the Jewish community (the Jewish lobby or pro-Israel lobby). Together, these factors mean that accounts of ethnic group impact on foreign policy in Canada are under-theorized and underdeveloped.[4]

First, most obviously missing in studies of Canadian ethnic groups and foreign policy, especially regarding the Middle East, are strong theoretical underpinnings. An effective conceptual framework facilitates understanding the conditions under which ethnic groups matter in foreign policy making, particularly over time. A strong theoretical framework would incorporate clear variables and, in particular, distinguish between the independent and dependent variables (on the importance of doing so, see Hermann 1978). Such studies must also explain whether they are about one particular foreign policy decision or about foreign policy more generally. Often there is no obvious distinction between these two, which leads to theoretical confusion and broad assumptions drawn from a narrow set of empirical evidence. This, in turn, leads to inaccurate conclusions about the impact of specific ethnic groups on policy.

There must also be clear definitions. What do we mean by "influence"? What does "success" or "failure" entail? It is important to include here the perception of success and failure. What government leaders might consider to be pro-Israel lobby successes, Jewish groups might not. Can we account for people's perception of influence as a factor that determines outcomes? How will ethnic group influence be coded—in terms of activity or outcome? More nuanced studies that address these questions are needed for a better understanding of ethnic groups and lobbying in Canada.

A second general problem exhibited by these types of studies relates to measurement of outcomes. This connects to the first point, particularly on the need for rigorous definitions, but also refers to the assessment of how much influence an ethnic group has. It is certainly true that ethnic groups have clearly had sway over specific government decisions. But does this signal a deeper, broader, more pervasive influence across time and issue areas? Why or why not? No answer is possible without an in-depth, sustained analysis of various foreign policy decisions. Only in this way can the confluence of elements involved in any one decision be penetrated.

Studies in Canada have focused mostly on Jewish groups, primarily because they are much better organized than Arab groups and because they have achieved some obvious successes from their active efforts. The general conclusions are that the pro-Israel lobby wields particularly significant influence on Canadian foreign policy toward the Middle East much of the time when it wants to (see Kirton and Lyon 1989). Interviews with former government officials also seem to support this perception. However, there are a number of academic studies, albeit dated, that contradict this assertion (see Goldberg 1990; Taras 1984; and various contributions in Taras and Goldberg 1989, especially Goldberg 1989). Fresh analysis is warranted.

A third problem, stemming from inadequate measurement standards, is the non-incorporation of situational variables. As David Dewitt and John Kirton (1983, 178) put it, "policy usually emerges as a consensus of opinion and analysis from diverse sources, and interest group intervention in the policy-making process is merely one of a number of stimuli." There are numerous factors that must be taken into account when studying a particular foreign policy decision, including the inclinations of a particular prime minister or foreign minister in office at the time; international, regional, and domestic developments; perceptions of other decision makers; national public opinion; and so on. Yet most studies in this area, chiefly those that point to the Jewish community's influence, take too little account of the multiplicity of factors at play.

For example, developments in the international system can raise or lower the priority of issues on the policy agenda. The September 11 terrorist attacks raised concerns about the activities of groups, such as Hizbullah, which could be deemed by Canada as terrorist groups, even if they resided and operated outside of Canada. America's forceful pursuit of and Canada's support for the "war on terrorism" helped raise the importance of this question and pushed Canada to list Hizbullah as a terrorist group, over the objections of Canadian Arab groups and despite the fact that previously Ottawa, like most of the European Union, had viewed Hizbullah as a militant but not a terrorist organization, and one that provided necessary social welfare and other services. Despite their efforts, Canadian Jewish groups were unable to convince the government to declare Hizbullah a terrorist group under Canadian law prior to September 11. It would be difficult, then, to code the listing of Hizbullah as a terrorist group as a success for Jewish groups without assessing the effect of September 11 on Canadian policy makers.

Accession by Stephen Harper to the office of prime minister is another example. Although, like most of his predecessors, he had little direct experience of the region, Harper came to office with strong personal religious beliefs, an inclination to support Israel, very clear ideas about terrorism and about the appropriate response to terrorist activities, and a desire to strengthen ties with the United States. He defended Israel's military response to Hizbullah and Hamas attacks in 2006 in near categorical terms. In fact, Canadian Jewish officials have remarked that they were surprised by the strength of Harper's defence of Israel and feared it might undermine their advocacy efforts vis-à-vis the other political parties.[5]

The absence of variables is also an important consideration. It is possible that an ethnic minority can "capture" policy toward a specific issue when the rest of the population does not care enough about that issue (Moore 2002, 84; Saideman 2002, 99–100).[6] In Canada, Jewish groups have effectively mobilized to promote their narrative and shape Canadian policy along their preferred lines. Although Canadians in general have views on the Arab-Israeli conflict, they do not feel strongly enough about it that they actively promote their views to politicians. In addition, as discussed below, the Arab community is far less capable in its own lobbying activity. Jewish groups have therefore had the field mostly to themselves, which has inevitably translated into more influence relative to other groups. This has implications for what is meant by the "success" of the pro-Israel lobby, and for the kinds of factors that decision makers must account for when formulating policy.

The final snag inherent in many studies on ethnic groups and their influence in Canada is a dearth of evidence combined with a lack of sustained analysis. First, much of the evidence used to support a particular study's conclusion is circumstantial, anecdotal, or not based on a wide enough set of sources. This is particularly so in studies on the Jewish community, where it is often asserted that Jewish groups wield substantial influence over policy related to Israel and the Arab-Israeli conflict. But there seems to be little in the way of in-depth study of these issues, which would require interviews with a number of Canadian policy makers (political and bureaucratic), representatives of Jewish groups, and other observers as well as primary documentary research. Instead, there are mostly assumptions and presumptions. In Canada, some studies of Jewish influence do point out that circumstances often contribute to their influence in some periods and on some issues over others. But, in the end, similar to the essay by John Mearsheimer and Stephen Walt (2006) on the impact of the pro-Israel lobby on U.S. foreign policy, many of these studies tend to come to the same sweeping (and thus inaccurate) conclusions as less empirically and analytically grounded studies: that the Jewish or pro-Israel lobby in Canada is a major determinant in all foreign policy issues related to Israel (e.g., Lyon 1992).

In one sense, these difficulties are inevitable in light of the issue being studied. Given the sensitivities surrounding the topic—including criticism of how policy is made—decision makers, mainly politicians, may be reluctant to be completely candid about how they arrive at their decisions, especially where policy change is concerned. Additionally, lobby groups may be hesitant about trumpeting their successes: too much publicity could undermine their effectiveness, and also raise concerns about the behavior of an ethnic minority in a multicultural country. These are some of the inherent challenges in attempting to measure and determine the impact of these communities, but that does not, or should not, automatically preclude efforts to debate the issue within theoretical frameworks and with empirical findings.

Second, most studies tend to be shorter pieces (article length) that, of necessity, can only focus on one decision or at most a few decisions. There is little room in these studies for in-depth and multi-case investigation. These pieces are important as building blocks for understanding the process of ethnic group influence, but they cannot substitute (although they often are assumed to) for the sustained analysis that comes only with a longer-term study incorporating a variety of situational variables, case studies, and research sources—in short, an extended, in-depth research agenda. To use the example of the Jewish community, very few studies actually compare Jewish lobby activity over time and account for differences in success and failure, and indeed levels of success. (Taras and Goldberg [1989] is a notable exception, but this is an edited volume with different chapters focuses on different case studies. See also Goldberg [1990].)

Some Theoretical Considerations

Redressing these theoretical and empirical problems through its own sustained analysis is beyond the scope of this chapter. However, it is useful to consider a theoretical framework that could go some way toward tackling the conceptual problems listed above. This section will draw on political science theories that examine domestic politics literature and international relations literature that highlight the power of non-materialist forms of influence and power (referred to as constructivism). These theories will help provide a more effective explanatory structure to investigate the impact of Canadian ethnic groups on foreign policy.

All governments in all countries are subject to pressure from domestic interests; even authoritarian states must respond to supporting elite groups, whether ethnic, tribal, religious, or economic. In order to understand this process, though, one must understand how much pressure can be exerted, when it succeeds and why, and when it fails and why. This chapter is concerned with domestic political actors—that is, the organized Jewish and Arab communities. These are groups that have constituted themselves with a physical location, budget, and professional staff; they are perceived by most of their communities and by Canadian policy makers as, to a greater or lesser extent, representative of their respective communities, and, indeed, they promote themselves as such. As active actors in the domestic political process, they matter for determining foreign policy.

Andrew Moravcsik (1997) provides the most rigorous theoretical statement on this. In essence, the argument is that government policies are not constructed in a vacuum; they are made by individuals and groups that compete in the political arena for positions of decision-making power. Once they achieve this power, they use their positions in government to translate their personal preferences and objectives into state policy (see also Berman 1998; Checkel 1997; Kingdon 1984).

In a democracy, however, these individuals and groups must remain responsive to the electorate. If they do not respond to their constituencies' demands and interests, they risk losing power at the next election (Bueno de Mesquita et al. 2003; Siverson 1998). Thus domestic activists have some room to operate and try to influence policy makers, if they can mobilize and present them with policy options. How much room is actually available is open to debate. Within the Canadian context, Denis Stairs (1970–71) and Kim Richard Nossal (1997, 129) have argued that while societal actors can force their concerns onto the foreign policy agenda and even set parameters on the range of policy options under consideration, they cannot dictate either the specific policy or its implementation. In contrast, John Kirton (2007) suggests that societal determinants will in fact influence specific policies and how they are formulated.

This question of whether domestic groups are able to influence foreign policy is not as important to understand as how they do. It is not enough to assert that groups compete for influence. As discussed above, one must understand the conditions under which they are effective in achieving their objectives. But one must also understand the process by which their preferences become policy. Here it is helpful to draw on constructivism, a conceptual-methodological approach now widely used in foreign policy analysis (for the most definitive statements on this approach, see Wendt 1999, 1992).

The study of state behaviour has been dominated by what are referred to as rationalist-materialist frameworks (Keohane 1988). These approaches assume that foreign policy is conditioned by national interests that are objectively derived from a state's interactions with other states at the level of the global system, rather than through the activities of its society. In this context, state behaviour is predicated on material considerations prevalent in international politics: the search for physical security or prosperity with respect to other states. There is little room in such analyses for any examination of the state itself and its domestic components.

But it should be obvious that a state's foreign policy is not always driven by external material motivations.[7] Moreover, not all states behave the same way under similar conditions, or maintain the same foreign policy over time. The starting point of constructivism is that material factors alone do not determine a state's actions, but rather how those factors are interpreted. In Alexander Wendt's (1992, 396–97) words, "people act toward objects, including other actors, on the basis of the meanings that the objects have for them. States act differently toward enemies than they do toward friends because enemies are threatening and friends are not" (see also Checkel 1998, 326; Wendt 1999, 24). Wendt's example is particularly cogent: during the Cold War, British nuclear missiles had a different significance for the U.S. than did Soviet missiles—the former were not perceived as threatening, while the latter were (Wendt 1992, 397; see also Jepperson, Wendt, and Katzenstein 1996, 34). It is not the objective capabilities that enemies have that make them enemies, but rather the nature of the relationship.

Thus social interactions are key to understanding how states act in the international system. Ideational factors (norms, ideas, culture, and identity) provide the parameters within which states conduct their foreign policies. The elastic nature of state interests leaves room for domestic actors to insert their own identities into the contours of foreign policy.[8] Most analyses using this methodology have focused on societal-wide cultural ideas or identities (see Katzenstein 1996). It must therefore be combined with a domestic politics approach. The confluence of these two insights is that Canadian identity becomes a battleground for competing narratives and interpretations of Canadian interests by domestic political actors, who seek to establish their ideas as the determining contours of Canadian foreign policy.

State behaviour is thus understood as being constantly constructed and reconstructed through the competition among groups and their differing interpretations of interests and identities, and in particular how to define interests and identity. Foreign policy, according to this constructivist model, is a dynamic process that gives greater weight to the contest of domestic actors. Foreign policy becomes a product of these groups' capacity to present their own preferences as the norm and render their interests as consistent with Canada's own national interests and values. This process of group contestation plays a significant role in determining the order of priorities in the policy process through which decisions are made about particular issues. The prioritization of certain issues over others is equivalent to the prioritization of certain identities over others and thus a designation of the range of policy options. In a multicultural society such as Canada, this competition for influence becomes a critical area of study.

This argument should not be taken too far. It should be obvious that a state's foreign policy is based on a number of factors, any one of which could carry greater weight than the others under specific developments and conditions. But, as a general point, identity is a battleground. Other factors often come into play: domestic groups do not operate in an empty field, and there are other players to compete with. As noted above, situational variables are always relevant. However, in trying to determine when, how, and how much influence an ethnic group has on policy making, the process that takes place as a result of the political competition among ethnic groups for the capacity to shape foreign policy is highly relevant, and should be the starting point for sustained analysis of ethnic groups in Canada, their lobbying efforts, and their consequent influence or lack of influence.

Advocacy by Organized Jewish and Arab Communities in Canada

Studies on the impact of ethnic groups in Canada on foreign policy making tend to focus on the substantial or dominant (or, in some views, overriding) influence of the Jewish community. This is natural, given that Jewish groups have for a long time been very attentive to Canadian policy toward the Middle East on issues related to Israel, and have proven quite willing to mobilize on such points. And it is true that Jewish groups have had more success in achieving their objectives than Arab groups have had; there is a real imbalance in the capabilities of these two communities when it comes to advocacy and influence in the policy process. But as already noted, there are empirical problems and incomplete evidence in these studies. Additionally, much of the literature, not including that published by advocacy groups themselves, is stale-dated (a situation that itself merits examination). This section seeks to provide some indication why extant studies are problematic from an empirical standpoint.

In the Middle East, Israel and Arab states have propagated dichotomous narratives and images of their conflict that underline their beliefs and their policies. The main contemporary points of differences regard the appropriate boundaries of Israel and a future Palestinian state, the disposition of Palestinian refugees, Israeli settlements in the occupied territories, the nature of security for people on both sides, and which party is responsible for preventing successful efforts at peace negotiations. These narratives are also utilized and promoted by the Jewish and Arab communities abroad, including in Canada, where they seek to shape Canadian identity and thus shape interests along lines favourable to their narrative.

The Arab community, for instance, has emphasized that Canadian identity is about law, a rule-based system, and the promotion of adherence to international legal structures and organizations. The policy corollary is that Canada should press Israel to abide by United Nations resolutions, such as Security Council (UNSC) resolutions 242 and 338, which for the most part call on Israel to withdraw from all or most of the West Bank and Gaza (see, e.g., National Council on Canada-Arab Relations 2006, 2004). This includes, for example, the argument that Canada should support the International Court of Justice's ruling against the Israeli construction of the separation barrier in parts of the occupied territory in the West Bank. The Jewish community, on the other hand, has emphasized that Canadian identity is based on its liberal democratic tradition. The policy corollary here is support for a fellow democracy (Israel) in the face of efforts to undermine its legitimacy by authoritarian Arab states and hostile entities (such as Hamas), both through international organizations and outside of them (see, e.g., Canada-Israel Committee 2006).

Many Canadians would likely subscribe to parts of both narratives and would not consider themselves partisan in doing so. Being pro-democracy does not necessarily mean being pro-Israel nor does being pro–international law necessitate being pro-Palestinian. But the example is representative of the domestic identity battles within Canada and their impact on Canadian foreign policy. While these identities, as part of Canadian identity, do not compete with each other, the manner in which they are emphasized and promoted by domestic communities does. This is where the struggle over influence comes in. As a constructivist theoretical model would underline, because these communities have different and opposing ideas about Canadian identity, they have different ideas about what constitute Canadian interests in the Middle East. Although both might argue for the same general or vague ideals—peace, democracy, international law—their understanding of how these ideas fit with specific national interests varies. Given the connection and interplay between Canadian values and interests in the region and their utilization by domestic groups, it is important to explore, in any study on this topic, who these groups are, what they believe, and what they advocate for.

Both communities have several organizations that represent them at an official level. Some of these concentrate chiefly on domestic issues in Canada, but all of them make statements on and offer suggestions about how their constituencies should react to Canadian policy in the international arena. At issue here are the organizations that, even though they may deal with domestic matters as well, focus primarily on Canadian policy toward the Middle East. In the Jewish community this includes the Canadian Council for Israel and Jewish Advocacy (CIJA), the Canada-Israel Committee (CIC), and the Canadian Jewish Political Affairs Committee (CJPAC).[9] Although all three organizations do focus on relations with Israel, they also deal more broadly with Canadian policy toward the Middle East insofar as it affects Canada's policy with regard to Israel, the Arab-Israeli conflict, and the Israeli-Palestinian conflict (CJPAC's primary purpose is to mobilize the Jewish community for political activity on issues of concern to the community).

The Arab community is represented mainly by the Canadian Arab Federation (CAF) and the National Council on Canada-Arab Relations (NCCAR).[10] Both organizations deal extensively with domestic issues, but both also stress that such work is closely connected to foreign policy. There is, for Canadian Arabs, a nexus among foreign policy, domestic policy, and identity. One Canadian Arab official pointed out that specific foreign policies also have implications for domestic policy: Canada's active support of American efforts in fighting terrorism has led to judicial and legal consequences for Canadian Arabs (and Muslims), such as racial profiling by law enforcement and transportation authorities.[11]

There is no doubt that the Jewish community is stronger, in relative terms, than the Arab community when it comes to the ability to mobilize and get its message heard in Ottawa. This is not to say that Canadian Arab groups are insignificant, but just that their organizational strength is weaker than Canadian Jewish groups. What is often missing in analyses of these groups' lobbying efforts, though, is the understanding that the Jewish community's capabilities are the natural outgrowth of a long historical process and that it is not the "fault" of the Jewish community that it is well organized and successful, while the Arab community is far less so. This is the explicit or implied conclusion of many studies on this issue.

The Canadian Jewish community is older and more established than the Arab community, and this fact has had profound effects on their respective organizational capacities. Jews began immigrating to Canada in greater numbers earlier than Arabs did. They had compelling reasons to relocate to Canada and build a new institutional life here, including the lack of their own country and widespread discrimination and persecution—and sometimes violence—in their countries of residence throughout Europe. Although Jews had been immigrating into Canada since the 18th century, the community's structure was really founded at the end of the 19th century and the beginning of the 20th century, when mass migration of Jews from Eastern Europe began (Taras and Weinfeld 1990, 667). In contrast, Arab immigration to Canada became heavier only after World War Two, and particularly beginning in the 1960s (Abu-Laban 1988, 104–05), but even then in smaller numbers. By the early 1990s, a second wave of Arab immigrants, many fleeing regional conflicts and repressive regimes, began arriving into Canada. The 2001 census estimated that there were approximately 200,000 Arabs living in Canada and 348,605 Jews (Statistics Canada 2001).[12]

The difference in age and size of the communities has had an important effect on their lobbying abilities: because Jews have had a longer period of time to acclimatize to the Canadian political system, they have been able to establish more sophisticated institutional structures to represent them at the political level and generate more resources to support them.[13] They have become much more comfortable engaging actively in the political process (Tulchinsky 1998), which has translated into greater influence in policy making.

For their part, many Arabs are either reluctant to become involved in politics or have not had a civic education in politics in their home countries. They are less experienced, particularly since many of their countries of origins are repressive autocracies with little or no capacity for societal involvement in policy making. Their status as newer immigrants has led many in the community to fear that actively promoting their causes will backfire on them and undermine their status in Canada.[14] This fear has been heightened post–September 11, particularly as many Canadian Arabs fear that their status as Canadians may not be respected by security and law enforcement officials. The experience of Maher Arar and the widened powers for issuing Canadian security certificates have had considerable effects on the community's self-censorship.

The age of the Jewish community is also important for another reason. The Jewish community has had more time to establish itself within Canada's economic system as well, and significant numbers of Jews have succeeded in this area. This has provided them with access to non-Jewish political leaders, giving those with an inclination to do so the wherewithal to lobby on behalf of Israel. Samuel Bronfman, heir to the Seagram's business empire and former president of the Canadian Jewish Congress, is often cited as an example (see Brown 2001; Goldberg 2001; Waller 2000).

In addition to its own efforts, the Jewish community has benefited from the sympathy many Canadian politicians have had for persecuted Jews and Israel, particularly in the years after World War Two. Lester Pearson, for example, who contributed much to the United Nations Partition Plan (and thus to legitimizing Jewish aspirations for their own state in Palestine) seems to have been heavily influenced by his "Sunday school" visions of the Holy Land and the role of the Jews in it (Bercuson 1985, 233). After the Holocaust, Canadian public compassion for Jewish survivors also played an important role in setting up a sympathetic public opinion, providing Canadian politicians more leeway to support the immigration of Jews into Palestine (Tulchinsky 1998, 239, 244, 270–74).

Many non-Jewish clergy supported the Zionist cause, as well as the establishment of some kind of Jewish homeland in Palestine for the survivors of the Holocaust. This also helped generate support among Canadian public opinion and the media (Bercuson 1985, ch. 1; Brown 2001, 121–29). The Arabs, given that they were not prominent in the bible and had not suffered genocide themselves, did not garner the same empathy for their communities' causes. More recently, Christian evangelical groups sympathetic to Zionist objectives have conducted their own pro-Israel advocacy (see, e.g., Arnold 2007). Public opinion does not normally determine foreign policy but it does have "a guiding or limiting influence on policy. Support permits or facilitates, while opposition limits or deters, policymakers' discretion" (Sobel 2001, 10). Thus Canadians' historical sympathy for persecuted Jews, and then by extension for Israel, was an important factor facilitating Jewish groups' early advocacy efforts.

Finally, notwithstanding the existence of small groups outside of the majority mainstream, most Canadian Jews have a strong affinity for and identification with Israel—particularly since the 1967 Arab-Israeli War. This applies as well to Israeli policy vis-à-vis the Arab-Israeli conflict (despite some private misgivings about some policies), which has translated into very strong support for Israel (Taras and Weinfeld 1990, 662; Waller 2000). This in turn has provided organized Jewish groups with an institutional, resource, and personnel base on which to draw in order to engage in lobbying, which is unmatched in the Arab community.

The Arab community also has a unifying cause and concern: Palestinian hardship under Israeli occupation of and military incursions into the West Bank and Gaza and as refugees in the wider Middle East. The historical narrative of Palestinians is reflected in al-Naqba (the Catastrophe—symbolizing an end to Arab hope for self-governance in the area of the former Mandate of Palestine and the resultant displacement of Palestinians). The existence of millions of Palestinian refugees and their aspirations for their own state is also a rallying call for many in the Arab community. Canadian Arabs have generally supported the Arab states' positions on the Arab-Israel conflict (Abu-Laban 1988, 108, 122–23), which have—at least until the mid 1990s, when they evolved toward acceptance of a two-state solution—been at odds with the Israeli and the Canadian Jewish position. Nevertheless, the Canadian Arab community is far from monolithic and is more divided along national, regional, and religious lines, which has actively prevented it from presenting a united front to policy makers.

In addition, Canadian Arab groups are hampered by their own political objectives and organizational deficiencies. Conversations with former government officials reveal the problems inherent in the former. For example, one civil servant who served in a variety of governmental offices noted that Jewish lobbyists would meet with him regularly to present the community's ideas on certain issues. In contrast, though, "almost never" did any representative from the Arab community do the same.[15]

Another former government official has noted that Arab groups continue to press Canada to adopt unrealistic policies toward Israel. In one meeting with Canadian Arab representatives, this official made this very point. Yet the response from the Arab spokesperson was that Canada should cut air links to Israel.[16] This was certainly not an option Ottawa was going to entertain, and so undermined the case the Arab lobbyist was trying to make to promote his community's identity and interests.

Since the Oslo Accords, international discourse about the conflict has been underlined by the idea that two states—an Israeli state that retains its Jewish character and a Palestinian state—is the only reasonable, effective, and feasible solution. Moderate Israelis and Palestinians have also adopted this proposal. The Canadian Jewish groups that deal with foreign affairs emphasize that they actively support this proposition.[17] Yet one Canadian Arab group representative, when asked about his organization's position on the right of return, supported the two-state solution, but then argued that any resolution of the conflict must also include the right of Palestinian refugees to return to their homes in Israel from where they were dispossessed during the 1947–49 Arab-Israeli War.[18] Given that some estimates of the number of Palestinian refugees reach six million or more, this would mean the end of Israel as a Jewish state. Arab Canadians could argue that some Canadian Jewish support for Jewish settlements in the West Bank pose a similar problem for Canadian policy makers, although this kind of backing is apparently no longer promoted at the official political level by the Canadian Jewish groups discussed in this chapter.[19]

Implications

Canadian foreign policy and identity are inextricably linked, as they are for all countries in the international system. The construction and maintenance of a particular identity, forged through domestic political interactions, profoundly affect a state's foreign policy. In the case of Canada, its identity as a country dedicated to the resolution of conflict through peaceful negotiation draws in large part on its perceived ability to act as a balanced, fair-minded interlocutor respected for its reputation by parties involved in a conflict. Nowhere is this clearer than in Canadian foreign policy in relation to the Arab-Israeli conflict. The complexities of the conflict combined with the emotional pulls on Arab and Jewish domestic elements within Canada render problematic the capacity for Canada to maintain its policy and identity as an impartial, fair-minded, and principled party. Preserving this identity is made more difficult when it comes to making concrete foreign policy decisions that touch upon the interests of these domestic groups, causing them to mobilize in an effort to shape Canadian foreign policy.

This chapter has raised questions about the current understanding of the process of ethnic group lobbying on foreign policy toward the Middle East. There are several theoretical and empirical problems inherent in existing studies on this topic. It has sought to provide some ideas and suggestions on how to improve explanations of this process, including more rigorous theoretical frameworks and in-depth, sustained empirical analysis. This section now turns to highlighting some preliminary implications from the exploration of this issue.

In order to formulate policy toward the Middle East, decision makers must take into account several factors. First, Canadian ethnic groups tend to engage in quieter, advocacy-type activities rather than the hard-hitting lobbying associated with interest groups in the United States (although this is not to say that Canadian groups cannot or have not done the same on occasion). This is partly the result of there being fewer access points in Canada for groups to influence officials, especially elected officials, on their policy decisions and the public service on its advice to government, the nature of the political system itself (greater party discipline, more power in Cabinet), and the fact that Canada has fewer direct interests in the Middle East and therefore the stakes seem less (see Taras and Weinfeld 1990, 674). This gives Canadian decision makers some insulation from lobbying, although not much. But it may be enough to affect the manner in which decisions are made.

Second, greater effort to understand domestic communities' identities and how they might shape Canadian identity is needed. Usually these identities, particularly of those groups that have mobilized on behalf of issues related to their kin states, are deeply held. Given that these groups are part of the Canadian cultural mosaic, help form and are formed by a broad set of Canadian values, and have become part of the landscape of citizenship, their views and ideas must be taken into account in the policy-making process (and usually they are). At the same time, they need to be heard but not necessarily heeded, because policy makers have an obligation to consider all the factors.

Finally, one ought not to ascribe more power to ethnic groups than they have in reality. There is no doubt that Jewish groups can have considerable influence on certain occasions and on important issues. Moreover, their long involvement in the Canadian political system, combined with a series of developments and external conditions favourable to their interests, have created an environment in which these interests are often taken into account even without active efforts on the community's part. But it should also be clear that Jewish groups' influence stems in part from the confluence of their activities with other factors that facilitate greater awareness of and resonance with their particular narrative of the Arab-Israeli conflict. In order to know where the limits of ethnic group influence lie, it is important to understand the conditions under which they matter more or less.

Notes

1 The authors would like to thank all the officials from the Jewish and Arab communities and former government officials who agreed to be interviewed for this chapter. Their comments are incorporated anonymously into the analysis.

2 The term "ethnic groups" is commonly used in the literature on this subject.

3 Interview by authors with former government official.

4 This is not to say that no effective studies exist. As an edited volume, Taras and Goldberg (1989) is probably the best book on the subject of ethnic groups and the Middle East, although there is no overarching theoretical framework. Goldberg (1990) is also a good source on situational variables. See also Noble (1985).

5 Interview by authors.

6 An example often cited is the Cuban-American community in the United States and policy on Cuba.

7 Some external interests are clearly important to all states, regardless of their specific domestic conditions—such as survival and minimal physical well-being (Jepperson, Wendt, and Katzenstein 1996, 60).

8 For good applications of constructivism to foreign policy, see Berger (1998), Duffield (1999), Hopf (2002), Katzenstein (1996), Ruggie (1997), and Telhami and Barnett (2002).

9 The Canadian Jewish Congress and B'nai Brith Canada, for example, are not mandated by the Jewish community to deal with foreign affairs, but they are attentive to Israel's concerns.

10 There are also Muslim organizations, such as the Canadian Islamic Congress, that share similar political goals with these Arab groups (e.g., supporting the Arab position on the Arab-Israeli conflict). See the Canadian Islamic Congress's web-

site at www.canadianislamiccongress.com. In addition, it has been widely recognized that the Palestine issue resonates in the broader Arab and Muslim worlds, both in the Middle East and beyond. See Standing Committee on Foreign Affairs and International Trade ([SCFAIT] 2004, 106).

11 Interview by authors.

12 It is difficult to get a precise number of the Arab population in Canada. Respondents to the 2001 census were able to use multiple listings: for example, one could identify as both an Arab and an Egyptian. In addition, small numbers of those who identified as "Lebanese," "Egyptian," "Iraqi," and so on could well have come from a non-Arab ethnic group from these countries.

13 However, some officials from Jewish groups have also commented on a lack of resources that has hampered some of their advocacy efforts.

14 Interview by authors with Canadian Arab leader.

15 Interview by authors.

16 Interview by authors.

17 Interview by authors.

18 Interview by authors.

19 Interview by authors with former government official.

References

Abu-Laban, Baha. 1988. "Arab-Canadians and the Arab-Israeli Conflict." *Arab Studies Quarterly* 10(1): 104–26.

Ansolabehere, Stephen, James M. Snyder Jr., and Micky Tripathi. 2002. "Are PAC Contributions and Lobbying Linked? New Evidence from the 1995 Lobby Disclosure Act." *Business and Politics* 4(2): 131–55.

Arnold, Janice. 2007. "Christians Must Stand with Israel, Evangelical Leader Says." *Canadian Jewish News,* July 12. On-line version. www.cjnews.com (July 16, 2007).

Bercuson, David. 1985. *Canada and the Birth of Israel: A Study in Canadian Foreign Policy.* Toronto: University of Toronto Press.

Berger, Thomas U. 1998. *Cultures of Antimilitarism: National Security in Germany and Japan.* Baltimore: Johns Hopkins University Press.

Berman, Sheri. 1998. *The Social Democratic Moment: Ideas and Politics in the Making of Interwar Europe.* Cambridge, MA: Harvard University Press.

Brown, Michael. 2001. "Zionism in the Pre-Statehood Years: The Canadian Response." In *From Immigration to Integration: The Canadian Jewish Experience: A Millennium Edition,* ed. Ruth Klein and Frank Dimant, 135–46. Toronto: Institute for International Affairs, B'nai Brith Canada.

Brunell, Thomas L. 2005. "The Relationship between Political Parties and Interest Groups: Explaining Patterns of PAC Contributions to Candidates for Congress." *Political Research Quarterly* 58(4): 681–88.

Bueno de Mesquita, Bruce, Alastair Smith, Randolph M. Siverson, and James D. Morrow. 2003. *The Logic of Political Survival.* Cambridge MA: MIT Press.

Canada-Israel Committee. 2006. "The Israeli and Canadian Political Systems: A Critical Comparison." www.cicweb.ca/relations/politics.cfm (August 2007).

Checkel, Jeffrey T. 1998. "The Constructivist Turn in International Relations Theory." *World Politics* 50(2): 324–48.

———. 1997. *Ideas and International Political Change: Soviet/Russian Behavior and the End of the Cold War.* New Haven: Yale University Press.

Dewitt, David, and John Kirton. 1983. *Canada as a Principal Power: A Study in Foreign Policy and International Relations.* Toronto: John Wiley & Sons.

Dietrich, John W. 1999. "Interest Groups and Foreign Policy: Clinton and the China MFN Debates." *Presidential Studies Quarterly* 29(2): 280–96.

Duffield, John S. 1999. "Political Culture and State Behavior: Why Germany Confounds Neorealism." *International Organization* 53(4): 765–803.

Goldberg, David H. 1989. "Keeping Score: From the Yom Kippur War to the Palestinian Uprising." In *The Domestic Battleground: Canada and the Arab-Israeli Conflict*, ed. David Taras and David H. Goldberg, 102–22. Kingston: McGill-Queen's University Press.

———. 1990. *Foreign Policy and Ethnic Interest Groups: American and Canadian Jews Lobby for Israel.* New York: Greenwood Press.

———. 2001. "The Post-Statehood Relationship: A Growing Friendship." In *From Immigration to Integration: The Canadian Jewish Experience: A Millennium Edition,* ed. Ruth Klein and Frank Dimant, 135–46. Toronto: Institute for International Affairs, B'nai Brith Canada.

Haney, Patrick J., and Walt Vanderbush. 1999. "The Role of Ethnic Interest Groups in U.S. Foreign Policy: The Case of the Cuban American National Foundation." *International Studies Quarterly* 43(2): 341–61.

Hermann, Charles F. 1978. "Foreign Policy Behavior: That Which Is to Be Explained." In *Why Nations Act: Theoretical Perspectives for Comparative Foreign Policy Studies*, ed. Maurice A. East, Stephen A. Salmore, and Charles F. Hermann, 25–47. Beverly Hills: Sage.

Hopf, Ted. 2002. *Social Construction of International Politics: Identities and Foreign Policies, Moscow, 1955 and 1999.* Ithaca: Cornell University Press.

Jepperson, Ronald L., Alexander Wendt, and Peter J. Katzenstein. 1996. "Norms, Identity, and Culture in National Security." In *The Culture of National Security: Norms and Identity in World Politics*, ed. Peter J. Katzenstein, 33–75. New York: Columbia University Press, 1996.

Katzenstein, Peter J., ed. 1996. *The Culture of National Security: Norms and Identity in World Politics.* New York: Columbia University Press.

Keohane, Robert O. 1988. "International Institutions: Two Approaches." *International Studies Quarterly* 32(4): 379–96.

Kingdon, John W. 1984. *Agendas, Alternatives, and Public Policies.* Boston: Little, Brown.

Kirton, John. 2007. *Canadian Foreign Policy in a Changing World*. Scarborough: Thomson Nelson.

Kirton, John, and Peyton Lyon. 1989. "Perceptions of the Middle East in the Department of External Affairs and Mulroney's Policy 1984–1988." In *The Domestic Battleground: Canada and the Arab-Israeli Conflict*, ed. David Taras and David H. Goldberg, 186–206. Kingston: McGill-Queen's University Press.

Lyon, Peyton. 1992. "The Canada Israel Committee and Canada's Middle East Policy." *Journal of Canadian Studies* 27(4): 5–24.

Mearsheimer, John J., and Stephen M. Walt. 2006. "The Israel Lobby and U.S. Foreign Policy." Working Paper No. RWP06–011. Harvard University. ksgnotes1.harvard.edu/Research/wpaper.nsf/rwp/RWP06–011/$File/rwp_06_0 11_walt.pdf (August 2007).

Moore, Will H. 2002. "Ethnic Minorities and Foreign Policy." *SAIS Review* 22(2): 77–91.

Moravcsik, Andrew. 1997. "Taking Preferences Seriously: A Liberal Theory of International Politics." *International Organization* 51(4): 513–53.

National Council on Canada-Arab Relations. 2004. "NCCAR Commends Foreign Minister Pettigrew for Voicing His Concern over Continuing Settlement Growth in the West Bank." August 25. www.nccar.ca/media_centre/08_25 _04.html (August 2007).

———. 2006. "PM's Statement on Middle East Reckless." December 21. www.nccar.ca/media_centre/12_21_06.html (August 2007).

Noble, Paul C. 1985. "From Refugees to a People? Canada and the Palestinians 1967–1973." In *Canada and the Arab World*, ed. Tareq Ismael, 85–106. Edmonton: University of Alberta Press.

Nossal, Kim Richard. 1997. *The Politics of Canadian Foreign Policy*, 3rd ed. Scarborough: Prentice Hall.

Ruggie, John Gerard. 1997. "The Past as Prologue? Interests, Identity, and American Foreign Policy." *International Security* 21(4): 89–125.

Saideman, Stephen M. 2002. "The Power of the Small: The Impact of Ethnic Minorities on Foreign Policy." *SAIS Review* 22(2): 93–105.

Shain, Yossi. 2002. "The Role of Diasporas in Conflict Perpetuation or Resolution." *SAIS Review* 22(2): 115–44.

Siverson, Randolph M. 1998. *Strategic Politicians, Institutions, and Foreign Policy*. Ann Arbor: University of Michigan Press.

Smith, Tony. 2000. *Foreign Attachments: The Power of Ethnic Groups in the Making of American Foreign Policy*. Cambridge, MA: Harvard University Press.

Sobel, Richard. 2001. *The Impact of Public Opinion on U.S. Foreign Policy since Vietnam: Constraining the Colossus*. Oxford: Oxford University Press.

Stairs, Denis. 1970–71. "Public and Policymakers: The Domestic Environment of Canada's Foreign Policy Community." *International Journal* 26(1): 221–48.

Standing Committee on Foreign Affairs and International Trade. 2004. "Report of
    the Standing Committee on Foreign Affairs and International Trade: Explor-
    ing Canada's Relations with the Countries of the Muslim World."
    cmte.parl.gc.ca/Content/HOC/committee/381/faae/reports/rp1423958/
    FAAE_Rpt01/FAAE_Rpt01-e.pdf (August 2007).

Statistics Canada. 2001. "Selected Ethnic Origins for Canada, Provinces and Ter-
    ritories." www12.statcan.ca/english/census01/products/highlight/ETO/
    Table1.cfm?Lang=E&T=501&GV=1&GID=0 (August 2007).

Taras, David. 1984. "Parliament and Middle East Interest Groups: The Politics of
    Canadian and American Diplomacy during the October 1973 War." *Mid-
    dle East Focus* 6(5): 17–24.

Taras, David, and David H. Goldberg, eds. 1989. *The Domestic Battleground:
    Canada and the Arab-Israeli Conflict.* Kingston: McGill-Queen's Univer-
    sity Press.

Taras, David, and Morton Weinfeld. 1990. "Continuity and Criticism: North Amer-
    ican Jews and Israel." *International Journal* 45(3): 661–84.

Telhami, Shibley, and Michael Barnett, eds. 2002. *Identity and Foreign Policy in
    the Middle East.* Ithaca: Cornell University Press.

Tulchinsky, Gerald. 1998. *Branching Out: The Transformation of the Canadian
    Jewish Community.* Toronto: Stoddart.

Waller, Harold M. 2000. "The Impact of the Six-Day War on the Organizational
    Life of Canadian Jewry." In *The Six-Day War and World Jewry*, ed. Eli
    Lederhendler, 81–97. Bethesda: University Press of Maryland.

Wendt, Alexander E. 1992. "Anarchy Is What States Make of It: The Social Con-
    struction of Power Politics." *International Organization* 46(2): 391–425.

———. 1999. *Social Theory of International Politics.* Cambridge, UK: Cam-
    bridge University Press.

Inland Refugee Claimants from the Middle East and Humanitarianism in Canadian Foreign Policy[1]

The United Nations reports that between 2005 and 2050 an estimated 98 million migrants will leave their home countries, and nearly a tenth of the flow will come to Canada—approximately 200,000 people annually, of which close to 14 percent will be refugees. Whether Canada is prepared to address the needs of asylum seekers, particularly those coming from the Middle East and seeking to be admitted as refugees according to the UN Convention Relating to the Status of Refugees, is a question that requires a clear address. This chapter suggests that although Canada has a strong track record in resettling refugees produced by crises in the Middle East, there is a weak relationship between parts of the Canadian refugee regime and the humanitarian objectives frequently articulated in Canadian foreign policy.[2] Specifically, this chapter makes a case for improving the system for determining the status of inland refugees—those who claim refugee status after entering the country—by using the information provided by refugee advocacy organizations and landmark appeal cases.

Refugee organizations have raised a number of specific problems with respect to Canadian procedures of inland refugee determination.[3] These concerns, which are already well known to Citizenship and Immigration Canada (CIC), are discussed here in terms of both the internal and international dimensions of Canadian policy, specifically with reference to Canada's commitment to humanitarian values and human security. In addressing the causes of Middle Eastern refugee flows, such as authoritarian regimes and widespread political violence, the chapter claims that the systematic observation of problem areas in inland refugee determination and appeal processes could complement current Canadian practices, which rely on official monitoring processes, international organizations such as the United Nations High Commission for

Refugees (UNHCR), and international human rights non-governmental organizations (NGOS) such as the Amnesty International. Overseas refugee problems have traditionally guided the institution of largely successful and wide-ranging resettlement programs. In contrast, a close examination of inland refugee acceptance and problem areas within this field reveals the workings of the refugee regime in Canada with its strengths and failings. It could also provide further insights into Middle Eastern societies. The independent status of the Immigration and Refugee Board (IRB), a major positive feature of the current system, does not preclude the development of processes and structures sensitive to judicial and political correctives. In other words, there is room for improvement and remedying of emergent problems.

Since Canada is an advocate of democracy and respect for human rights in the Middle East, it makes sense for the IRB to seek information from other government departments on the performance of Middle Eastern governments on this score and, in turn, for its decisions to be utilized as a source of information in other parts of the state as well as by the government. The judicial appeal process already reveals the dynamism involved in Canadian understanding of the plight of Middle Eastern refugees who arrive of their own accord. Inland refugee claimants come to Canada's doors as a result of ongoing as well as acute crises and thus the criteria for the evaluation of their applications are complex. However, there are ways to address the criticisms raised by asylum seekers and refugees concerning Canada's inland refugee determination process while preserving its strong foundations.[4] The chapter concludes that the sustained engagement of relevant offices and government departments with the Canadian public in these matters would foster an environment of consultation, open debate, and better results.

Canada's Refugee Policy

From a foreign policy point of view, a key concern about the Canadian immigration and refugee regime pertains to its priorities. If these priorities and their application comply with humanitarian values and the doctrine of human security, a strong reciprocal relationship can be confirmed. If, on the other hand, there are problem areas whereby the humanitarian mandate of the refugee regime is unduly overshadowed by other concerns or failings of the bureaucracy, it would be apt to conclude that the message Canada delivers about humanitarianism in the national and international arenas is a mixed one. In this section, the underlying principles of the Canadian refugee regime will be discussed in order to discern the application of humanitarian principles in Canadian bureaucracy in the specific area of inland refugee determination.

The current Canadian immigration and refugee regime is informed by the 2002 *Immigration and Refugee Protection Act* (IRPA), which is implemented in combination with the decisions of the Supreme Court of Canada, federal courts, trial courts, and the IRB.[5] This immigration and refugee system has three main components. The social component refers to state facilitation of family reunification and permission for members of the nuclear family unit to immigrate with principal applicants. The economic component shapes the body of regulations pertaining to immigrant selection, including the acceptance of skilled workers and business immigrants. The humanitarian component relates to Canada's international obligations in the area of humanitarian and international public law. Humanitarian principles embedded in related international conventions guide Canada's actions in deciding claims for protection made by people arriving spontaneously in the country, as well as for the arrangement of government-assisted and privately sponsored refugee settlement and protection programs abroad. These provisions are considered proof of Canada's commitment to international efforts to provide assistance to those in need of humanitarian aid, resettlement, and safe havens. They are also mechanisms through which Canada provides direct protection for individuals with a well-founded fear of persecution based on race, religion, nationality, political opinion, or membership in a particular social group, as well as those at risk of torture or cruel and unusual treatment or punishment. This chapter addresses this last, humanitarian component of the Canadian immigration and refugee regime with a focus on inland refugee applicants arriving from the Middle East.

Until 1976, the admission of inland refugee claimants was mainly shaped by ad hoc measures. The 1976 *Immigration Act* embedded the UN refugee convention definition in Canadian legislation and created a legal framework for the determination of the cases of people claiming refugee status at the border or on Canadian territory. In 1987, with the introduction of Bill C-55, Canada's refugee regime underwent a significant series of reforms. With the creation of the IRB in 1989, this process reached its nadir in terms of perfecting the regime's regularization. The procedures outlined for the IRB are distinct from the practices Canada utilizes for its overseas identification and selection of refugees for resettlement purposes. However, both streams of refugee admission adhere to the basic humanitarian principles defined in international.

Inland refugee determination processes have important repercussions for internal and international political debates over the performance of successive Canadian governments and Canadian bureaucracy in meeting Canada's obligation to protect victims of humanitarian crises and systemic human rights abuses. In many ways, public opinion regards inland refugee acceptance as a test for Canadian humanitarian practice on home turf. This is despite the fact that decisions regarding inland refugee claimants have been deliberately put into the hands of the independent body of the IRB.

The original Canadian form of refugee acceptance, dating back to the early 1950s, is resettlement. In this framework, refugees and people falling into other humanitarian categories are brought to Canada for permanent resettlement. The government of the day sets regional and situational targets for resettlement programs, which respond to regional crises and shifts in UNHCR's priorities. Political judgment, foreign policy considerations, and the principle of international burden sharing play a direct role in the setting of Canada's resettlement targets. Once set in motion, these programs operate out of the visa sections of Canadian embassies abroad. Selected refugees and displaced people are then settled through a variety of mechanisms including government assistance, private sponsorship, joint assistance, host families, and the women-at-risk program.

The government, the judiciary, and Parliament have a considerable impact on how appeals of rejected inland refugee claims are dealt with. Various government departments also have direct say in the setting of general guidelines concerning the safety and security of the Canadian public in cases for removing inland refugee claimants. Furthermore, as the history of the IRB and the changes made to asylum-related regulations and refugee law indicate, when the system cannot respond to cases that may fall outside the existing legal-bureaucratic framework, the negotiation for change often involves consultations with refugee groups and advocacy organizations. In summary, there has been a noteworthy component of political and advocacy interventions in the inland refugee determination stream of the Canadian refugee regime. Political judgment, policy measures, and international humanitarian principles all interact in shaping the Canadian refugee regime, as can be seen in the government's issuance of policy directives and overseeing of regulations as well as in judicial interventions and the overturning of decisions. This chapter suggests that regularized consultations and monitoring of problem areas also play and should continue to play a role in the updating of the system.

As a signatory to international agreements including the Convention Relating to the Status of Refugees, the International Covenant on Civil and Political Rights, and the Convention Against Torture and Other Cruel, Inhuman or Degrading Treatment or Punishment, Canada continuously reflects on its humanitarian commitments in shaping and maintaining its refugee policy. Canada embarked on a strong program of resettlement following World War Two and, since the 1980s, has significantly increased the expediency and evenhandedness of its acceptance process for inland refugees. And yet there are differing perceptions of the efficacy and fairness of Canada's refugee regime. Some suggest Canada is fair in its approach and argue that it strives to secure a balance between facilitating the movement of people in need and exercising effective border controls. In opposition, conservative voices insist that the current refugee regime poses a challenge to Canada's public and national security. Meanwhile, a growing body of scholars, legal practitioners, and advocacy organizations posit that, while striving to fulfill its international humanitarian commitments, Canada's primary priority has been to ensure the selection of the kinds of refugees whose absorption into Canada's economy and society would be easier (Aiken 2000). The argument that Canada is more concerned with the participation of asylum seekers in its economy and society rather than with saving lives and providing sanctuary is a recurrent one. It points to the dilemma that western liberal democracies face in terms of balancing the ideally unconditional requirements of humanitarianism and their socioeconomical viability. In the resettlement category, there are programs designed to assist refugees to adjust and re-establish their lives in Canada and to curb the possibility of creating an underclass. Meanwhile, how well a person will do after admission to Canada as a refugee does not enter the decision-making process at the IRB level. Overall, refugee integration is a public concern and guides much of the debate in Canadian politics on refugees under the banner of absorption capacity. Variant interpretations of the working principles of the Canadian refugee regime constitute a second area of political debate in which the bureaucratic process, policy measures, and humanitarian principles seem to coexist in tension. While bureaucrats argue that refugees are not selected based on Canada's absorption potential and they are helped to integrate afterward, scholars and the general public often hold different points of view about the selection process and about the success rate of refugee integration.

In addition to these two areas of political debate on the refugee regime, there are three clusters of problems identified by refugees, advocacy organizations, and legal scholars in the field of inland refugee determination. As already mentioned, conditions applied to inland stream of refugees who arrive spontaneously at Canadian borders emanate from international conventions. Problems pinpointed by stakeholders do not stem from the rules per se but from their specific interpretations by IRB judges. In addition, lengthy appeal processes, consequences of rejection such as deportation orders, and delays in the processing of permits and visas due to security clearance are among the issues that are raised in order to improve the system. Acknowledging the importance of this set of concerns, CIC added a section to its website in 2006 and noted that stakeholders who work directly with refugees have raised questions relating to five key areas of Canada's refugee programs. These are identified as "the Canada-U.S. Safe Third Country Agreement, the Refugee Appeal Division, the Private Sponsorship of Refugees Program, family reunification, and individuals who benefit from a stay of Temporary Suspension of Removals" (CIC 2006b). These concerns were long flagged by refugees, their legal representatives, and advocacy organizations.

The second set of concerns about the inland refugee stream is raised by immigration scholars. Once accepted to Canada based on an IRB decision, inland refugee claimants (now officially recognized as Convention refugees) are allowed to work with a permit, receive social assistance, attend elementary and secondary school, and obtain essential and emergency public health care. They are entitled to apply for permanent residence (landed status) in Canada and eventually for Canadian citizenship. Compared to those who never make it to this stage of recognition, they are protected from deportation to any country where they fear persecution. Until they have landed status (a process that can sometimes take years), successful refugee claimants cannot sponsor family members and often remain separated from a spouse and children for extended periods. They cannot get a bank loan, work in certain professions such as in education and health care, or travel across international borders. As they are not yet citizens, they cannot vote either.

In addition to those people whose lives are on temporary hold, there has also emerged a refugee claimant population whose applications were refused but who continue to remain in the country despite deportation orders. Since the 1990s, Canada is estimated to have accumulated half a million non-status people living and working in its midst.[6] Along with illegal immigrants, such "clandestine refugees" find work in the construction and hospitality industries and live on the edges of Canadian society.[7] This is a noted difference compared to the situation of refugees who arrive from abroad under the refugee settlement program and benefit from programs and mechanisms available to them. In this area, successful inland refugee claimants have been asking for help from the Canadian government. Failed refugee claimants who became non-status people, on the other hand, wait for periodic amnesties to legalize their existence.

The final problem area in inland refugee stream, this time revealed by Canadian human rights and refugee lawyers, concerns changing rules of for security clearance that inland refugee claimants must go through. IRPA contains a provision called the Pre-Removal Risk Assessment (PRRA), which permits an asylum seeker whose application has been turned down to apply for a review before being deported. In most cases, the risk assessment is broad, including the risk to life, cruel and unusual treatment, or punishment. If protection is granted, the concerned individual is allowed to apply for permanent residency. In specific cases, including those inadmissible to Canada because of concerns over security (such as individuals with links to organized or serious crimes and those who have violated human or international rights), the PRRA criteria are narrowed in accordance with Canada's acknowledgment of its post–World War II international obligations concerning war criminals and perpetrators of genocide. While it is possible to apply for consideration to stay in Canada on humanitarian and compassionate grounds, this process is expensive and rarely successful.[8] Those who fail at this stage or whose hearings have not been concluded often remain in limbo for years. As testimonies of refugee applicants and human rights lawyers indicate, some individuals in this category do not have proven links to organized or serious crimes. Contrary to common assumptions, they have not violated human or international rights and then slipped through the system either. On the contrary, advocates assert that many of the impending cases relate to whether the person whose claim to have suffered from persecution would fit into the Convention criteria and, if not, whether it is safe to return them back to their home country. In other words, the dilemma is what to do in situations where there is reasonable doubt of persecution either at the time of the person's application or upon his or her possible deportation, and the case is not strong enough to merit the entitlement of refugee status and the protection such status entails.

In the light of these problem areas identified by various stakeholders in the inland stream of the Canadian refugee regime, the remainder of this chapter presents three groups of Middle Eastern refugees and the public claims they and others made on their behalf. The aim of this exercise is to illustrate the point that there is room for improvement based on political dialogue, judicial reviews, and policy initiatives in the inland refugee determination process despite the quasi-judicial and independent nature of the IRB. Furthermore, the chapter makes the case that such re-evaluation practices are necessary for establishing the legitimacy of Canada's claim to have embraced humanitarian principles in its refugee regime at home (inland stream) and abroad (resettlement stream). Refugee claims and problem areas indicated by other stakeholders point out possible weak points in the system and indicate solutions. By paying attention to these, Canadian policy makers would benefit from valuable feedback about the home-based component of the system they have invested so much in. They would also gather additional information to help set future guidelines for action in the area of humanitarianism in the Middle East and elsewhere.

Middle Eastern Refugees in Canada

Canada has one of the highest per capita admission rates for immigration applications among western states. It has, on average, offered residency to about 200,000 immigrants and refugees per year over the past decade. In 2006, the UN report on migration and development ranked Canada seventh among 28 countries that in 2005 hosted 75 percent of all international migrants (United Nations General Assembly 2006). The majority of Canada's immigrants and refugees come from Asia, particularly China, India, and the Philippines. Sizeable numbers of immigrants arrive from the Middle East (see Table 11-1). Many refugees fleeing to Canada have also once called the Middle East their home (see Table 11-2); albeit not the largest groups of refugees, their numbers are increasing as war escalates and authoritarian rule is further entrenched throughout the region (see Table 11-3). There are roughly 750,000 Muslims living in Canada today, a significant increase from the 580,000 Muslims recorded

TABLE II–I

Permanent Canadian Residents from Africa and the Middle East

Country	1996	1997	1998	1999	2000	2001	2002	2003	2004	2005
					Number					
Iran	5,833	7,486	6,775	5,909	5,617	5,746	7,889	5,652	6,063	5,502
United Arab Emirates	2,289	2,812	1,826	1,755	3,084	4,523	4,446	3,321	4,359	4,052
Algeria	1,721	1,608	1,916	2,034	2,529	3,009	3,030	2,786	3,209	3,130
Lebanon	1,809	1,246	1,230	1,397	1,681	2,070	1,722	2,601	2,673	3,122
Morocco	836	1,040	1,187	1,768	2,557	3,951	4,057	3,243	3,471	2,692
Israel	2,546	2,108	1,917	2,427	2,601	2,479	2,605	2,366	2,857	2,549
Saudi Arabia	2,495	3,293	2,022	1,581	2,030	3,564	2,538	2,042	2,111	2,364
Egypt	2,418	2,031	1,320	1,416	1,737	1,915	1,634	1,929	2,051	2,061
Iraq	1,839	1,919	1,395	1,397	1,384	1,597	1,365	969	1,140	1,316
Kuwait	1,449	1,476	1,177	739	1,222	1,713	947	1,074	917	1,140
Top 10 source countries	23,956	26,042	21,339	21,487	25,173	31,060	30,920	26,925	29,758	28,887
Other countries	12,539	11,757	11,258	12,072	15,736	17,179	15,420	16,755	19,773	20,390
Total	36,495	37,799	32,597	33,559	40,909	48,239	46,340	43,680	49,531	49,277

Source: Citizenship and Immigration Canada (2006a).

TABLE 11–2

Canada: Annual Flow of Humanitarian Population by Selected Countries

Source countries	1997	1998	1999	2000	2001	2002	2003	2004	2005	2006
Mexico	983	1,083	1,068	1,310	1,599	2,017	2,541	2,761	3,340	4,678
United States	316	235	246	346	408	860	2,649	2,986	1,300	1,498
Pakistan	1,197	1,742	2,464	3,145	3,048	3,296	3,363	739	558	560
Israel	401	306	203	226	437	533	508	388	282	428
Turkey	184	279	479	1,026	1,582	996	357	237	243	234
Iran	1,159	757	774	735	660	289	271	338	300	183
Algeria	795	778	508	413	511	106	62	62	44	53
Top 10 source countries	12,106	12,499	21,785	18,073	22,549	17,053	16,918	14,055	10,335	11,887
Other countries	12,621	13,013	16,679	19,785	22,199	16,582	13,689	10,562	8,568	9,493
Total	24,727	25,512	38,464	37,858	44,748	33,635	30,607	24,617	18,903	21,380

Source: Citizenship and Immigration Canada (2006a).

TABLE 11–3

Canada: Permanent Residents from the Middle East by Category

Source area	1996	1997	1998	1999	2000	2001	2002	2003	2004	2005
Family class total	68,359	59,979	50,898	55,277	60,612	66,795	62,304	65,129	62,260	63,352
Africa and the Middle East	20,234	23,121	19,284	18,999	23,414	30,706	30,604	25,384	27,591	28,649
Economic immigrants	125,370	128,351	97,911	109,255	136,299	155,719	137,861	121,047	133,745	156,310
Africa and the Middle East	8,665	7,975	7,662	8,503	10,338	9,663	8,824	9,536	12,593	11,439
Refugees	28,478	24,308	22,842	24,398	30,092	27,919	25,124	25,984	32,687	35,768
Africa and the Middle East	422	642	488	222	101	61	525	1,293	1,445	1,562

Source: Citizenship and Immigration Canada (2006a).

in the 2001 census. In this group, an estimated 10 percent to 15 percent are refugees.[9]

Middle Eastern refugees have different experiences in Canada compared to immigrants arriving from the same region. They must navigate the unique circumstances originating from their distinct status as unwanted or targeted people prior to seeking asylum. Furthermore, they often struggle to carry forward a message to the world at large that injustices rendering them as asylum seekers continue to affect their homeland. Third, Islamophobia in Canada has added to a feeling of suspicion and unease concerning the presence of Middle Eastern immigrants and refugees.[10]

Refugees from the Middle East must also deal with inter-communal conflicts related to their marginal status and claims within the Muslim diaspora. This is partially due to the fact that refugee organizations and advocacy groups have become increasingly involved in wider Canadian debates on multiculturalism and citizenship. Moreover, it is often argued that refugees are politically more involved compared to immigrants because of their attentiveness to issues "back home" where they have "unfinished business" (Safran 1991; Sheffer 1994; Basch, Schiller, and Blanc 1994; Cohen 1996; Smith and Guarnizo 1998; Al-Ali et al. 2001; Portes 2001; Saideman 2001; Adamson 2002; Ogelman, Money, and Martin 2002). Refugees are generally more engaged in transnational politics as part of their advocacy and public awareness activities. Consequently, they are suspected to experience a higher degree of dual loyalty compared to immigrants. However, this is more often the case for refugees who entertain a scenario of return. Refugees from the Middle East, such as Iranians, Palestinians, or Kurds, have little or no hope of return. Middle Eastern refugees in Canada are a small sample of discarded populations in the region whose organizational activities are led by their struggle for recognition of chronic human rights abuses in their home countries (see Suhrke 1995). Educated professionals from these communities act as public intellectuals and discuss Middle Eastern politics, Islam, authoritarian nationalism, and the ailments that produce forced migrations and systemic political violence in the region to Canadian audiences. At the lay level, on the other hand, grassroots refugee organizations take part in private sponsorship programs and constitute a small but critical constituency advocating the recognition of authoritarian features of many of the existing regimes in the Middle East.

By publicly speaking about their ordeal, refugees often find themselves in a head-on collision course with their brethren from their home countries who arrived and settled in Canada as immigrants. Muslim immigrant communities are concerned with the recognition of and legalized respect for their ethno-religious identity. For many, the problems of their society of origin should not be discussed in the already skeptical environment in their adopted homes. Consequently, refugees are often blamed for exhibiting "dirty laundry" and inconvenient truths that provide no benefit for immigrants from the Middle East settled in the West. In effect, some refugee advocacy groups are even accused of furthering the alienation of Middle Eastern immigrants due to the negative image of the region they may foster. Canadian policy makers should remain alert to these tensions between refugee and immigrant communities from the Middle East. To prove this point, it is worth noting that none of the publicly recognized Muslim organizations with wide membership in Canada address the refugee issue or refugee concerns in their mandate, programs, or activities. To assume that there can be a single, all-encompassing platform representing interests and concerns of both migrants and refugees from the Middle East is to ignore these important differences. Needless to say, successive Canadian governments have identified problems in the Middle East without being told about them by refugee claimants. This, however, is not a valid argument for refusing to observe closely what unfolds within Canada among refugee communities. Many inland refugee claimants bring the news of the region to Canada at a potential cost to their own lives. Their plight reveals systematic abuses that often fall beneath the radar of foreign policy makers due to their regular nature—as opposed to the crisis situations leading to resettlement programs. Canadian policy makers could not learn about these realities from immigrant groups from the Middle East, whose immediate organizational interests are largely related to identity politics and equal opportunity claims.

Specifically, refugee claimants' cases heard by the IRB and various Canadian courts provide valuable internal information about the state of affairs in the Middle East. Their testimonies include a wealth of documents of the kind used by leading human rights NGOs such as Amnesty International. Thus an examination of landmark cases and categorical examination of the IRB's positive decisions pertaining to refugees from the Middle East could be helpful in determining long-term humanitarian goals and foreign policy priorities of the Canadian government in the region. This is not to suggest that testimonies of refugees produced before the IRB and the courts are to be trolled through in the offices of the foreign ministry. Rather, the recommendation is for other governmental departments to pay regular attention to landmark hearings and decisions within the Canadian refugee system, as well as to the activities and public statements of refugee organizations from the Middle East. These may provide early warning about systemic human rights abuses abroad as well as problems within the refugee protection system in Canada.

The Case of Palestinian Refugees

The case of Palestinian refugees and their plight in the Middle East has a history of almost 60 years. Since the mid 1990s, a small but steady number of Palestinian refugees has been seeking asylum in Canada as inland refugee claimants, in addition to those who arrive as immigrants. Although some refugee claimants have been successful in remaining in Canada, none has been granted Convention refugee status. Instead, positive decisions have been rendered based on humanitarian and compassionate grounds. Where applications have been denied, the Palestinians in question faced deportation to the Middle East. This latter situation raised public concern and led to a wide network of alliances among advocacy organizations active in social justice issues as well as in the area of immigration and refugee law. Currently, there are an estimated 100 Palestinian refugee applicants in Canada facing possible deportation if their requests for Convention refugee status are denied. Asylum seekers and advocacy organizations argue that the consequences of deportation would be grave. Advocates for Palestinian refugees' rights point out that in Lebanon, in particular, Palestinian refugees are systematically prevented from owning property, working in select professions, receiving proper health care, and accessing higher education. Intensified conditions of disadvantage and second-class citizenship of Palestinian refugees inside Lebanon's refugee camps are underlined as a real peril. Israeli military occupation, public insecurity, and the poverty faced by Palestinians in the West Bank and Gaza are also widely cited on Palestinian refugee applications as reasons for their request for refugee status in Canada.

The public debate surrounding the case of three elderly Palestinian refugee claimants who found sanctuary in a Montreal church exemplifies this ongoing situation. Originally from (pre-1948) Mandate Palestine, the claimants spent most of their lives moving among refugee camps throughout the Middle East. In 2001, feeling that the violence was too intense in Lebanon, they fled the Middle East and arrived in Canada where they claimed refugee status. Their claim was rejected in 2003 and appeals proved unsuccessful. In January 2004, CIC asked the claimants to present themselves for deportation that February. In mid January, the three Palestinians sought refuge at the Église Notre-Dame-de-Grâce, whose members unanimously decided to support their case and stop their imminent deportation to the refugee camp of Ein el-Helweh in Lebanon. The three were granted permission to stay in Canada on humanitarian and compassionate grounds after taking sanctuary in the church for a year.

The Case of Refugees from Iran

Since the 1979 Islamic revolution in Iran created a religious-based state ideology that many Iranians, particularly the western-oriented secular elite favoured by the former shah and members of socialist, feminist, and labour movements, have fled to the West in search of refuge. In recent years, CIC has repeatedly claimed to have no evidence of any danger inflicted upon failed refugee claimants deported to Iran. However, the case of Haleh Sahba, a women's rights activist deported from Vancouver in 2005, has proven otherwise. It has been widely reported that she was detained in Iran for 26 hours and subjected to extensive questioning after being deported from Canada. Sahba's story has become a rallying call for a number of refugee advocacy groups and organizations. It led to public statements and organized activities supporting the plight of refugees from Iran. The involved groups and organizations expressed a general concern about refugee claimants from Iran whose applications have been rejected and who await deportation.

Iranian refugees are one of the better-organized communities both in Canada and abroad. The Vancouver chapter of the International Federation of Iranian Refugees, for example, is a community-based group with several hundred members and supporters. Members took a strong stance against government statements that Iran did not constitute a threatening environment for failed refugee claimants facing deportation. Their past efforts included the establishment of private sponsorship agreements for Iranian refugees. (To sponsor a refugee, one must agree to provide basic emotional and financial support for up to a year to enable the refugee to adjust and settle in Canada.) Partnerships with eligible sponsors in Canada led to the resettlement of at least 16 families during the Iranian refugee crisis in Turkey in the 1980s. At present, there are an estimated 20 Iranian asylum seekers facing imminent deportation from Canada. They are political dissidents, scholars, and activists. Refugee groups and advocacy organizations actively support such cases at the national and international levels by increasing awareness of authoritarian aspects of the regime in Iran.

Refugees from Iran have also been active in Toronto-based Canadian Centre for Victims of Torture.[11] Although the original impetus for the centre came from Chilean, Argentinean, and Uruguayan torture victims arriving in Canada during the late 1970s, Iranian refugees and torture victims jailed and oppressed in the immediate aftermath of the Islamic revolution also played a significant role in the furthering of the centre's mandate. The centre was established as a non-profit facility to help refugee survivors overcome the lasting effects of torture and war. To date, it has treated an estimated 14,000 victims and is a world leader in this field.

The Case of Kurdish Refugees

With no state to call their own, the Kurdish people are scattered among a number of Middle East countries. Kurdish refugees come from southeast Turkey, northeast Iraq, and east-central Iran, as well as the northeastern corner of Syria and the southern border regions of Armenia. Comprising the largest stateless people in the world, the Kurds in the Middle East range from estimates of 10 million to 35 million people. Since World War II, their situation has been fraught with political conflict, violence, and armed confrontation. In recent years, they suffered marked losses from the Iran-Iraq War (1980–88), the first Gulf War (1990–91), the uprising against Iraq that followed the first Gulf War, the continued military conflicts in Turkey (since the 1990s), and the American-British occupation of Iraq (2003 to present). As a result, an estimated three million Kurds have been forced to flee their homes and seek refuge throughout the region, in Europe, and overseas. A small group of rural Kurdish refugees in the wake of the first Gulf War were brought to Canada as part of refugee resettlement programs. However, the majority of Kurdish refugees arrived in Canada spontaneously and went through the inland refugee determination system. During the 1980s, Kurdish refugee claimants began to arrive mostly from Europe. During the late 1980s and 1990s, the majority of refugee hearings for Kurdish applicants resulted in positive decisions. A second group of Kurdish immigrants arrived in Canada again as political refugees in the 1990s. These claimants were originally from Turkey and Iraq. They entered the U.S. first and continued to Canada via land border crossings. Both groups of Kurdish refugees have been active advocates for the plight of Kurds in the Middle East and have found support within the Canadian legal community on issues such as the official documentation and recognition of the suffering of Kurds in the region.

Canadian human rights and refugee lawyers currently cite two successful appeal cases concerning Kurdish refugees Sami Durgun and Suleyman Goven. These are considered to have significantly challenged the PRRA criteria and the application of the IRPA with a broad mandate. In particular, Goven's lawyers took issue with the appeal process and its long-term consequences. Goven is a Kurd from Turkey who was granted refugee status in Canada in 1991. He then applied for permanent residency but was kept in limbo for 13 years. His application remained pending due to accusations of terrorist activity in his country of origin. Although the Security Intelligence Review Committee cleared these allegations in 2000, Goven was not granted permanent resident status until a lengthy legal process that ended in September 2006. Consequently, he was unable to travel outside of Canada to see his family. In addition, while eligible for full employment, his social insurance number informed potential employers that he did not have permanent status (because it began with the number nine) and he was not permitted to pursue further education. Rather than being a singular incidence of a bureaucratic mistake, Goven's case is accepted as a landmark legal appeal that led to revisions in the applications of definition of terrorism, in particular with regard to refugee claimants from the Middle East.

Lessons Learned from Middle Eastern Inland Refugee Applicants in Canada

Activities and public interventions of refugees from the Middle East in Canada demonstrate that although Canada's refugee regime is generally fair and well structured, there emerge periodic difficulties and problems in its application. In this chapter, at least three problem areas have been noted as exemplified by the experiences of inland refugee claimants from the Middle East. These persistent issues have led refugee organizations and advocacy groups to focus their energy on short-term and individual solutions first and foremost. A number of legal rulings pertaining to the appeal of refugee-related decisions ensued as a result, some of which are now regarded as landmark cases in Canadian law, such as the Goven case.

Refugee advocacy organizations have also been instrumental in resolving some individual deportation cases by staging public awareness campaigns to familiarize Canadians with the plight of refugees from the Middle East. For instance, Iranian refugee organizations have proven that establishing alliances with international networks and government offices is both possible and highly beneficial in raising awareness and gaining support. The case of Palestinian refugees, on the other hand, demonstrates the need for issue-specific agendas and strong legal guidance in questioning IRB decisions. Lacking in these strengths but having gained public sympathy, the plight of Palestinian refugees has not yet found a legal address. Palestinian claims to systemic human rights abuses has so far resulted in ad hoc solutions to individual cases. The case of Kurdish refugees from the Middle East also supports this observation. Is the IRB prejudiced in the case of special groups of refugees from the Middle East? In the case of Palestinian refugees, is it misapplying the UN organizational distinction between the mandates of the UNHCR and the United Nations Relief and Works Agency for Palestine Refugees in the Near East (UNRWA)? These questions are waiting for an answer that appears to be beyond the capabilities of the IRB itself. It is also likely that once Canadian policy makers make a decision concerning the plight of Palestinian refugees, similar to the introduction of gender-based prosecution clause, they set the tone for the adoption of regulatory standards on the issue.[12] Meanwhile, Canadian bureaucracy alone should not be burdened with this responsibility, and judicial as well as political consultations could be sought to remedy the ongoing deadlock on these matters.

During the last 25 years, direct engagement between refugee organizations, Canadian advocacy groups, and legal practitioners on the one hand and politicians, government officials, and courts on the other has resulted in a number of significant changes to Canada's refugee regime. Refugee advocacy efforts helped, in part, broaden the coverage of the *Immigration Act* in 2001. The previous act contained only provisions relating to claims for Convention refugee status. Other grounds for protection have been developed over time by way of added regulations, administrative discretionary practices, and references to case law. This was a major development noticed at a global level. However, it would be a mistake to assume that perfection has been achieved. As discussed in detail, there are a number of problem areas identified by refugee organizations and advocacy groups. Canada on occasion deports individuals to countries with weak or poor human rights records, Canada's utilization of the safe third-country clause raises concerns, and security clearances of asylum seekers and backlog of appeal cases create legal limbo for many. These concerns can be potentially hazardous to Canada's reputation as a global forerunner on human rights and refugee protection. Although Canada has a fairly robust reputation in this area, there remains the real issue of whether the current workings of these policies inadvertently result in people who merit protection being denied it. Redressing policy weaknesses is crucial in the light of the fact that Canada widely endorses the principle of human security and adheres to humanitarian values in international politics.

The human security principle has been described by the Department of Foreign Affairs and International Trade (DFAIT) as a people-centred approach to foreign policy, which recognizes that lasting social stability cannot be achieved until people are protected from state-led threats to their individual rights and safety (see Chapter 3). Canada's current human security agenda includes the protection of civilians and public safety. Most refugee appeals are launched precisely with reference to these two principles. In this regard, there is a direct, but largely unrecognized, connection between the stated aims of Canadian foreign policy and its refugee regime. The experiences of inland refugee claimants can be seen as a potent test case for the efficacy of Canadian foreign policy, albeit in home territory.

Currently, refugee groups and advocacy organizations point particularly to the potential repercussions of the Safe Third Country Agreement endorsed by Canada and the U.S. in December 2004. This agreement does not allow refugees to make a claim if they have already passed through another country where they could have sought refuge. Needless to say, the UN Convention does not provide asylum seekers the right to "shop around" for the most advantageous country to press their claim for protection. However, variations in refugee regimes ascribed by different countries, as evidenced during the disasters concerning Jews during World War II, indicate that the knowledge of a neighbouring country exercising xenophobic or otherwise lower standards of refugee acceptance should lead to precaution in terms of orchestration of common policies. The European Union, which is taken as the model for the Safe Third Country Agreement, has system-wide principles in place that guarantee even-handed treatment of asylum seekers. No such coordination has thus far materialized in the Canada-U.S. case. Opponents of the Canada-U.S. agreement thus argue that it forces inland claimants to seek protection in a country currently engaged in the detention of asylum seekers in jails alongside convicted criminals. People from the Middle East are particularly at risk of potential dragnet exercises. Another concern is that the U.S. and Canada have different policies pertaining to refugee admissions. In the past, numerous claimants have been recognized as legitimate refugees in Canada after having been refused in the United States.

The definition of organized criminality, which has undergone changes in the post–September 11 era, is also identified as a problem for Middle Eastern refugee claimants. Although the Convention specifically withholds protection from criminals, the common worry expressed by refugee organizations is that undefined charges of terrorism and links to terrorism could be used, and indeed have been used, against refugee claimants. This concern points to the relationship between the larger context of Canadian foreign policy measures and the specifics of the Canadian refugee regime. Policy makers should pay attention to those who are directly affected by the framework within which this relationship materializes in order to secure the efficacy of Canada's humanitarian mandate for victims of human rights abuses. Screening out terrorists and criminals who pose a danger for Canadian safety and security is both ethical and necessary. The issue presented here is not about ignoring standard precautions used to this end, a tradition started with the exclusion of war criminals and members of the mafia. Rather, it concerns the curbing of excessive and unforeseen effects of new security measures instituted in the aftermath of September 11, which inadvertently produce victims who have no involvement with international crimes. This is the significance of the Goven case. A person who is admitted as a Convention refugee to Canada based on the inland refugee determination criteria and who subsequently obtained security clearance should not have been denied the right to settle in Canada legally as a permanent resident based on a quasi-legal interpretation of a new security act *ex post facto*.

A final issue for the inland refugee stream in Canada, again illustrated by the case of Middle Eastern refugees, concerns the classification of types of persecution, including gender-based persecution. Historically, the definition of a refugee did not take gender-based persecution into account. Since the 1980s, however, Canadian refugee policy has come to recognize it as a valid claim. In 1993, after the Nada case and others, Canada became the first country to issue guidelines on female refugee claimants fleeing gender-based persecution. Since then, countries including the U.S. and Australia have adopted their own administrative guidelines, and others such as Sweden amended legislation to recognize gender-based persecution. This transformative change within the Canadian system and its wide-ranging international repercussions were influenced in part by cases of female Iranian refugees. Since the establishment of the Islamic revolutionary government in Iran, scores of women have fled their homeland fearing persecution by their government. Their refugee claims constituted some of the most compelling cases heard in Canada. The oppression or persecution that women face in Iran has been recognized as an institutionalized practice supported by a plethora of laws and policies devised to abrogate the basic rights of women. Public statements by refugee organizations and advocacy groups have repeated recognized the fact that women often face different types of human rights violations than men and can have different reasons for fleeing. Idealism and humanitarian convictions resulting from evolving departmental values among Canadian bureaucrats, operational monitoring, and feedback from Canadian overseas operations played a crucial role in the institution of these changes. However, the public voice of refugee organizations on this issue should not be underestimated. Much elaborate policy work and many bureaucratic consultations on gender-based persecution and directives on how Canada should respond to it in the form of manual instructions, referral systems were no doubt influenced by the legal and public claims made by asylum seekers themselves. Perhaps some would argue that CIC would have launched its gender–based persecution program regardless of outside factors and public involvement on the issue. This point of view attributes omnipotency and powers of undue proportions to Canadian bureaucracy in understanding the plight of refugees from Middle East and elsewhere.

The Canadian refugee regime responds to and learns from refugees and asylum seekers while providing invaluable humanitarian service to them. This chapter advocates the steady furthering of this interchange in the light of current concerns raised by refugee groups such as those arriving from the Middle East, advocacy organizations, and Canadian refugee and human rights lawyers. It does not at all suggest that refugees are the only ones whose voices matter in the institution and maintenance of Canada's refugee regime.

However, it also refrains from the self-referential understanding of the bureaucratic organs of the Canadian state, a tendency that puts an undue onus on the shoulders of selected government departments and their employees for a matter that concerns and reflects the opinions and choices of the whole Canadian society—how to provide humanitarian protection to people fleeing persecution and threats who arrive at the borders of Canada. Consultations such as those conducted by CIC in the form of standing committees that discuss issues flagged by refugees themselves are a sure sign that the front-line workers feel the pressure and strive to find workable solutions. It is important to think further in that direction and aim for possible synergies among different departments within the bureaucracy as well as consultations with advocacy groups and refugee organizations in an effort to iron out the causes of recurrent problems and to detect new ones before they become systematic issues. The common response to such suggestions is to point out the much required independence of the IRB's Refugee Protection Division. However, the IRB's stance is a conditional one. It is not an autonomous political body in whose affairs the state or the society cannot intervene. It is a quasi-judicial bureaucratic formation instituted to serve a specific function. Surely, it has done a very good job for almost two decades. What is needed now is for CIC to continue to consult with the government, other government departments, and public stakeholders in order to step in areas where the IRB alone cannot solve the issue, or where the refugee law may have fallen silent, or where different parts of the refugee regime may not be working in full synchronization especially with the introduction of new security measures in the post–September 11 era. This is not to argue that Canada has failed in its humanitarian commitments in the area of inland refugee determination. On the contrary, identification of problem areas and their direct address are a sure sign to Canadian society as well as to an international audience that Canada takes these commitments very seriously.

The 2002 Government Response to the Report of the Standing Committee on Citizenship and Immigration, which provided a critical examination of the regulations under the new IRPA, amply proves these points (CIC 2003). The dialogue resulting from this round of consultations led to a series of improvements in Canada's immigration and refugee regime. At the very least, the process provided a public venue in which open discussion took place and the government responded to concerns and criticisms with a clear rationale. It is wrong to assume that the Canadian public knows why the government and different parts of Canadian bureaucracy make certain decisions in contentious cases or what rationale it uses to solve problems. It is equally wrong to shelve public concerns in fields that are deemed in the trust of Canadian bureaucracy. Whether such concerns were raised by refugee organizations themselves or by advocacy and professional groups in Canada, they should be monitored and receive a public address.

Internationally, Canada has set the tone for the refugee determination system in the past as an ideal model for its streamlining and regularization, as well as in the area of rendering a broader interpretation of the UN Convention. Therefore, it already has the credentials to offer internationally applicable solutions to problems such as legal limbo, weaknesses in the area of job placement and integration of inland refugee claimants, the disconnect between refugee determination and security clearance procedures, the situation of non-status people, and systematized documentation of refugee cases to identify chronic issues in refugee-producing regions. This last suggestion is perhaps the most contentious one, as the IRB does not attend to clusters of cases but discusses individual applications. However, Canadian refugee regime regulations direct the IRB to make decisions based on classes and identified types of persecution. The expansion of this list had tremendously positive outcomes for refugee applicants in the past. Further updates and changes should be considered in the light of the information that other government departments such as

DFAIT could provide in terms of emergence of regional crises and changing international conditions. The judiciary already steps in as an ongoing corrective to the IRB. However, to wait for the courts to indicate recurrent mistakes and omissions is a costly and slow route to follow for ensuring that the Canadian refugee regime's inland admissions stream functions in a responsive and dynamic way to tackle the demands created by new refugee waves. The Middle East is a microcosm upon which this chapter tested some of these observations.

Conclusion

Refugee advocacy groups and organizations need access to governmental and international organs to negotiate their demands for wider access to asylum for remaining refugee claimants and to spread the message of their plight (Shain 1989, 1999; Shain and Barth 2003; Shain and Britsman 2002; Shain and Sherman 2001). Consequently, refugees' public involvement can be unique because of their ability to adapt and reconfigure existing political forums to influence policy measures and challenge bureaucratic decision-making processes. In the case of Middle Eastern refugees, Kurdish inland refugees claimants sought legal remedies for the betterment of their treatment and for avoiding pitfalls of new security measures, Iranian refugees established networks of support for private sponsorship programs and made repeated legal cases for the widespread recognition of gender-based persecution, and Palestinian refugees sought public support for the acknowledgment of their unusual international status. As these cases illustrate, refugees should be considered as political actors, albeit reluctant ones. The dilemma they pose is that despite their public engagement, they have little, if any, influence in mainstream politics and policy-making circles. As non-voters, they are considered unimportant compared to immigrant communities. As recipients of bureaucratic services, they have little if any influence over institutions within which such offices are situated. And yet issues determining their engagement with the Canadian public have global and Canadian significance in the area of humanitarianism. To view such challenges to policy as irrelevant would be a mistake. Improvements to the existing system are not only possible, but, in the current global context, they are also highly desirable. With reference to the specific case of refugees from the Middle East, given the current status quo in international politics, improvements in Canadian recognition of humanitarian needs in the region in the form of balanced refugee policies and well-informed practices on Canadian soil would add significantly to Canada's global credibility as an even-handed player in the field of global human rights advocacy.

Notes

1 The author would like to thank Mordechai Wasserman, Michelle Millard, Bessma Momani, Paul Heinbecker, and Michael Molloy for their advice, comments, criticisms, and input during the preparation of this chapter. Relying on their expertise in Canadian refugee law, refugee advocacy, Canadian foreign policy measures, and Canadian bureaucracy, she hopes to have avoided common pitfalls in her analysis of the Canadian refugee regime.

2 Canadian refugee regime is defined as the sum total of refugee selection and admission standards, refugee status determination and protection systems, and appeal processes when applicable.

3 Statistics compiled by Citizenship and Immigration Canada ([CIC] 2005, s.3[b]) indicate that for the base year 2004, under the category of protected persons, Canada admitted 7,411 government-assisted refugees, 3,155 privately sponsored refugees, and 15,901 inland claimants, and, 6,945 people were admitted based on humanitarian and compassionate grounds. The total, including family reunification cases, amounts to close to 40,000, of which about two thirds come through inland refugee admissions.

4 The term "asylum seeker" is the legal nomination for a person who seeks protection from persecution and threats to his or her life. Although Canada refers to inland refugee claimants as people who seek refugee status or as refugee claimants, international refugee law identifies this group as asylum seekers, who then become refugees if their claims are accepted on grounds related to the UN Convention Relating to the Status of Refugees. Throughout this chapter, these three terms are used interchangeably depending on the context.

5 In particular see *Immigration and Refugee Protection Regulations*, SOR/2002–227, which came in force (with some exceptions) on June 28, 2002.

6 Demetrios Papademetriou (2005) at Migration Policy Institute in Washington, DC makes this claim in *The Global Struggle with Illegal Migration: No End in Sight*. His findings are supported by Luin Goldring at York University, among others.

7 For detailed numbers and estimates, see Jimenez (2003). Ontario's construction secretariat reported 76,000 illegal immigrants in its construction sector alone. Many of these workers are asylum seekers whose refugee status applications have been denied. There are at least 36,000 refugees waiting for deportation, and a standard rate of 8 percent out of the 800,000 or so work and student visa holders overstay their visas per year. In addition there is a backlog of 53,000 disputed refugee cases. Unlike the U.S. with 8 million non-status workers formally acknowledged by the government, Canada pays little public attention to non-status people in its midst.

8 If recognized by the IRB, on the other hand, a refugee may apply for status as a landed immigrant. In addition to paying set fees, refugee applicants must also produce "satisfactory" identity documents, meet health requirements, and undergo security checks.

9 For the actual numbers and recent trends, see IRB (2006, s.2).

10 For trends in the settlement of Muslims in Canada, see Statistics Canada (2003).

11 The first such centre was founded in Copenhagen, Denmark, in 1982. It has now

grown into the International Rehabilitation Council for Torture Victims, an independent, international health professional organization that promotes and supports the rehabilitation of torture victims and works for the prevention of torture worldwide.

12 The clause on gender-related persecution was in part adopted because of the landmark case of an asylum seeker from Saudi Arabia named Nada, who refused to wear a veil, and who was initially denied refugee status. The panel that heard the case advised Nada that she "would do well to comply with the laws of her homeland." In January 1993, the Canadian government announced it would allow Nada to stay in Canada but only on humanitarian grounds. Finally in March 1993, amid public outcry over Nada's case and several other well-publicized incidents regarding the plight of women who had made unsuccessful refugee claims based on gender-related persecution, Canada adopted Guidelines on Women Refugee Claimants Fearing Gender-Related Persecution.

References

Adamson, Fiona B. 2002. "Mobilizing for the Transformation of Home: Politicised Identities and Transnational Practices." In *New Approaches to Migration? Transnational Communities and the Transformation of Home*, ed. Nadje Al-Ali and Khalid Koser, 155–68. London: Routledge.

Aiken, Sharryn. 2000. "Manufacturing Terrorists: Refugees, National Security, and Canadian Law." *Refuge* 19(3): 54–73.

Al-Ali, Nadje, Black, Richard, and Koser, Khalid. 2001. "The Limits to 'Transnationalism': Bosnian and Eritrean Refugees in Europe as Emerging Transnational Communities." *Ethnic and Racial Studies* 24(4): 578–600.

Basch, Linda, Schiller, Nina Glick, and Blanc, Cristina Szanton. 1994. *Nations Unbound: Transnational Projects, Postcolonial Predicaments, and Deterritorialized Nation-States.* Longhorne, PA: Gordon and Breach.

Citizenship and Immigration Canada. 2002. "Building a Nation: The Regulations under the Immigration and Refugee Protection Act." Government Response to the Report of the Standing Committee on Citizenship and Immigration. www.cic.gc.ca/english/resources/publications/response/response.asp (August 2007).

———. 2005. "Departmental Performance Report 2004–2005." www.tbs-sct.gc.ca/rma/dpr1/04–05/CI-CI/CI-CId4502_e.asp#sec_3_B (August 2007).

———. 2006a. "Facts and Figures 2005." www.cic.gc.ca/english/resources/statistics/facts2005/permanent/13.asp (August 2007).

———. 2006b. "Fact Sheets on Refugee Issues." www.cic.gc.ca/english/about/laws-policy/responses.asp (August 2007).

Cohen, Robin. 1996. "Diasporas and the Nation-State: From Victims to Challengers" *International Affairs* 72(3): 507–20.

Immigration and Review Board. 2006. "Report on Plans and Priorities 2006–2007." www.tbs-sct.gc.ca/rpp/0607/IRB-CISR/irb-cisr02_e.asp (August 2007).

Jiminez, Marina. 2003. "200,000 Illegal Immigrants Toiling in Canada's Underground Economy." *Globe and Mail*, November 15, A1.

Ogelman, Nedim, Money, Jeannette, and Martin, Philip. 2002. "Immigrant Cohe-
sion and Political Access in Influencing Host Country Foreign Policy."
SAIS Review 22(2): 145–65.

Papademetriou, Demetrios. 2005. "The Global Struggle with Illegal Migration: No
End in Sight." Washington, DC: Migration Policy Institute. www.migra
tioninformation.org/Feature/display.cfm?id=336 (August 2007).

Portes, Alejandro. 2001. "Introduction: The Debates and Significance of Immigrant
Transnationalism." *Global Networks* 1(3): 181–93.

Safran, William. 1991. "Diasporas in Modern Societies: Myths of Homeland and
Return." *Diaspora* 1(1): 83–99.

Saideman, Stephen. 2001. *The Ties That Divide: Ethnic Politics, Foreign Policy,
and International Politics*. New York: Columbia University Press.

Shain, Yossi. 1989. *The Frontier of Loyalty: Political Exiles in the Age of the
Nation-State*. Middletown, CT: Wesleyan University Press.

———. 1999. *Marketing the American Creed Abroad: Diasporas in the U.S. and
their Homelands*. Cambridge, UK: Cambridge University Press.

Shain, Yossi, and Aharon Barth. 2003. "Diasporas and International Relations
Theory." *International Organization* 57(3): 449–79.

Shain, Yossi, and Barry Britsman. 2002. "The Jewish Security Dilemma." *Orbis*
46(1): 47–72.

Shain, Yossi, and Martin Sherman. 2001. "Diasporic Transnational Financial Flows
and Their Impact on National Identity." *Nationalism and Ethnic Politics*
7(4): 1–36.

Sheffer, Gabriel. 1994. "Ethno-National Diasporas and Security." *Survival* 36(1):
60–79.

Smith, Michael P., and Guarnizo, Luis E., eds. 1998. *Transnationalism from Below*.
New Brunswick, NJ: Transaction.

Statistics Canada. 2003. "Longitudinal Survey of Immigrants to Canada: Process,
Progress, and Prospects." www.statcan.ca/english/freepub/89-611-XIE/
89-611-XIE2003001.pdf (August 2007).

Suhrke, Astri. 1995. "Refugees and Asylum in the Muslim World." In *The Cambridge Survey of World Migration*, ed. Robin Cohen, 457–59. Cambridge,
UK: Cambridge University Press.

Agata Antkiewicz is Senior Researcher at the Centre for International Governance Innovation, where she oversees economic governance projects. She holds an MA in economics, specializing in international trade and international relations from the University of Economics in Wroclaw, Poland. Antkiewicz's authored or co-authored articles have been published by the *World Economy*, *Review of International Organizations*, *Canadian Public Policy*, *Third World Quarterly*, and *National Bureau of Economic Research.*

Michael Bell is Paul Martin Senior Scholar in International Diplomacy at the University of Windsor. He is also co-director of the Jerusalem Old City Initiative. In 2007 he completed two years as chair of the donor committee of the International Reconstruction Fund Facility for Iraq. Bell spent 36 years in the Canada's Department of Foreign Affairs and International Trade, serving as ambassador to Jordan (1987–90), Egypt (1994–98), and Israel (1990–92, and 1992–2003).

Rex Brynen is a professor of political science at McGill University, and author, editor, or co-editor of eight books on regional security and political development in the Middle East. In addition to his academic work he has served as a member of the policy staff of the Department of Foreign Affairs and International Trade and as a consultant to the Privy Council Office, the Canadian International Development Agency, the International Development Research Centre, the World Bank, and others.

Nergis Canefe is an associate professor of political science at York University, an SJD candidate at Osgoode Hall Law School, and resident faculty at the Centre for Refugee Studies. Her areas of expertise are political violence, nationalism studies, minority rights, diaspora politics, and crimes against humanity.

Janine A. Clark is an associate professor in the Department of Political Science at the University of Guelph. She is the author of *Islam, Charity, and Activism: Middle-Class Networks and Social Welfare in Egypt, Jordan, and Yemen* (Indiana University Press, 2004) as well as numerous articles on political Islam. She is also co-editor of *Economic Liberalization, Democratization and Civil Society in the Developing World* (St. Martin's Press, 2000).

Nathan C. Funk is assistant professor of Peace and Conflict Studies at the University of Waterloo's Conrad Grebel University College, with previous appointments at American University and George Washington University. His publications on intercultural dialogue and Middle East policy include *Peace and Conflict Resolution in Islam* (University Press of America, 2001), *Ameen Rihani: Bridging East and West* (University Press of America, 2004), and *Making Peace with Islam* (forthcoming).

Ronald Harpelle of Lakehead University's Department of History is a specialist in 20th-century British West Indian immigration and settlement. He has been commissioned, with Bruce Muirhead of the University of Waterloo, to write an intellectual history of the International Development Research Centre.

Paul Heinbecker was a former chief foreign policy advisor to Prime Minister Brian Mulroney, ambassador to Germany, and permanent representative of Canada at the United Nations. He is currently the director of the Laurier Centre for Global Relations and a distinguished fellow at the Centre for International Governance Innovation, both in Waterloo. He is the co-editor of *Irrelevant or Indispensable? The United Nations in the 21st Century* (Wilfrid Laurier University Press, 2005) and a frequent writer in journals, magazines, and newspapers and commentator on television.

Tami Amanda Jacoby is acting director of the Centre for Defence and Security Studies, and associate professor of political studies at the University of Manitoba. She has published in the areas of Middle East politics, gender studies, terrorism, and Canadian foreign policy. Her two most recent books are *Women in Zones of Conflict: Power and Resistance in Israel* (McGill-Queen's University Press, 2005) and *Bridging the Barrier: Israeli Unilateral Disengagement* (Ashgate Publishing, 2007).

Paul Kingston is an associate professor of political science and international development studies at the University of Toronto, Scarborough. His work focuses on the history and political economy of development in the contemporary Middle East and he is currently completing a book on civil society, non-governmental organizations, and advocacy politics in postwar Lebanon.

Michael Molloy spent 35 years in the Canadian foreign service specializing in refugee policy and operations. Assignments abroad included Lebanon, Syria, and Jordan. From 1993 to 1996 he was advisor to Refugee Working Group. He was ambassador to Jordan from 1996 to 2000 and Canadian Special Coordinator for the Peace Process and chair of the Refugee Workig Group from 2000 to 2003. In retirement he continues to work on "final status" issues including Jerusalem and the Palestinian refugee problem.

Bessma Momani is an assistant professor in the departments of political science and history at the University of Waterloo and a senior fellow at the Centre for International Governance and Innovation. She has a monograph entitled *IMF–Egyptian Debt Negotiations* (American University in Cairo Press, 2005), is co-author of *Twentieth Century World History: A Canadian Perspective* (Nelson Education, 2006), and has published articles in over a dozen political and economic journals.

Bruce Muirhead teaches Canadian history at the University of Waterloo. He has published in the area of international financial relations and international trade. This chapter, written with Ron Harpelle, is his first foray into the complicated world of the Middle East.

Brent E. Sasley is an assistant professor in the Department of Political Science at the University of Texas at Arlington. His previous book, *Redefining Security in the Middle East* (University of British Columbia Press, 2002), was co-edited with Tami Amanda Jacoby, and his next book on the politics of governing in the Middle East will be published in 2008. His research focuses on Middle East security and, more broadly, on foreign policy analysis. His current project centres on the role of emotions in foreign policy decision making.

Sallama Shaker is Egypt's former assistant minister of foreign affairs for the Americas and ambassador of Egypt to Canada. Since January 2007, she is visiting professor at Claremont Graduate University in South California. She has a PhD from the School of International Services at the American University in Washington, DC and has authored *State, Society, and Privatization in Turkey, 1979–1990* (Woodrow Wilson Center Press, 1995).

David Sultan was born in Cairo in 1938 and immigrated to Israel in 1949. After receiving an MA from the Hebrew University of Jerusalem, he joined Israel's Ministry of Foreign Affairs in 1964. As a diplomat with 40 years' experience, he has served as Israeli ambassador to Egypt, Turkey, and, in 1996–2000, to Canada. In the Ministry of Foreign Affairs he also served as head of the Middle East and Peace Process Department.

Marie-Joëlle Zahar is an associate professor of political science at the Université de Montréal. Her research focuses on conflict resolution and post-conflict peace building. Her work on the Middle East has appeared in *Critique Internationale, International Journal,* and *Conflits dans le monde,* as well as in a number of edited collections. She is currently completing a manuscript on political dynamics in post–civil war Lebanon and their impact on reconstruction and the sustainability of peace.